Victor C. de Munck is Associate Professor in Anthropology at the State University of New York (SUNY).

Ljupcho Risteski is Associate Professor in Ethnography and Anthropology at Ss. Cyril and Methodius University in Macedonia.

MACEDONIA

The Political, Social, Economic and Cultural
Foundations of a Balkan State

Edited by
Victor C. de Munck
and
Ljupcho Risteski

BLOOMSBURY ACADEMIC
LONDON • NEW YORK • OXFORD • NEW DELHI • SYDNEY

BLOOMSBURY ACADEMIC
Bloomsbury Publishing Plc
50 Bedford Square, London, WC1B 3DP, UK
1385 Broadway, New York, NY 10018, USA
29 Earlsfort Terrace, Dublin 2, Ireland

BLOOMSBURY, BLOOMSBURY ACADEMIC and the Diana logo
are trademarks of Bloomsbury Publishing Plc

First published in Great Britain 2013 by I. B. Tauris
This paperback edition published in 2021

Copyright © Victor C. de Munck and Ljupcho Risteski, 2013
Copyright of Individual Chapters © Victor A. Friedman, Ilka Thiessen, Violeta Duklevska Schubert, Davorin Trpeski, Burcu Akan Ellis, Galina Oustinova-Stjepanovic, Shayna Plaut, Rozita Dimova, Joseph Moldow, Anastasia Karakasidou, Jonathan Matthew Schwartz, Victor C. de Munck and Ljupcho Risteski, 2013

Victor C. de Munck and Ljupcho Risteski have asserted their right under the Copyright, Designs and Patents Act, 1988, to be identified as Author of this work.

All rights reserved. No part of this publication may be reproduced or transmitted in any form or by any means, electronic or mechanical, including photocopying, recording, or any information storage or retrieval system, without prior permission in writing from the publishers.

Bloomsbury Publishing Plc does not have any control over, or responsibility for, any third-party websites referred to or in this book. All internet addresses given in this book were correct at the time of going to press. The author and publisher regret any inconvenience caused if addresses have changed or sites have ceased to exist, but can accept no responsibility for any such changes.

A catalogue record for this book is available from the British Library.

A catalog record for this book is available from the Library of Congress.

ISBN: HB: 978 1 8488 5936 4
PB: 978 1 3502 4177 0

Typeset by Newgen Publishers, Chennai

International Library of Historical Studies, vol. 87

To find out more about our authors and books visit
www.bloomsbury.com and sign up for our newsletters.

CONTENTS

List of Captions vii
Map viii
List of Contributors ix

Introduction 1
Victor C. de Munck and Ljupcho Risteski

1. A Tantrum from the Cradle of Democracy: On
   the Dangers of Studying Macedonian 22
   Victor A. Friedman

2. 'EU as Future?': From a Macedonian Viewpoint – The Multiple
   Ways of Being European in Macedonia and Not Being
   in Europe 44
   Ilka Thiessen

3. 'My Faith, My Nation': Exploring the 'Natural'
   Affinity between Orthodox Christianity and
   National Identity in Macedonia 65
   Violeta Duklevska Schubert

4. Nationalism and the Use of Cultural Heritage:
   A Few Post-Socialist Macedonian Examples 89
   Davorin Trpeski

5. Conceptualizing Gender in Macedonia 109
   Victor C. de Munck and Davorin Trpeski

6. Is It Just a Song That Remains? Reflections on Turkish
   Minorities in Macedonia 136
   Burcu Akan Ellis

7. Why a Gypsy in Macedonia Does Not Know
   'Correct' Islam 162
   Galina Oustinova-Stjepanovic

8. Absent Roma, Imported Interest: 'Roma' as Subject
   and Agent in the Republic of Macedonia 191
   Shayna Plaut

9. Topography of Spatial and Temporal Ruptures:
   (Im)materialities of (Post)socialism in a Northern
   Town in Macedonia 210
   Rozita Dimova

10. Africa : Europe : Albania : Macedonia – a Zero-Sum Game,
    Ecological Fallacy Theory of Ethnic Divisiveness 233
    Victor C. de Munck and Joseph Moldow

11. National Purities, Ecological Disasters: Greek Modernity
    and the War on Nature 258
    Anastasia Karakasidou

12. 'Kapka po kapka' (Drop by Drop): Civil Society and Rural
    Ecology in the Prespa Lake Region of Macedonia 277
    Jonathan Matthew Schwartz

    Index 298

LIST OF CAPTIONS

All photos supplied by the author

Photo 1. Victor de Munck with taxi driver

Photo 2. Skopje Plaza with Millennium Cross

Photo 3. View of Old Town from the Stone Bridge

Photo 4. Vendor at Bit Pazar

Photo 5. Victor Friedman and thug – eye to eye

Photo 6. Street in the Old Town

Photo 7. Local grocery store

Photo 8. Mother and daughter baking bread

Photo 9. Family cleaning onion harvest

A MAP OF MACEDONIA

LIST OF CONTRIBUTORS

Victor C. de Munck is Professor of Anthropology at SUNY New Paltz. He is also Chair of the department. De Munck has conducted fieldwork in Sri Lanka, on cultural change using an ecological perspective; Lithuania, the United States and Russia on a comparative study of cultural models of romantic love; Macedonia on kinship and family among Macedonians and Albanians. He is a cognitive and cross-cultural anthropologist and has published extensively on issues of cultural models, cultural theory, methods, gender, romantic love and identity. He is currently writing a book on cultural models and a cross-cultural psychology textbook, as well as preparing papers on the relationship between globalization, social structure, the Human Development Index and what humans really want. He is a co-editor of the *Journal of Globalization Studies*.

Rozita Dimova is Senior Research Fellow in the Department for South Slavic Languages and Cultural Studies (Institute for Slavistics) at Humboldt University – Berlin, working on her habilitation project on borders in southeastern Europe. After receiving her PhD in Anthropology at Stanford University in 2004, Dimova was a postdoctoral research fellow at the Max Planck Institute for Social Anthropology in Halle (2004–06). Her fields of specialization include materiality, aesthetics, space, consumption and transnational regimes of humanitarianism. A guest co-editor of the forthcoming issue of *History and Anthropology* (Winter 2012, vol. 23) entitled 'Contested Nation-building within the International "Order of Things": Performance, Festivals and Legitimization in South-Eastern Europe', Dimova is currently completing a book manuscript on aesthetics and politics in the Balkans.

Burcu Akan Ellis is Assistant Professor of International Relations at San Francisco State University. Originally from Turkey, she works on issues of identity and migration in the Balkans and southeast Europe, especially among the Albanian populations. Her previous book *Shadow Genealogies: Memory and Identity among Urban Muslims in Macedonia* was published by East European Monographs in 2003 and is being translated into Albanian. Her recent publications include articles on the Albanian diaspora in *Balkanistica*. She holds a PhD from American University's School of International Service.

Victor A. Friedman is Andrew W. Mellon Professor in the Department of Slavic Languages and Literatures and the Department of Linguistics at the University of Chicago, where he also holds an associate appointment in the Department of Anthropology, and he is Director of Chicago's Center for East European and Russian/Eurasian Studies. He is a member of the Macedonian Academy of Arts and Sciences, the Academy of Sciences of Albania, the Academy of Arts and Sciences of Kosova, Matica Srpska, and holds the '1300 Years of Bulgaria' jubilee medal. He has thrice been awarded the Golden Plaque from the University of Skopje, from which he also holds the degree of Doctor Honoris Causa. In 2009 he received the American Association of Teachers of Slavic and East European Languages' Annual Award for Outstanding Contributions to Scholarship. During the Yugoslav Wars he worked for the UN as a senior policy and political analyst in Macedonia and consulted for other organizations. He has held Guggenheim, Fulbright-Hays, ACLS, NEH, and other fellowships. His books include *Macedonian* (2002), *Turkish in Macedonia and Beyond* (2003), *Studies in Albanian and Other Balkan Languages* (2004), a scholarly edition of Aleko Konstantinov's *Bai Ganyo* (2010) and *Očerki lakskogo jazyka* (2011).

Anastasia Karakasidou is a social anthropologist. She received her doctorate degree from Columbia University in 1992. Her specializations are themes of nationhood and identity, religion and ideology, gender and social stratification, narrative and history, and anthropological theory. She has published a book titled *Fields of Wheat, Hills of Blood: Passages to Nationhood in Greek Macedonia, 1870–1990* (University of Chicago Press, 1997), as well as a number of articles on the ideology of nationhood in Greece and the Balkans. Since 1999, Karakasidou has been involved in the study of chemical pollution, the vulnerable human body and cancer as a disease of modernity. She has been conducting a cross-cultural study on discourses of cancer by exploring different cultural understandings of the disease and examining its narration and imagery in three diverse settings: the United States, Greece and China.

Joseph Moldow received his BA in Anthropology from the State University of New York at New Paltz. He is currently working on an article on how countries with small populations (like Macedonia) can successfully compete in a global marketplace if they don't have economically valued natural resources (e.g. oil, a beautiful shoreline), and another article on the fall relationship between the Human Development Index and economic growth, both in collaboration with Victor de Munck.

Galina Oustinova-Stjepanovic is Research Officer at University College London and Fellow at the University of Edinburgh. She is interested in anthropology of religion, especially Islam, and the issues of godlessness, enlightenment and political experiments. She is currently working on a series of articles about failure to perform religion, atheism and unwanted religion in Macedonia.

Shayna Plaut is completing her PhD thesis at the University of British Columbia. Her area of research is on the intersections of journalism, human rights and social change with transnational populations. She is also interested in the growing industry of donors and foundations and how this influences ideas of agency and activism. Prior to returning to graduate school, Plaut taught courses on human rights at Columbia College, Chicago, where she honed her interest on the intersections of media, culture and transnational activism. Plaut has conducted activism and academic work in Macedonia, Hungary, the UK, Kosovo and Sapmi – the traditional land of the Saami people. Plaut has published in *The International Journal for Human Rights* as well *Alternatives: Global, Local, Political* and contributed to various edited volumes. She has conducted extensive research on Romani media and civil society since 2001 and served in a variety of volunteer leadership positions with Amnesty and Amnesty USA addressing human rights issues in the Balkans, including assisting in the design and implementation of a research mission in 2006. From 2000 to 2003, she was the Human Rights Education Coordinator for the Midwest Region of Amnesty International USA. Plaut received her MA from the University of Chicago and her BA from Antioch College.

Ljupcho S. Risteski received his PhD degree in Ethnology at the Institute of Ethnology and Anthropology at Sts Cyril and Methodius University in Skopje, Macedonia, in 2002. Since 1998 he has worked at the Institute, and was promoted to Associate Professor in 2002. His main topics of research are: traditional folk cultures in the Balkans, as well as post-socialism and the transition of southeastern European and Balkan societies, nationalism, symbols and nation-building processes, and socially marginalized groups. He has published extensively on these issues in Macedonian as well as international journals.

Violeta Duklevska Schubert received her PhD in 2001 from the University of Melbourne. Her doctoral thesis, 'Too Many Men' focused on Macedonian kinship and the plight of ageing bachelors in changing rural societies. Violeta is currently a lecturer at the University of Melbourne in anthropology and development studies in the School of Social and Political Sciences. She has published papers on a range of issues relating to Macedonia culture including 'Dynamics of Macedonian kinship: contextualizing ideologies and pragmatics of agnation' in *Journal of Mediterranean Studies* Volume 15:1 (2005); 'Refusing to Sing: Gender, Kinship and Patriliny in Macedonia' (2005) in *The Australian Journal of Anthropology*, 16:1 (2005), 62–75; 'Waiting for Marriage' in G. Hage (ed.) *Waiting* (2009, Melbourne University

Press); 'Equilibrium, chaos and Macedonian nationalism' in G. Hage & E. Kowal (eds) *Force, Movement, Intensity: The Newtonian Imagination in the Humanities and Social Sciences* (2010, Melbourne University Press).

Jonathan Matthew Schwartz is Associate Professor Emeritus at the Institute of Anthropology, University of Copenhagen. He conducted an action research project with 'guest workers' in Denmark during the 1970s. As a result of this project, he became acquainted with emigrants from several ethnic groups who had emigrated from the Prespa Lake region of Macedonia. As a result his research turned to local and ethnic communities in the Prespa Lake region and subsequently shifted from 'labor migrants' to 'ethnic refugees'. In the most recent phase of field research, his focus has been on NGOs engaged in the environment. Schwartz has written, introduced and edited many publications in Danish. Among his publications in English are: *Reluctant Hosts: Denmark's Reception of Guest Workers* (1985), *In Defense of Homesickness: Essays on Identity and Locality* (1989) and *Pieces of Mosaic: an Essay on the Making of Makedonija* (1996); the last was recently translated into Macedonian (2010). Schwartz writes poetry and fiction and, in his retirement, also volunteers as a cook in a Copenhagen literary cafe.

Ilka Thiessen is Professor of Anthropology at Malaspina University-College located in British Columbia, Canada. She has written extensively on Macedonian culture and identity. Her book *Waiting for the Macedonians* (2006, University of Toronto Press) has become a must read for all Macedonian specialists.

Davorin Trpeski holds a PhD in ethnology (2010) from the Institute of Ethnology and Anthropology at Ss. Cyril and Methodius University in Skopje. He has contributed to several international projects concerning the interpretation of cultural heritage in Macedonia and southeast Europe. He has worked on research projects through the Marie Curie Institute, CEEPUS and Helmut Kohl fellowship programmes. Currently, Trpeski is Assistant Professor at the Ss. Cyril and Methodius University in Skopje in the fields of political anthropology and the anthropology of cultural heritage.

INTRODUCTION

Victor C. de Munck and Ljupcho Risteski

In this new edited volume on Macedonia, we aspire to present an empirically diverse and rich set of papers, most of which are an outgrowth of research conducted in Macedonia from 2007 to 2011. The only other English edited volume was published in 2000 by Pluto Press and consisted of seven chapters, five of which focused as much on Greece as on Macedonia. This earlier work, edited by Jane Cowan, was primarily drawn from anthropologists who worked in Greece and were drawn to the Macedonian conflict (Danforth 1995; Schwartz, also this volume).

The common metaphor for the earlier edited volume was 'inflection', as described by Keith Brown and Jane Cowan, the authors of the Introduction. By this they meant to direct the focus away from the singular to the plural: that the 'perspective' of a people or nation or anything else often 'depends on where one stands' (Cowan and Brown 2000: 21). Their goal was, in short, to emphasize the 'Macedonian multiplicity' (ibid: 22) that they viewed as both urgent and necessary for the creation of a viable nation-state considering that wars had broken out in the Balkans after the dissolution of Yugoslavia. The question at that time was, 'Could Macedonia serve as a model of a successful multicultural Balkan country or would it too be sucked into the vortex of 'interethnic fratricide'?[1] This is a question just as relevant 11 years later and is the inspiration for this current set of chapters.

While interethnic and Greek-Macedonian tensions remain as complicated and important as ever, much has happened to shift the emphasis to Macedonia as a more 'self-confident', independent and multicultural nation. The answer to the question asked above seems to be a qualified 'yes, it can serve as a model of a sustainable multicultural Balkan country'. In this volume we advance to the second step, examining the reasons for the 'qualified yes' above and the problems related to creating a successful state.

We start with Macedonia as a nation whose independence and nationality are still often magnets that draw the focus of researchers and heated discussions. However, instead of discussion on the construction of the nation-state as we find in Cowan (2000) and earlier works on Macedonia (Brown 2003; Thiessen 2007; Rossos 2008), here the focus is more on real people who have to deal with pollution, economic struggles, and the 'tangentiality' between their lives and those of relevant others – Western Europeans, other ethnicities, the employed, polluters, and the opposite sex among others. Also, many of the authors in this volume look at how Macedonia is becoming part of a larger whole – i.e. the European Union – and how it deals with the realities that modernity brings. Further, instead of discussing other ethnicities in the abstract, many of the chapters in this volume deal with minority ethnicities in the concrete. Thus, it is not only their relationship to the Macedonian majority that is important, but also how they forge intra-community links in terms of their own unique history, economic and political and socio-cultural conditions.

When one reads about all the differences within Macedonia, and the nation's attempt to articulate a nationalistic dialogue with Western Europe as well as its neighbours (Brown 2003; Cowan 2000; Thiessen 2007), we acquire a much more subtle picture of multi-ethnic Macedonia than had previously been developed. It is no longer just the question of whether these different ethnic groups can live together in one nation. The volume aspires, just as the people of Macedonia, to better understand varied and multilayered relationships between the different relevant groups within national boundaries and to understand both how they work together and what separates them.

The theoretical mélange of anthropology has often been taken to indicate fragmentation and intellectual schisms. Perhaps this assessment is correct; on the other hand, when the common focus of our discipline is members of a culture or groups of cultures, we are not talking about rocks or animals governed by instinctive and predictable mechanisms that can be fully represented by a single paradigm. Instead, our focus is on a rational-irrational, logical–emotional creature that reflects on him/her self and who, without an *a priori* collective blueprint much less a plan, collectively constructs socio-cultural systems. Further, these systems emerge from the dynamic intersection of environmental forces, contacts with other cultures, linkages to supra-cultural regional or world systems, the effects of its own subsystems on each other, and the actions of unique individuals.

Such an ambitious discipline requires many theories and methods to capture even a momentary speck of this moveable, local–global feast. In this sense, we believe this work is true to the goals and nature(s) of anthropology. The contributors to this volume are collectively exploring the question of cultural identity and its ramifications for constructing a cohesive functional multicultural nation. Can groups who claim distinct cultural identities and heritages coexist as one nation – here primarily Macedonians, Albanians, Roma and Turks? Alternatively, can groups who claim overlapping cultural heritages but trace distinctly different identities (i.e. Macedonia and Greece) coexist peacefully? Is the Balkanization of cultures a Frankensteinian mistake leading to chronic misunderstandings, conflicts and warfare, or is there a solution by which Balkanization can become a source of multicultural strength? Macedonia seems to be a test case for the rest of the Balkans. From this perspective, this volume serves as an updated assessment of how Macedonia is doing.

Each chapter is a report on the nature of Macedonian culture(s) in action. The method predominantly relied on by the authors is that of participant observation. Ilka Thiessen, Anastasia Karakasidou, and Jonathan Schwartz write eloquently of the strength of this method. Underlying participant observation is the recognition that the informants, the people we are studying, make meaning and are the experts on what happens in their society. The participant observer follows their lead, eavesdropping, so to speak, 'among the natives'. The concern with our informants' experiences and how they understand their experiences links us to Cowan (2000), where the people in their inflected variety were the subject of study.

We continue with the theme of multiculturalism but instead of the focus being solely on Albanians and Greeks, we have two chapters on the Roma, one on Turks, one on gender, and one that focuses on Aegean Macedonians not only as a minority in Greece, but as local activists for environmental reform. In addition to questions of ethnicity, Karakasidou and Schwartz examine environmental issues in two chapters, and Victor de Munck and Davorin Trpeski explore constructions of Macedonian gender in another. The authors range in theoretical approach from an objective/scientific mode of analysis to historical, ethnographic, historical materialist/Marxist, and interpretivist/postmodern approaches. In this sense, we can say that this volume is inflected in practice as well as theory.

The 'Greek problem' remains an important one, but rather than a subject that dominates as it did in earlier approaches, we have just two chapters that vividly deal with this problem – the opening paper by Victor Friedman, and the chapter by Karakasidou on 'Greek Macedonians'. However, these two chapters are thematically more 'contemporary' and distinct from the earlier Greek-Macedonian papers. Friedman explores a group of Greek nationalist thugs who broke into a meeting celebrating the publication of a Macedonian-Greek dictionary and who threatened the author and other participants. His vivid description and comparative reflections on Greek and Macedonian nationalism show how far Macedonia has come in becoming a relative beacon of multiculturalism and democracy in the Balkans. Karakasidou remembers how, as a young student, she was caught up in the popular concern with nationalism; in reviewing her ethnographic notebooks, she noticed that a hitherto neglected textual vein of pollution, water shortages and sickness was also present. She praises the ethnographic method (i.e. participant observation) as a means of detecting what is important to 'the natives' as well as to the anthropologist; in so doing, she portrays the twin pull on almost all field anthropologists of academic fashion and the impulse to

INTRODUCTION 5

advocate for the people whose lives and homes you enter while doing fieldwork.

Taking on the role of interlocutors we discuss the chapters in this volume in order to find common themes, angles of interpretation, antiphonies between authors and, metaphorically, to point out some of the jewels that shine through these pages. We hope that this long look provides a means to recognize connections between individual papers and to view the volume as a whole.

Karakasidou writes about Macedonian Greeks and the problems encountered by environmental degradation due largely to modernization. The problems she poses don't have borders in today's world. The responses by locals to political and technological manipulations of nature that threaten their health and welfare provides a window to our own locales and, consequently, to the global 'us' as well. We begin here, though her chapter is one of the last chapters, because it is her epiphany and turn from nationalism to environmental pollution that signals both the difference and continuity between this and earlier approaches to Macedonia. She tells a story of environmental pollution in the village Mavrorahi, a 'depopulated' Macedonian Greek village initially populated by refugees from the Pontos region (now northeastern Turkey) in the 1920s. Water issues have been at the centre of environmental issues; it has both been scarce where it had been plentiful, and it has been contaminated on a far-reaching scale. During her fieldwork from 1988 to 1990, her focus had been on nationalism and how the power of the Greek nation-state radiated out from the centres to the margins in order to create both a homogeneous nationality and a uniform recognition of the power of the state. A turn in her ethnographic reading of her material and experiences occurred in the late 1990s when she returned and became cognizant of information on pollution in water, air and earth, and how many of her friends and most important informants had died of various cancers between 1990 and 1997. There was a self-epiphany when she recognized that while her gaze had been on the nation-states' production of hegemony, just out of the corner of her eye she had noticed and recorded residents' concerns with pollution. In retrospect, Karakasidou realized that, in her research on the nation-state, there was a subtext that she had not paid enough attention to at the time. In rereading her ethnographic notes, she shifted her more recent work towards the subject that also and perhaps more directly impacts on the life of all Greeks, regardless of ethnicity – pollution and environmental degradation.

Davorin Trpeski provides examples of how the cultural elite assist the state in producing a cultural heritage by which the people of a nation can espouse their common ancestry and their uniqueness. His chapter is one of the few in this volume that directly tackles the question of nation-making with reference to the 'Macedonian question'. Loring Danforth framed the issue as well as anyone when he wrote:

> From an anthropological perspective the Macedonian Question in its current form can be seen as a conflict between two opposing nationalist ideologies, both of which reify nations, national cultures and national identities; project them far back into the past; and treat them as eternal, natural and immutable essences. The anthropology of nationalism must dereify the nation; it must deconstruct national cultures and identities. These tasks can be accomplished by analyzing the process of nation formation, the process by which nations, national cultures and national identities are constantly constructed and reconstructed from pre-existing cultural forms (1993: 7).

In Trpeski's analysis, the reifying of nationalism is done wryly. His analysis seems to rely on a surrealistic trope, or style of argumentation, that does not directly criticize. Rather, it introduces us to the claims of those who espouse the purity of Macedonian identity until these fantastic creations shatter, like oversized sculptures, under their own weight. He presents arguments that become, for the rational reader who is not fervently seeking ethnic purity, ever more unbelievable.

Trpeski and Karakasidou seek to de-reify the inherent mystification of nationalism and power by relying on archival and ethnographic material to offer an ironic depiction of this venture as it swings, sometimes, between verity and absurdity. Both provide paradigms, though of a different nature. Trpeski remains more true to the theoretical recipe of nationalism as 'essentialized ethnicity' offering a two-course meal that ultimately leads the reader to question the relationship between rationality and irrationality in 'nation-making'. Karakasidou shunts nation-making aside in favour of her ethnographic sensibility to listen to what her informants have to say about their lives rather than what she wants to hear about nation-making. The difference is not only one of varying interests but also, I believe, one of time depth in that Karakasidou's work covers more than 20 years of participant observation in the field from the early 1980s to 2010.

Her reflections on nationalism are ironic because she comes to recognize that nationalism is a project of people other than a single villager or a group of townspeople of Greece. While individuals may focus, some of the time, on the grandeur or authenticity of their heritage, the majority of working-class individuals, most of the time, are concerned with their health, their crops and herds, where the water went, and why medical wastes are now being dumped in their backyard. Nationalism, as Trpeski and Karakasidou show, is the work of the cultural elite, academics and politicians; how people accept these productions is more problematic.

Ilka Thiessen's account is similar to those above; like Karakasidou, she has been visiting her main field site, Skopje, and her informants who are female electrical engineers for over a decade. She is a veteran of the ethnographic venture and is at home in Skopje with her informants (most of whom are also her friends). She uses some of her cultural capital in her paper by making an argument that the Macedonians are no longer 'waiting' either for themselves or for Europe but are 'making' Macedonia European or Europe Macedonian on their own. The key conceptual lever she uses is 'tangentiality' – a polyvalent term that she uses much the same as Cowan and Keith Brown use 'inflected'. Tangentiality refers to 'all things that are perpendicular to unity'. An example of this is the way the West associates Macedonia with war, crime and chaos, which inevitably leads to 'micro-' and 'macro-security concerns' by the West and Westerner, and which are 'insulting' to her informants.

Her chapter is a broad-ranging discussion of numerous tangentialities, contrasts or oppositions, things perpendicular to each other and hindering a presumed unity. Some she discusses are: (1) how Europe sees the Macedonian borders as areas rife with extortion and other crimes; (2) that the EU seems to have an 'Anglo-Saxon' model rather than a socialist model planned for Macedonia, yet the Macedonians she has interviewed favour a 'Swedish/German' sort of socialism and democracy; (3) by extension, she suggests that many Macedonians reject the 'post socialist' label placed on them, preferring socialism to a US style Darwinian capitalism; (4) offering a unique interpretation of the millennium cross overlooking Skopje as a cynical symbol of Macedonia's desire to join the (Christian) European club, rather than a seemingly singular religious symbol; (6) illustrating that Macedonians are better exemplars than Europeans of the Western image of female beauty as slender and elegantly dressed fashion models. In all these ways, Macedonians are at 'right angles' to the West. As we follow Thiessen, we note that she points to a reduction if not dissolution of aggression between Albanians and Macedonians, with both redirecting their hostilities towards Western Europe. She is not denying ethnic tensions but seems to be asserting that both Albanians and Macedonians have as their geopolitical and socio-cultural focus Europe and not each other. Thiessen suggests that the people of Macedonia are more concerned with how Macedonia fits into Europe and not with how it fits together as one nation.

Violeta Schubert's ethnographic eye focuses on the Orthodox Church as it helps shape national identity. While many authors note the importance of the Orthodox Church in Macedonia, there have been few articles looking at it specifically and it is typically not a subject of ethnographic study on Macedonia by foreign researchers. Fortunately, this major omission is redressed by Schubert's highly knowledgeable analysis of the history and contemporary role of the Church in Macedonia. She shows us how the Church retains its place in the hearts and minds of Macedonians. Her chapter traces the history of the Macedonian Church from the time of the brothers and priests Cyril and Methodius, who translated the Bible into Old Slavic by creating a Slavic writing system between AD 863 and 869. They were also responsible for the emergence of an independent Slavic Orthodox Church. Like Trpeski, Schubert provides a historically descriptive analysis of nationalism focusing on how religion, language and ethnic identity combine to make a potent recipe for nationalism. Unlike Trpeski's contemporary revisionist accounts, Schubert's descriptions of these linkages are generally acknowledged and accepted and show how history serves as a rich reservoir for the construction of nationalist ideology. She examines the mechanisms by which such concepts are tied together to promote a nationalist ideology. For instance, she describes how the separation of language was used first as a means to create a Slavic identity in the Balkans. It was then used to tie language to an orthodox religion in which Greek, the Church language, was replaced with Slavic and thus the Slavic Church separated from the Greek. One can see the same strategy at work when the Macedonian Church was separated from the Serbian Church, so that rather than being marginal members of a wider Serbian identity, Macedonians could feel a 'subjective sense of belonging' to their own orthodox tradition (Borowik 2006: 275).

Schubert views modernity through the eyes of villagers in a small town outside Bitola within the context of Church, family and tradition. Modernity has two key loci: the first is the 'insipid means by which the young seek to find their place in it'; the second, an entailment of this 'insipidness', is the somewhat timid, but nonetheless 'radical', redefining of the moral authority of Church, family and kinship. Modernity is not a matter of consumption, accessing Europe, nor the penetration of power regimes into the environment, health and everyday lives of people. It is rather an undermining of the 'traditional' social order by putting the self first. In the rural region where Schubert worked there were 'too many men' living with their anxious mothers. The younger women migrated to cities or emigrated. This is in part a result of traditional inheritance practices, whereby the land and family wealth go to the sons who stay home after marriage while the daughters move to their husband's homestead. While this inheritance practice is no longer legal, families still find ways for daughters to relinquish their inheritance rights. It is also easier for daughters to find jobs or spouses in the cities or abroad, whereas sons earn their income from the family land or business. With the chronically high unemployment rate in Macedonia hovering between 30 and 40 per cent over the last decade, there are few economic incentives for the sons to leave. While 'tradition' and the absence of jobs in the city may keep sons at home, modernity tempts them to the unencumbered life and a rejection of marriage, family, and Church as part of the 'natural order of things' that shapes their lives. Schubert views modernity as a counterpoint to the traditional order. However, rather than reifying and establishing a dichotomy between them, she describes existing tensions within the everyday lives of Macedonians as they seek to accommodate both the values of the Orthodox Church and modernity.

Friedman's chapter was sparked when he spoke at a meeting in Athens promoting a Macedonian-Greek dictionary authored by Vasko Karadža, a Greek author and translator who died in 2003. During the meeting, Greek nationalist thugs interrupted Dr. Friedman's speech, threatening violence, and verbally abused the crowd and then left before the police arrived. His chapter vividly describes the moment, its historical background and its aftermath in the United States. In the process Dr. Friedman, the world's foremost authority on Balkan languages (especially Macedonian), provides a pithy and scholarly historical depiction of why the Macedonian language (*Makedonski*) and people (*Makedonci*) are historically distinct from Bulgarians and Serbians. He provides historical evidence to show that, prior to the 1960s, Bulgarians considered Macedonian to be a language distinct from Bulgarian, and then, for nationalistic reasons, Bulgarians reversed course and claimed that Macedonian was a dialect of Bulgarian. Additionally, he provides evidence that *Makedonci* perceived themselves as a distinct people and language in the nineteenth century and that neither were, as some have claimed, 'Tito's invention'.

Friedman uses the concept of 'erasure' for analysing the more recent claims that question the historical distinctiveness of the Macedonian language and national identity and that call for the erasure of Macedonian as well as other minority identities in Greece. Greek national policies avow a one nation, one language, one ethnicity state. The Macedonian-Greek dictionary denies the singular ('uninflected') claim by recognizing a Macedonian linguistic, if not ethnic, minority within the territory of the Greek nation. Activities by individuals such as those Friedman and his colleagues encountered are a product of the 'one nation' espousal. Friedman notes how ironic it is that France and Greece have refused to ratify the European Charter on Minority and Regional Languages, thus implicitly averring that there are no ethnolinguistic minorities but only French and Greek speakers who are citizens of their respective countries. He goes on to write that, among the Balkan countries, only the Republic of Macedonia 'preserves the kind of nineteenth century multilingualism that underlies modern ideas of multiculturalism'.

The strains between Greece and Macedonia, the focus of Friedman's chapter and important to Karakasidou's narrative, should be understood not only with regard to the dispute over the name but also over language and human rights issues regarding the Macedonian Greeks. The Republic of Macedonia certainly is no threat to Greece (or, for that matter, Bulgaria) nor is there any intention by the Republic to extend its territories to its former size. Nonetheless, for Greece and Bulgaria to proclaim a 'one nation–one ethnicity–one language' model requires the 'erasure' of the historical and present-day reality of a Slavic Macedonian population, as well as other minority populations, within its borders.

The Macedonian state, its culture and people are not controversial; the people of Macedonia are, like most citizens of most nation-states, simply trying to make a living in difficult times. There should no longer be a question over who the Macedonians are or what they are waiting for. We take as given the presence of the nation-state and its inhabitants. This is not to say that there are not internal problems and ethno-nationalist responses within the Republic of Macedonia towards its own minorities. In fact internal problems, particularly those related to minority groups, are the focus of study by most of this book's contributors. However, while the editors cannot speak for all the authors, we see these problems within the context of Macedonia as a nation-state, much as one would see internal ethno-nationalist problems within any other nation-state.

Finally, much to the credit of the Republic of Macedonia–with all its flaws and problems of corruption, economic inequalities, undocumented inhabitants (mostly Roma and Albanian refugees from Kosovo), environmental problems, and chronically high unemployment rates–it must be noted that during both recent Bosnian and Kosovo wars Macedonia opened its borders to thousands of refugees. Further, in the Macedonian Constitution, Macedonia is recognized as an ethnically pluralistic country that, particularly after the Ohrid Framework in 2000, has worked hard to implement affirmative action policies to benefit minorities. Shyana Plaut and Burcu Ellis take some exception to this statement by noting that the government's attention is focused on the Albanian minority to the neglect of Turks and the Roma.

An interesting perspective on Macedonian problems of multiculturalism and conflicts between its ethnic groups is presented by Ellis. She makes the point that the Turks are under-represented and identified either with the Ottomans as historical villains or as a 'docile third leg of international relations'. She mentions the continuing diffusion of Turkish customs, foods, and especially popular culture into Macedonian and particularly Albanian cultural patterns. Thus, despite the 'invisibility' of the Turkish community, Turkey itself is not invisible and in fact is perceived to be a loyal ally of Macedonia.

Ellis writes that the most important impact on Turks in Macedonia was the policy of free migration back to Turkey that started in 1953. Apparently this was part of a Yugoslavian view that nationalism also meant that people would prefer to reside in 'their ethnic homelands'. Between 1953 and 1968 approximately 200,000 people (not all ethnic Turks) migrated under this policy (Ellis citing Kirisci 1996). The mass migrations left the Turks who remained in Macedonia 'psychologically displaced'.

Ellis points out that, ironically, because of the results of affirmative action policies and quota systems, ethnic minorities find themselves in competition with each other. Not unlike India's affirmative action policies designed to redress historically embedded structural inequalities against *Dalits* (untouchables), ethnicity ironically increases in socio-economic saliency as a very result of the government's success in dealing with past wrongs. Further, she argues that, in practice, the Ohrid framework targeted Albanians while other minorities with less than 5 per cent of the Macedonian population are neglected and marginalized.

To Turks, particularly those who immigrated back to Turkey, Macedonia is thought of as a 'lover lost' (Ellis). While Ellis muses about the invisibility of the Turks, she also writes about the important political and economic support Turkey has provided Macedonia and how 'things-Turkey' are generally associated with high culture and considered desirable. In particular, Macedonian Turks have opened about 40 NGOs to tap into Turkish funding for aid on issues such as women's education, inheritance, poverty, diet, developmental projects and so forth.

In a positive sense, the Turkish homeland serves as a gateway to power, goods, educational and economic opportunities. In a negative sense, Turkey serves as a locus that leads to a pervasive sense of psychological displacement for Macedonian Turks as they identify with a homeland that is neither theirs (i.e. Turkey) nor extant (the days of the Ottoman Empire). She suggests that, through the new activism buttressed by the close political and economic ties between Turkey and Macedonia, a new identity may emerge rooted in the Balkan homeland and not in Turkey. However, she notes that this will most likely happen only when ethnicity ceases to be the axis along which the salient social, economic and political divisions are demarcated.

The Roma (or Romani) are another important minority in Macedonia. Census figures place them below the Turkish community in numbers; this is, frankly, impossible to believe. It may well be that many of the Roma define themselves as 'Albanians' or 'Turks' to escape the stigma identified with being Romani or to obtain benefits that may come with being Albanian or Turk. Even taking these numbers into account, there are many thousands of undocumented Romani and, as Plaut mentions, estimates of their population vary wildly from a low of 60,000 to a high of 200,000.

Plaut's chapter is intriguing and similar to Ellis' study of Turks in that both rely on historical as well as ethnographic data, and both point out that there is a deep gulf between the multicultural proclamations of the state and its practice. Plaut's analysis is much more critical, largely because the Roma in Macedonia are not the remnants of a dominant colonizing population, but of an ethnic group that has historically been the most stigmatized in Europe.

The problem of improving the situation of the Roma, as Dimova, de Munck and Moldow show, is compounded by the failure of the government to help create a growing and stable economy. Plaut suggests that the government substitutes bold statements, conference meetings, generous symbolic gestures, and support for a plethora of social research to fill the vacuum left in the absence of a robust economy. Gestures of exaggerated concern such as academic conferences and reports are used as substitutes for real internal economic and educational assistance. Few seem to notice, since foreign NGOs and other aid agencies fill part of the gap between word and deed. Plaut, who has conducted ethnographic and archival research with the Roma and NGOs and has experience with Macedonian government projects, digs a bit deeper. She suggests that the attention of foreign governments on Macedonia and on the Roma has led to a tendency by the Macedonian government to expect that others (foreign NGOs and governments) will do their work for them. Some might even suggest that this borders on a dependency on outside intervention. The government's enthusiastic building of symbolic bridges to reach out to the Roma has led to 'smoke and mirror' development. Plaut's chapter is a Jonathan Swift-like indictment of the government's feigned interest in improving the lot of the Roma. She concludes by arguing that there should be greater activism from the Roma, and there should be both internal and external pressures to hold the state accountable for providing its citizens with basic human rights.

Plaut's and Galina Oustinova-Stjepanovic's chapters on the Roma are as different as night and day. While one speaks of the issues that affect most Romani – poverty, marginalization, lack of educational opportunities, unemployment and domestic violence, the other looks at Romani Sufis as 'failed mystics'. Here, we have sedentary, urban Romani seeking to follow in the Turkish Sufi tradition of the local *tekkes* (or Sufi lodges) led by a *shaykh* (a *pir* or leader-teacher). The story that Oustinova-Stjepanovic tells is a remarkable one for all its wealth of backstage ethnographic material, the kind of thick description that brings the hopes, dreams and pathos of the Roma families and members of the *tekke* into your own mind's eye and sensibility.

Oustinova-Stjepanovic begins with a rich history of Gypsies (the term she uses instead of Roma) in Macedonia/Yugoslavia. Her story swims, so to speak, in the same river of history as Ellis, where the main occupants and head of the tekke she is studying were originally Turks, most of whom, in the 1950s, immigrated to Turkey. The vacuum they left was quickly filled by Gypsies who took over both as dervishes and as the *shaykh*, or leader, who founded the current line of shaykhs. The current shaykh, Mehmed, is the third in the tekke's line of succession. Shaykh Mehmed saw theological learning and education to be a road to modernity and to the empowerment of not only the dervish families but to the 'Roma nation'.

Oustinova-Stjepanovic's ability to be included in what is an exclusively male space and activity, the tekke and dervish rituals and practices, is impressive. Victor de Munck tried for months to participate in tekke rituals without success, even as he regularly accompanied a barber on circumcision rites to Romani houses that included tekke members. Oustinova-Stjepanovic adds to the work of Ellis, Plaut, Trpeski, and Karakasidou with her ethnographic examples and insights. Within the mystic context she touches on a variety of themes discussed by other contributors such as cultural heritage, the continuity of traditions, becoming modern, education, erasing minority status, political activism and nation-building.

Rozita Dimova's work, influenced by the writings of Walter Benjamin, concerns the historical use of space and architecture as they mark not heroes and famous historical events to be commemorated, but what is left 'unsaid' – ideological conflicts inscribed in the spaces and architecture, which she reads to reveal tensions, exploitation and coercion. Her eyes are trained to read space and buildings in historical time and to read the lives that are etched in and inhabit those spaces, both then and now. Her analysis is reminiscent of Ismail Kadare's (2005) novel, *The Three-Arched Bridge*, a story narrated by a monk about a bridge that was being built in the fourteenth century. The bridge builder's efforts are sabotaged each night, it seems, by the river naiads. The town's people and traders who contracted him are anxious for him to complete his mission. Finally, a sacrificial man is plastered into the masonry and the bridge holds. For both Dimova and Kadare, there is a merging of history, architecture and the unsaid anxieties of ordinary folk.

Dimova recounts the rich multicultural history of Kumanovo, which was first a village, then a Turkish town. After the Turks left, the Albanians moved in, and then waves of Macedonians came around the turn of the twentieth century, so that now approximately 60 per cent of the town's residents are of Macedonian ethnicity. As roads and train routes were built, the city became a thriving manufacturing centre attracting entrepreneurs from different countries (including Greeks and Serbians), regions, ethnic groups and families that were marked by particular specialties (e.g. cheese makers, butchers, label makers, etc.). As a result of this dynamic history, the spaces of Kumanovo have been and still are 'literal and symbolic battlefields' where ideologies and the people who uphold or are resigned to them have been in 'constant struggle'. Among these conflicting elements Dimova cites Islam and Christianity, capitalism, socialism and late capitalism. She writes about these struggles from a historical-materialist perspective, pointing out, in tour-guide fashion, different buildings and spaces and exposing their unsaid meanings.

She concludes that the contemporary nationalist discourse, both by Albanians and Macedonians, is 'that Macedonians live on one side of the main street, Albanians on the other, or Roma people live in the ghetto near the small river'. Yet she finds this discourse of difference to be 'imaginary' because members of both groups, when they can build and furnish their houses and cafes in the same ostentatious ways, live in mixed neighbourhoods and share similar imaginary but inverted nationalist discourses of each other. She notes that class underlies much of the mutually accusatory ethnic narratives, and again, this is inscribed in the unplanned parts of the city that all people, regardless of ethnicity, characterize as 'wild' and 'uncivilized' or 'dangerous', yet each ascribe to the other.

Victor de Munck and Joseph Moldow come to similar conclusions as Dimova though by a far different route. Indeed they start their chapter with a quote from an Albanian unemployed taxi driver sitting in the *Bit Pazar* (a large bazaar in Skopje) who points out that 'this side of the river' (meaning the Albanian side) is 'Africa' and 'that side is Europe'. In fact his claim is wrong or, as Rozita might write 'imaginary', for on 'this side' also live Turks, Romani and many Macedonians, just as they do on the other side. Nevertheless, the visible public spaces in Skopje immediately on the other side of the *Kamen Most* (stone bridge) that 'unites' the two sides are marked as Modern, European and Macedonian on one side and Ottoman, Muslim, Albanian and Turkish on the other. Without recourse to Benjamin's theoretical framework or Dimova's historical material eye, de Munck and Moldow describe the distinctions in spatial features of the two sides of the Vardar River including the obligatory assignment of Christian domination as singularly signified by the Millennium Cross overlooking Skopje (see Photo 2; de Munck and Moldow). Yet their chapter is not about space but about perception. Unlike the other authors of this work, de Munck and Moldow rely on a positivist position in which surveys and semi-structured interviews are taken at face value and their aggregate patterns are analysed through statistical procedures. The import of this study, as well as that of de Munck and Trpeski's study on gender, is that scientific methods can also be applied successfully to the ethnographic/anthropological enterprise, as they reveal non-obvious cultural patterns.

The study on Albanian-Macedonian perceptions of each other utilizes four free-association lists in which four different samples of Albanians and Macedonians are asked to list characteristics they identify with their own ethnicity. Then they are asked to list those characteristics that they associate with the other ethnicity. The results of these tasks provide rich fodder for interpreting how Albanians and Macedonians characterize themselves and each other. De Munck and Moldow use three theoretical concepts to interpret their data. First they rely on a zero-sum game analysis of the data – identified with George Foster's (1965) 'image of the limited good' in anthropology; second they use an ecological fallacy approach – which is based on people assuming that the character of an individual mirrors group characteristics; third they use relative deprivation, which refers to individuals expecting more than they receive and therefore directing their wrath towards a scapegoat responsible for this injustice.

The authors suggest that interethnic hostilities are not a product of historical events or cultural factors – even though the rationale, expressive content and narratives each invokes against the other and uses to construct a self-image are shaped by culture and history. Instead, de Munck and Moldow argue that hostilities and tensions between Albanians and Macedonians are a result of the confluence of three theoretical elements: a zero-sum image of limited if not constant resources (which in fact is the situation in Macedonia); the psychological mechanism of the ecological fallacy by which any real or imagined misbehaviours and undeserved fortunes which befall a member of the other group are generalized to the entire group; relative deprivation – the conceptualized distance between what one expects should be one's position in life versus one's actual standing in life.

This theoretical framework is used to describe the negative profiles each group constructs of the other. More importantly, they further argue that this implies that cultural sensitivity-driven educational or practical programmes will be ineffective at ameliorating interethnic tension. Instead, they argue that only a clearly merit-based means for hiring, with equal access to resources by all groups and a growing economy, can resolve interethnic tensions. Their argument explores some of the underlying conditions that foster ethnic divisiveness rather than the nationalistic discourses that express those divisions.

Jonathan Schwartz went to the Lake Prespa region for the first time in 1977 and has returned 16 times, the last being in 2010. Over this period, he has witnessed both a drop in water elevation of the lake and a decline in the quality of the water. He supported his impressionistic observations with data: according to a 2009 UNDP report, the water had receded 7.1 meters since 1975, and water quality likewise has declined. The purpose of his chapter is to find out why. The lake borders Greece, Macedonia and Albania. Greek farmers grow 'prespa' bean plants in the area of the lake and Macedonians grow apples exclusively. Both sides consume massive quantities of water for irrigating their crops and, as one would expect, blame each other for excessive use of water. Schwartz, like Karakasidou, praises the potential for anthropologists to act as both researcher and activist, particularly through engagement with local NGOs. In 1995, he set out to investigate whether the Soros Open Society or any other NGOs had conducted any work or made their presence felt in the Prespa region, and they were not to be found.

Schwartz and Karakasidou are kindred spirits not only in that their research experiences have led them to look at environmental issues and to advocate for NGOs as well as local residents, but both narratives show the wisdom gained from working in the same region for over 20 years. Going to a new place requires exerting all that initial energy again each time. Indeed, many of the researchers here show that there is a huge advantage in 'coming home' to a familiar region, knowing the territory, people and places. One's work expands beyond the task at hand because one can listen to what people said in the past and thread it with what people say in the present. It is through this greater depth that we can follow Schwartz's affable account of how he solved, in part, the answer to his question. He was able to find out about NGOs through a local radio DJ, and talk with local farmers and schoolchildren about a new farming technique of watering called 'drop by drop'. His account, in the end, is optimistic as he informs us that economic realities, local issues, the beginnings of eco-tourism, new technologies for watering orchards, and the input of NGOs have all led to a recent increase in the Lake Prespa water table.

Summary

Like Plaut, Oustinova-Stjepanovic conducted her research with the Roma, though she uses the term 'Gypsies'. The two studies encompass, in a sense, the range of studies that are possible in anthropology and more generally the social sciences. To this we add Friedman's work on nationality and language, which provides a case study lesson in how words bringing people together are indeed mightier than fists propelling them apart.

Schubert's historical account of splintered Orthodoxy in the Balkans and Macedonia shows how combining modernity with the sacred yields the profane quandary of 'too many men'. Dimova's historical-material analysis of the inscriptions of power via ethnicity on spaces, artefacts and architecture informs us that the material world does not so much dissimulate as reveal the mechanisms of power for those trained to see them. Trpeski describes how cultural heritage is constructed through a reactive nationalism materialized largely through neighbourly hostilities. Karakasidou's 20-year embrace of a town and village in northern

Greece leads to a multilayered account of nationalism, modernity, the environment, and cancer. The casual intimate scope of Schwartz's return to Lake Prespa allows us to eavesdrop on his investigations into the sources of water pollution and reasons for the drop in the lake's water level. Thiessen creates a zen koan, finding Europeanness in Macedonia and its reverse, Macedonianness in Europe. In so doings, she de-essentializes them both, leaving people making themselves into their own images with the symbolic and material productions of the other. The systematic survey-driven reports by de Munck and Trpeski on Macedonian conceptions of gender, or the former's co-authored piece with Moldow on Albanian and Macedonian conceptions of each other, show that there is room for a scientific account of cultural dynamics. In this volume we find the massive breadth and depth of the anthropological endeavour, recalling with a Cheshire cat smile the truth of Eric Wolf's remark that anthropology is the most scientific of the humanities and the most humanistic of the sciences.[2]

Notes

1. This is a modification of Stanley Tambiah's (1986) use of the phrase 'ethnic fratricide'.
2. Though not all the writers are anthropologists, all relied on the anthropological method of first-hand experience, intimate encounters, and a privileging of the 'native's' account over the expert's without diminishing either.

References

Borowik, I. 2006. 'Orthodoxy confronting the collapse of communism in post-soviet countries'. *Social Compass.* vol. 53, no. 2, pp. 267–78.

Brown, Keith 2003. *The Past in Question: Modern Macedonia and the Uncertainties of Nation.* Princeton: Princeton University Press.

Cowan, Jane (ed.) 2000. *Macedonia: The Politics of Identity and Difference.* London: Pluto Press.

Cowan, Jane and Keith Brown 2000. 'Introduction: Macedonian inflections'. In *Macedonia: The Politics of Identity and Difference,* Jane Cowan (ed.) (pp. 1–27). London: Pluto Press.

Danforth, Loring M. 1993. 'Claims to Macedonian Identity: the Macedonian Question and the Breakup of Yugoslavia'. *Anthropology Today* (9): 3–10.

Ellis, Burcu 2003. *Shadow Genealogies: Memory and Identity Among Urban Muslims in Macedonia*. Boulder: East European Monographs, Columbia University Press.

Foster, George M. 1965. 'Peasant Society and the Image of Limited Good'. *American Anthropologist*, V 67(2): 293–315.

Kadare, Ismail 2000. *Elegy for Kosova: Stories*. New York: Arcade Publishing.

——. 2005. *The Three-Arched Bridge*. New York: Arcade Publishing.

Kirisci, Kemal 1996. 'Refugees of Turkish Origin: Coerced Immigrants to Turkey since 1945'. *International Migration* 34(3): 385–412.

Rossos, Andrew 2008. *Macedonia and the Macedonians: A History*. Stanford, CA: Hoover Institution Press.

Tambia, Stanley J. 1986. *Sri Lanka: Ethnic Fratricide and the Dismantling of Democracy*. Chicago: University of Chicago Press.

Thiessen, Ilka 2007. *Waiting for the Macedonia: Identity in a Changing World*. Peterborough, On: Broadview Press.

Working Group of Minority Issues 2004. 'Shadow Report on Minority Issues', Skopje, Macedonia.

1

A TANTRUM FROM THE CRADLE OF DEMOCRACY: ON THE DANGERS OF STUDYING MACEDONIAN

Victor A. Friedman

İt ürür, kervan yürür. 'The dog barks, the caravan goes on.'
— Turkish proverb

Introduction[1]

When I was a first-year graduate student in Slavic linguistics at the University of Chicago in 1971 and one of my professors, Zbigniew Gołąb, asked me if I would like to go to Macedonia that summer to study Macedonian (at the Fourth Annual Seminar for Macedonian Language, Literature, and Culture in Ohrid), I happily accepted the suggestion.[2] I had no inkling that 38 years later I would find myself in Greece, assaulted by thugs for speaking about a dictionary of that language written by a man born in Greece.[3] I wish to explore here that violent, anti-Macedonian incident, which occurred in Athens on 2 June 2009. I shall argue that such intimidation proceeds directly from Greece's refusal to uphold the European values for which it receives credit by being known as the 'cradle of democracy'. Moreover, this policy of intimidation is long-standing and is promulgated by Greeks and their allies in the United States. Finally, Greece's intimidation and denial of its ethno-linguistic minorities stands in direct contrast to the situation in the Republic of Macedonia, where the multilingualism so valued by the European Union (EU) is both practised and protected by law.

The Speech

I went to Athens on 2 June 2009 for the book launch of the first Modern Greek-Macedonian Dictionary to be published in Greece (Karaděa 2009). The promotion took place on the main floor of the building of the Foreign Press Association in the city centre. The first part of the promotion proper was presented by Riki van Boeschoeten, a Dutch anthropologist who has been teaching at the University of Thessaly (Volos) for many years. Dimitris Lithoksoou, writer, and Thanasis Parisis, President of the Greek Committee of the European Bureau of Lesser Used Languages (EBLUL), were also on the podium and participated in the book launch. Riki's speech, which applauded the publication of the dictionary and its furthering of Greece's multilingual heritage, alluded to the fact that Greeks have been trying to eliminate other languages in the Balkans for centuries, by citing the same verses in Daniil's *Tetraglosson* (1802) – a quadrilingual manual aimed at Hellenizing European Turkey's Christians – that I have also cited (Friedman 2008b):

> Albanians, Bulgars, Vlachs and all who now do speak
> An alien tongue, rejoice, prepare to make you Greek.
> Change your barbaric tongue, your customs rude forego,
> So that as bygone myths your children may them know.[4]

In a letter/report dated 6 June describing the event Riki wrote:

> This dictionary is a much needed guide for cultural mediation between standard Greek and standard Macedonian. It grew

out of the author's long-standing work as a translator (he has translated major works of Greek literature including Seferis, Ritsos and Kavafis into Macedonian) and his love for the two languages in his life, Greek and Macedonian. Just before his death in 2003, he handed over the material to members of the Rainbow Party with the wish to see his work published in Greece. This last wish was fulfilled this month when the Greek-Macedonian dictionary was printed in Salonica by the Zora press. In his foreword Mr. Karadzas expressed the wish that the dictionary may contribute to a better understanding between the Greek and Macedonian people by improving their linguistic skills.

I reproduce now the exact text of my speech. I do so, since it was in the course of this speech that I was assaulted for reasons alluded to in the speech itself:

The publication in Greece of Vasko Karaděa's Modern Greek-Macedonian dictionary by the publishing house Zora is an important step in the normalization of Greek relations toward one of its own linguistic minorities, and also, we might hope, toward one of its neighboring states, the Republic of Macedonia. Please note that when I refer to the Republic of Macedonia by its constitutional name, the name under which it is recognized by the country of which I am a citizen, the United States of America, I am speaking as a private individual, but one whose views happen to coincide with United States foreign policy in this respect. In so doing, I am exercising the right to free speech that is expected of democratic nations. Unfortunately, in the past, my right to free speech in the Hellenic Republic has been questioned by Greek academics just for mentioning the Macedonian language, as happened at an international conference in Thessaloniki in 1994. Let us hope that such days of intolerance are past.

The fact that the promotion of a Modern Greek-Modern Macedonian dictionary is taking place here in Athens has a dual significance. On the one hand, as the capital of the Hellenic Republic, Athens is Greece's most important city. Thus, a promotion in the nation's capital can be presumed to have national significance. On the other hand, the fact that the promotion is taking place here and not in Thessaloniki, where the dictionary was published and which is, in addition to being Greece's second largest city, also the urban center closest to the districts where the majority of Greece's Macedonian-speakers live, means that speakers of Macedonian are less likely to be present.[5] One might even wonder if the City of Thessaloniki would permit such a promotion, since less than three years ago, on September 29, 2006, at the inauguration of Latvian collector Juris Cibuls' exhibition of primers in Thessaloniki, the Deputy Mayor for Culture and Youth of that city ordered the organizers to take the Macedonian primer out of the show case so that it could not be displayed [p.c. Juris Cibuls]. But perhaps times have changed. Let us hope so. The fact that recently Greece is reported to have attempted to ban the name of the Macedonian language from official EU communications, however, leaves me less than optimistic.

The story of this dictionary is a part of the story of Greece's Macedonian-speaking minority. It is a painful story, and one that the majority of Greek citizens are unaware of, owing to the semiotic process that anthropologists Susan Gal and Judith Irvine have identified with the term *erasure* (Gal and Irvine 1995). They define *erasure* as the elimination of differences and complexities for the purpose of some hegemonic process such as, for example, the formation of a nation-state or a standard language. When used in the formation of a standard language, itself often the vehicle of a nation-state, erasure applies to the complexities inherent in differing dialectal systems. When applied to the formation of a nation-state, erasure can refer to the elimination from public view of regional differences, but also, as is the case in the formation of the Greek nation-state, of linguistic minorities. Thus, for example, under the Metaksas dictatorship in Greece in the 1930s, and again in the 1950s after the Greek civil war, even the speaking of Macedonian was banned, and, as described by, among others, anthropologist Anastasia Karakasidou (1997), villagers were made to swear they would no longer speak their native language. My co-promoter Prof. van Boeschoeten has also documented this process in the form of bilingual jokes, in which word plays between Macedonian and Greek are set in the context of Macedonian being a forbidden language (Van Boeschoeten 2006). Greek author Tasos Kōstopoulos (2000) has documented precisely this phenomenon in his book *Ē Apogogeumenē Glōssa* [The forbidden language]. This shameful history of the Hellenic Republic's treatment of its linguistic minorities should be acknowledged and repudiated rather than ignored and forgotten. Perhaps this dictionary will help bring such acknowledgment about.

This brings us to the memorial to Vasko Karaděa by the members of Vinočito which precedes the foreword and the dictionary itself. Vasko Karaděa was born in the village of Dembeni in 1923 in what was then the Greek state, and the village's name was translated into Greek and officially renamed Dendohorion in 1926. Mr. Karaděa left Greece in 1949 as a political emigrant and eventually settled in Skopje, in what was then the Socialist Republic of Macedonia. Although some political emigrants with the same sort of background as Mr. Karaděa's were granted amnesty and allowed to return to Greece in 1982 according to law no. 1266 of that year, the law contained a clause limiting its effect to those who were Greek by *genos* (in Modern Macedonian *rod*). Thus, Mr. Karaděa and other Macedonians and other non-Greeks were forbidden to return to the state in which they were born simply because they were born of non-Greek parents on territory that had become part of the Greek state. In the United States and in the rest of the EU, such a clause is considered racist. The memorial closes with the statement that the dictionary is an answer to the stance of the Greek regime that Macedonian – supposedly – does not exist. Given that the Macedonian language does indeed exist, and that its speakers on what is now Greek territory are documented as referring to it as *makedonski* over a hundred years ago, it is bizarre indeed to meet otherwise well-educated people who cannot accept the existence of this language in Greece as well as beyond its borders.

But let us return for a moment to the process of erasure and how it contributes to the formation of standard languages. Both standard Macedonian and standard Greek, like standard Albanian, standard Bulgarian, standard French, standard English, and virtually all other standard languages, have eliminated or absorbed dialectal differences in order to create these unified standards. The creation of a standard, however, does not necessarily entail the elimination of dialects. Dialects are the repository of the culture and history of their speakers, and – especially in the case of marginal and isolated dialects – of precious information about earlier stages of a language or the possibilities of how a system can change over time. In 2003, the value of dialects was recognized by UNESCO in its Convention for the Safeguarding of Intangible Cultural Heritage, which Greece ratified in 2007. At this point in time, the Macedonian dialects of Greece are moribund. Few fluent speakers are under the age of forty. Moreover, many speakers do not refer to their dialects as Macedonian, which is hardly surprising after so many decades of persecution. Sometimes it is claimed that these are not dialects of Macedonian but rather separate languages. On the one hand, we can note that dialects such as those of Florina and Edhessa in Greece are so close to those of neighboring Bitola and Gevgelija in neighboring Macedonia that calling them separate languages does not have a basis in the linguistic data. On the other hand, if we accept the argument that the Macedonian dialects of Greece are a separate language or separate languages, then their documentation is all the more urgent, since they are on the very brink of extinction.[6] Either way, it is to be hoped that the Greek government will permit linguists to document these dialects before they disappear without the police harassment that, unfortunately, continues to instill fear in speakers and obstruct researchers.[7]

The Tantrum

I was reading my paper in English and Riki was translating into Greek as I read. Just as Riki finished translating, 'documentation is all the more urgent, since they are on the very brink of extinction', about a dozen thugs dressed in black and wearing the kind of huge, round combat helmets that riot police wear burst into the room screaming and yelling.

All but two of them took up positions by the doors so that no one could escape. Two large louts – one bearded, one bald – were screaming at us on the podium and at the audience *'Oli ekso!'* (Everybody out), and *'Prodhotes!'* (Traitors) *'Edo einai Ellada'* (Here is Greece) – cf. the motto that was used on placards banning the speaking of Macedonian and Vlah that were posted all over Greek Macedonia in the 1950s – and shouting various threats and obscenities. They identified themselves as belonging to Hrisi Avgi (Golden Dawn), a Greek fascist political party that has won seats in Greek elections. I decided that if they were going to beat me up I would try to get a picture of it, and pulled out my camera and started snapping. The bearded thug took a swing at me with his combat helmet (photo number 5), but the bald thug stopped him before he could actually bash my head in, which was clearly his intent. Apparently the thugs were under orders to bark but not bite. We did not know this at the time, however. They kept screaming and yelling and making menacing gestures, but did not actually come up onto the podium. One of them screamed at me 'Sign me this book', in English using the intonation that one would use to scream 'I'm going to smash your head in'.

At about this point, one of them then turned the video camera to face the wall (it was recording the event) and then ripped the banner off the podium that had the name of the book in Greek and Macedonian. Another ripped out the wires that the TV cameras were attached to. There were several more minutes of screaming and yelling and crashing, and to those seeing the video which showed only the blank wall, it was unclear whether the thugs were smashing things or people. A friend of mine who saw the video on YouTube, before he knew we were safe, compared the effect to that of the Blair Witch Project. After a few more minutes of abuse and vandalism, the thugs left, taking the display copy of the dictionary with them. (They did not, however, actually destroy it in our presence.) Although we did not know it at the time, the thugs turned left upon leaving the building, and one minute after they were out of sight of a hand-held video camera carried by a spectator, a group of riot police came walking towards the building from the same direction as that taken by the thugs. According to Riki van Boeschoeten's letter:

> Nobody was arrested, but later the commander of the police force told me they had accompanied them to the nearest metro station. [. . .] The attitude of the Greek riot police that night raises serious doubts, to say the least, about their ability to protect academic freedom and freedom of expression, a basic human right guaranteed by the Greek Constitution. It confirms the claims made by serious newspapers, such as Ta Nea, about the close relationships between part of the Greek police force and neo-fascist groups such as the Golden Dawn (see report published by Ta Nea on 17/04/2004).

After a few minutes of discussion, we resumed the promotion and I finished my speech. After it was all over, we stayed in the building for a while not knowing whether it was safe to leave. The riot police also got angry when I photographed them. There was no reaction or coverage in the Greek press, and the US Embassy did not respond to the complaint I lodged.

The Complicity of Scholars in the United States

It was a sufficiently sad commentary on the state of Greek Studies in the United States that when an American member of the Modern Greek Studies Association (MGSA), an organization whose litserv is hosted by the University of California at Irvine, posted one of the videos of the assault, not one Greek member of that organization condemned the actions of the thugs. Instead, on 19 October 2009, the MGSA distributed an ugly and hysterical call encouraging readers to pressure the

University of Utah into cancelling the Seventh Macedonian-North American Conference on Macedonian Studies that was held at the University of Utah on 5–7 November 2009. Although the call did not originate with the MGSA, its unedited and unmoderated distribution by them gave academic support to the barrage of faxes, emails, letters and phone calls that inundated the offices of the Provost and President at Utah demanding that the conference be cancelled. Fortunately, the University stood its ground on principles of academic freedom, and they also provided security to prevent a recurrence of the June incident. Greek members of the fascist organization Stohos came all the way from New Hampshire to disrupt the meeting but were, fortunately, prevented from doing so.[8] Instead, they intimidated one of the participants into not contributing to the conference volume. That participant wrote: 'I am sorry, but I do not intend to publish my presentation. I think that I can NOT change the minds of the Greek nationalists...and can make more enemies...and I still need to have an open door especially to [the names of the places have been omitted to protect the author, VAF].'[9] The entire incident is illustrative of the extent to which American Modern Greek Studies has been compromised and of how the field promotes interests that oppose academic freedom. It also illustrates the extent to which Greek policy attempts to disrupt the normal functioning of Macedonian studies as well as the extent to which Greek academics are complicit with the fascist side of Greek politics.

Why Do They Hate Us?

The title of this section is a quotation from an ethnic Macedonian in 1994 during one of the illegal Greek embargos. The man was a neighbourhood shopkeeper in Skopje. Like many other Macedonians, he liked Greek music, had enjoyed shopping trips to Salonica and had vacationed along the Aegean coast. He was expressing genuine bewilderment at the vehemence of Greece's attacks on Macedonian language, identity and political stability. His attitude was not an isolated one in the Republic of Macedonia at that time. A tiny country with approximately one-fifth the population, one-fifth the area of

Greece and with a military budget that is approximately 1 per cent that of Greece's, what threat could such an entity possibly pose to a member of NATO, the EU, the Eurozone, etc.? There is a Macedonian folk expression *se buni kako Grk u aps*, which can be roughly translated as 'He's protesting noisily like a Greek under arrest,' the implication of which is that the one who is guilty makes the most noise protesting his innocence. In the case of Greek policy towards the Republic of Macedonia, the issue is that Greece does not want to admit the existence of the Macedonian ethno-linguistic minority on its territory, much less the history of the policies of state terror directed at that minority (Rossos 1991, 1994, 1997, 2008). This government policy of denying ethnic identity, and Greece's history of oppressing its Macedonian minority (see Human Rights Watch/Helsinki 1994 & note 8), gives tacit support to political parties like Hrisi Avgi and fascist organizations like Stohos.[10]

Over the last four decades I have published extensively on the structure of the modern Macedonian language's grammar (Friedman 2003a, 2003c, 2002, 1993b, 1977), dialectology (Friedman 2008a, 2008c), and standardization (2004, 2000a, 1998, 1993c, 1989, 1985a). Elsewhere I have also examined the rise of modern Macedonian identity in the nineteenth and early twentieth centuries (Friedman 2008b, 2003a, 2000b, 1999), the politics of the transition from Yugoslav to independent Republic (Friedman 2005, 1996, 1993a), as well as the Macedonian language's relations with both neighbouring non-Slavic and historically related Slavic languages (Friedman 2007, 2004, 2003b, 1995, 1986, 1985b). The following basic facts will suffice for the purposes here. They are amply documented in the aforementioned works as well as in works by other scholars cited there.

The Slavic dialects that gave rise to modern Macedonian are part of a South Slavic continuum that runs more or less contiguously from the Julian Alps to the Black Sea and the Gulf of Salonica. I have discussed the rise of a Macedonian language and identity distinct from Serbian and Bulgarian in detail in the works cited above. Suffice it to say here that these dialects have been spoken for well over a thousand years in part of the territory that was awarded to Greece in 1913 by the Treaty of Bucharest at the end of the Second Balkan War. Prior to

1912–13, the territory had been part of the Ottoman Empire for more than five centuries, although it became the site of overlapping claims and insurgencies (including an autonomist one that rejected Serbian, Greek and Bulgarian claims) in the late nineteenth century. Some of the speakers of the Slavic dialects in the Ottoman vilayets[11] of Selânik, Manastir and Üsküp (Kosova) began referring to their language as *makedonski* (Macedonian) in the nineteenth century, which is when Greek speakers began referring to their language as *ellinika* (Hellenic) after having called it *romaïka* (Roman) for over a thousand years.[12] However, whereas the Greek, Bulgarian and (now former) Serbo-Croatian languages were successfully established during the course of the nineteenth century and underwent various types of elaboration (and in the case of Serbo-Croatian, disintegration) during the twentieth, Macedonian was not allowed to develop officially on any of the territories where it was spoken until 1944.

In 1944 Macedonian was established as the official language of what eventually became the Republic of Macedonia. It was also an official minority language in Bulgaria 1946–48, and it continued to be recognized as distinct by Bulgarian Slavists until at least 1968 (Lekov 1968: 51, 126–27, 168–70). Significantly, in Albania, even after the 1948 Tito-Stalin break, Macedonian continued to be taught as a minority language through grade four among the Macedonian-speaking Christians of southeastern Albania (but not among the Macedonian-speaking Muslims further north). The suppression of Macedonian prior to 1944 has resulted in numerous claims that Macedonian identity (and the language that went with it) was 'invented' by Tito in 1944 (cf. Troebst 1994 vs Friedman 1999).[13] Such claims must willfully erase or discount the published evidence of authors such as Pulevski (1875: 48–49), Misirkov (1903: 132–35) and Upward (1908: 202–06), all of which make it clear that at least some of the speakers of Slavic dialects in what is today both the Republic of Macedonia and Greek Macedonia called their language *makedonski* (Macedonian) and themselves *Makedonci* (Macedonians) well before World War 1.

More recently, additional evidence has come to light of the widespread feeling of a Macedonian identity separate from Serbian,

Bulgarian and Greek during the period before World War 1. As Brown (2010: 824) observes:

> For these journeys [of migrant labor between Macedonia and North America – VAF] left archival traces in which migrants and returnees are recorded in passenger manifests as members of a Macedonian race or people. According to Greek, Bulgarian and Serbian nationalist narratives, then and now, as well as the 'scientific' categories of 'race or people' in use by the Immigration Bureau, this term should not appear. Yet in thousands of records, so regularly that its meaning demands explanation, people emerge from U.S. immigration stations classified as Macedonian, and thereby representing a strikingly concrete challenge to those who deny that such sentiment was even thinkable at the time.

Brown also refers in a footnote to his unpublished paper *'Friction in the archives: Nations and negotiations on Ellis Island* (NY), 1904–10' presented at the Tenth Annual Conference of the Council for European Studies in Chicago in March 1996, but he does not attempt to supply an explanation that he says these records demand.

Sterjovski (2008), however, gives the figure of 8,608 as those declaring themselves Macedonian at Ellis Island between 1897 and 1924, and he supplies some of the names of the passengers and their villages. The overwhelming majority of these Macedonians have clearly Christian Slavic names, e.g. Lazar Konstantinov (Vrbnik), Risto Stojan (Prespa), Stojan Gligor (Šulin). There are also some names that are Aromanian, e.g. Dušis Papaleta (Moskopole), and there is at least one Muslim, Abedin Raman (Trebeništa), in Sterjovski's list, which is only a small fraction of the total. It is possible that some Albanian and Greek speakers were also in the mix. While it is too late to track down any of these individuals and ask them what they were thinking, one thing is completely clear: they knew about the categories 'Greek', 'Bulgarian' and 'Serbian' and, therefore, chose to reject those designations, and they emigrated at a time when we have documentary evidence that Macedonian speakers were trying to articulate an identity that was different from all three of those. At the same time, we have evidence that some people were trying to articulate both an ethnic and a regional sense of Macedonian identity (Pulevski 1875: 49).

Brown (2010: 818) writes that prior to 1990 anthropologists writing on Macedonia 'treated identity issues only in passing'. While this is true, it says more about what anthropologists were (not) aware of, or what their own discipline's interests were, than it does about what was going on in Macedonia from 1944–91. Only five anthropology dissertations in the United States dealt with the Republic of Macedonia, and their themes were music and interpersonal relationships.[14] The dissertations on Greek Macedonia were mostly about folklore and ritual and treated the region as Greece, as the Greek government would have wanted. Moreover, the anthropologists themselves could only conduct their fieldwork in Greek, so there wasn't much about identity questions that they could have explored. Meanwhile, throughout this period Macedonian language and identity were subject to numerous attacks from Greek and Bulgarian academics (Andriotes 1957; BAN 1978). The attacks did not stop at publications. In 1981 at a conference in Sofia, Bulgaria, I was summoned to the office of a Bulgarian colleague who, in kindly tones, threatened me with being declared *persona non grata* in Bulgaria if I continued to write about Bulgarian and Macedonian as separate languages. In 1989, Roland Schmieger, who was doing dialectological research in the village of Nestram (Greek Nestorion), was summoned to the local police station and his tapes were confiscated and destroyed (Šmiger 1998).[15] The examples of such intimidation are legion, but what is striking about them is that they focus on language. It is the Macedonian language that Bulgaria insists is a dialect of Bulgarian, and that Greece insists does not exist at all.[16] Macedonian independence in 1991 raised the stakes with the Republic's new international visibility, and thus precipitated new and more egregious – and, as seen above, also violent – attacks on Macedonian identity, language and scholarship. At their most basic, Greek and Bulgarian attempts to erase or absorb Macedonia and/or Macedonian have an almost unbroken record going back to the nineteenth century.[17]

In certain respects, nineteenth-century thinking remains operative in the twenty-first. At the same time, post-1991 international structures such as the EU have proven remarkably incapable of establishing more modern ideas in its southeastern periphery. It would appear that this is because the models that produced French, Herderian and Greek nationalism – among others – are still operative. It is thus no accident that France has refused to ratify the European Charter on Minority and Regional Languages, declaring all citizens of France to be French.[18] In the same way, Greece insists that all citizens of Greece are Greek, and that therefore it has no ethno-linguistic minorities.[19] At the same time, it is distinctly ironic that the one Balkan nation-state that is the most 'contested', i.e. the Republic of Macedonia, is the only one that preserves the kind of nineteenth-century multilingualism that underlies modern ideas of multiculturalism. Of all the challenges to the Republic of Macedonia's sovereignty – and there are such from all of its neighbours in various respects (Friedman 2010) – the most damaging has been Greece's successful flouting of international law and convention, insofar as Greece's success has given fuel to nationalist politicians in the Republic of Macedonia.[20]

Greeks who claimed to deplore the action of Hrisi Avgi, and simultaneously expressed offence at my comment that I was not surprised when the attack occurred, basically want to have their cake and eat it too, or, as the Macedonians say, *em volkot sit, em ovci na broj* (have the wolf be full and the sheepfold complete). Greece's continued successful campaign against Macedonian language and identity is nothing less than a more civilized-appearing continuation of the campaign of terror directed against Macedonian language and identity from the late nineteenth century onward in what became Greek territory after the Treaty of Bucharest in 1913 (Lithoksoou 1998). Greek nationalists are committed to destroying Macedonian language and identity. Treating such nationalists as rational interlocutors is like Neville Chamberlain's declaring 'peace in our time'. A 'compromise' on the so-called name issue, i.e. a Macedonian capitulation to Greek demands that it give up its constitutional name, is no more likely to end Greece's attack on Macedonian language and identity than the Munich Agreement was to prevent World War II. This is because more is at stake than the name of a country. Unless Greece succeeds in destroying Macedonian language and identity on its territory, it might have to admit that its state – like most states – is not mono-ethnic.

Conclusion: Macedonia Is Not Greece

This section takes its title from an ad campaign mounted by the Greek government shortly after the Republic of Macedonia declared independence. The slogan of the campaign was 'Macedonia is Greece', and the Greeks went so far as to obtain or pay for permission to hang banners with this slogan on all the lampposts of the downtown stretch of Chicago's Michigan Avenue, a popular tourist destination and the main thoroughfare connecting the north and south sides of the city. At issue is not the Republic of Macedonia's 'right' to the name Macedonia. At issue is not even Greece's own shaky identity vis-à-vis Western Europe (see Herzfeld 1986). Rather, there is a dangerously volatile combination of seeking to erase the past and of distracting public consciousness from the largely economic problems of the present. The result is a combustible environment eminently suitable to neo-fascist parties like Hrisi Avgi. In fact, to this day, both Greek Macedonia and the Republic of Macedonia remain multilingual. The difference is that while multilingualism is legally protected, and even encouraged, in the Republic of Macedonia, it is discouraged and persecuted in Greece.[21] It is for this reason, if for no other, that Macedonia is most emphatically not Greece.

Notes

1. The research on which this article is based was conducted over many years with support from the following grants and organizations: American Council of Learned Societies (2000–01), National Endowment for the Humanities (2001), Slavic and East European Language Resource Center at Duke University (2003), Research Center for Linguistic Typology at LaTrobe University (2004), Fulbright-Hays (2008–09), John Simon Guggenheim Foundation (2009). None of the opinions expressed herein are the responsibility of any of these organizations. All translations are my own except where noted.
2. For a bibliography of Gołąb's work, including that on Macedonian, see Friedman et al. (1997).

3. Note that a legal definition of assault is the following: 'an intentional act by one person that creates an apprehension in another of an imminent harmful or offensive contact'.
4. The translation appears in Wace and Thompson (1913: 6). The Greek original, which is what Riki read, is the following:
Ἀλβανοὶ, Βλάχοι, Βούλγαροι, Ἀλλόγλωσσοι χαρῆτε,
Κ'ἐτοιμασθῆτε ὅλοι σας Ῥωναῖοι νὰ γενῆτε.
Βαρβαρικὴν ἀφήνοντες γλῶσσαν, φωνὴν καὶ ἤθη,
Ὁποῦ στοὺς Ἀπογόνους σας νὰ φαίνωνται σὰν μῦθοι. (Daniil 1802: 7)
The verses appear as part of the introduction to a quadrilingual manual by an Aromanian Hieropriest named Daniil of Moschopolis (now Voskopoja in Albania). The purpose of the manual, quite unlike that of Karadža's dictionary, was to eliminate all languages other than Greek which were spoken by Orthodox Christians on what was then still Ottoman territory.
5. I later learned that in 2006, at the promotion of the reprinting of a 1925 Macedonian primer (Vinožito 2006), which had originally been published in Athens, the venue had to be surrounded by riot police to protect the promoters. This primer was published as part of Greece's fulfillment of its obligations to its Macedonian minority under the Treaty of Lausanne (1923). Although the primer, which used the Latin alphabet, was never actually used, its publication is a demonstration of the fact that the international community was more effective in making Greece conform to international norms – at least in appearances – prior to the 1930s, when the excesses of the Metaxas dictatorship against Macedonians went unremarked and unpunished.
6. It was just as I finished this sentence that the thugs from Hrisi Avgi entered, threatened the audience, assaulted me, vandalized the podium, and then left. Riot police appeared exactly 70 seconds later from the same direction whither the thugs had left. The incident can be viewed on YouTube at http://www.youtube.com/watch?v=2hVZYz_gH5k. Another clip http://www.youtube.com/watch?v=_QXj4fXgEmw has Macedonian subtitles and shows the thugs leaving and the police arriving from the same direction (both accessed 9 April 2011).
7. The final paragraph of the speech, which was read after the thugs had left, was the following:

> Vasko Karadža's Greek-Macedonian dictionary was a labor of love. Moreover, it was arguably the labor of a man who loved both the Greek and the Macedonian languages. In the memorial, Vinožito writes that they are preparing a Macedonian-Greek version of the dictionary. Like the current volume, this will be an important step in creating mutual understanding among people

who wish to learn one or the other standard language. At the same time, let us hope that the Macedonian dialects still spoken on the territory of the Hellenic Republic, some of which are closer to standard Macedonian than others, will also be able to receive the scholarly attention they deserve before they disappear.
8. I did not learn the affiliation of these Greeks until after the event. One of the participants in the conference learned of it and informed me.
9. The participant's paper was, in fact, basically a report on Kōstopoulos (2000), which documents the oppression of the Macedonian language in Greece. The participant characterized the book as 'speaking truth to power'. Unfortunately, based on Greece's depressing record towards its Macedonian minority, the participant is quite jutified in fearing that merely publishing an English-language summary of a book published in Greek in Greece that documents Greece's oppression of its Macedonian minority could result in persecution in Greece.
10. See also Rougheri (1998).
11. A vilayet was the largest administrative unit at the end of the Ottoman Empire.
12. As the heir of Rome, the Byzantines called themselves 'Romans' and associated the term 'Hellene' with paganism. Hellenophones retained these usages until the nineteenth century. See Herzfeld (1986) on that transition.
13. Macedonian literature was permitted as 'dialect' literature in the first Yugoslavia (as Serbian) and Bulgaria (as Bulgarian) during the interwar period. In Greece, however, it was proscribed. Speakers were jailed, tortured, and made to take oaths abjuring their native language.
14. The five dissertations were these: David B. Rheubottom, 'A Structural Analysis of Conflict and Cleavage in Macedonian Domestic Groups' (PhD diss., University of Rochester, 1971); Nahoma Sachs, 'Music and Meaning in a Macedonian Village' (PhD diss., Indiana University, 1975); John C. Grossmith, 'Marginality and Reproductive Behavior among the Albanian Minority in Yugoslav Macedonia' (PhD diss., University of North Carolina, Chapel Hill, 1977); Christopher Marshall, 'The Aesthetics of Music in Village Macedonia' (PhD diss., Cornell, 1977); George H. Ford, 'Networks, Ritual, and 'Vrski': A Study of Urban Adjustment in Macedonia' (PhD diss., Arizona State, 1982).
15. In his introduction, Šmiger thanks the Greek police for teaching him to always make back-up copies.
16. Although the Bulgarian government officially recognized the Macedonian standard language as the official language of the Republic of Macedonia in February 1999, it still considers all Macedonian dialects to be dialects of

Bulgarian. Bulgarian dialect atlases such as Kočev (2001) still show all of Macedonia as Bulgarian, the Bulgarian press and diplomatic corps declare the Macedonians of Albania to be Bulgarians, and Bulgaria officially gives Bulgarian passports (which have EU travel abilities) to any ethnic Macedonian willing to declare him/herself to be an ethnic Bulgarian.

17. In this regard, see especially Nastovski's forthcoming study of how Greece's current policies towards Macedonia continue those of the Greek fascists during and after World War II. See also Rossos (1991, 1994, 1997).
18. See Weber (1976: 67–94).
19. Greece's denial of the existence of its minorities has even penetrated the world of American men's magazines. The November 2006 issue of *Maxim* featured a photo-spread of international 'Miss Maxim's, each a scantily clad and provocatively posed representative of a different country with a putative quotation from the model and a 'hometown fact' about the country such as the difference between Holland and Netherlands, the number of bulls killed annually in bullfights in Spain, and the number of tons of radioactive dust released in the 1986 Chernobyl disaster. The hometown fact for 'Miss Maxim Greece' was the following: 'According to the Greek government there are no ethnic divisions in Greece' (p. 176).
20. Greece's embargoes and passport defacings were in defiance of international law, the blocking of the Republic of Macedonia's name has no justification in international law.
21. Although Turkish is permitted in Greek Thrace, the government insists that these Turkish speakers are 'Muslim Greeks' and linguists even refer to Turkish in Greece as *Mousoulmaniká Thrákēs*, i.e. 'Muslimish of Thrace' (*Ellēnikē dialektologia* 5[1996–98]).

References

Andriotes, N.P. 1957. *The Confederate State of Skopje and Its Language*. Athens: Argonaut.

BAN [Bǎlgarska akademija na naukite] (ed.) (1978). *Edinstvo na b„lgarskija ezik v minaloto i dnes*. ['The unity of the Bulgarian language in the past and today'] reprinted in *Blgarski ezik* 28(1), 3–43.

Brown, Keith 1996. 'Friction in the archives: nations and negotiations on Ellis Island', 1904. Paper presented at the Tenth International Conference of Europeanists. Chicago, March 1996.

——— 2010. 'From the Balkans to Baghdad (via Baltimore): labor migration and the routes of empire'. *Slavic Review* 69: 816–34.

Daniil Moskhopoleōs, Mihali Adami Hadži 1802. *Eisagōgikē Didaskalia*. ['Introductory instruction'] Venice: Nektarion Bishop of Pelagonia.

Friedman, Victor A. 1977. *The Grammatical Categories of the Macedonian Indicative*. Columbus: Slavica.

—— 1985a. 'The sociolinguistics of literary Macedonian'. *International Journal of the Sociology of Language* 52: 31–57.

—— 1985b. 'Aspectual usage in Russian, Macedonian, and Bulgarian.' *The Scope of Slavic Aspect* (UCLA Slavic Studies, Vol. 12), ed. by Michael Flier and Alan Timberlake, 234–46. Columbus: Slavica.

—— 1986. 'Evidentiality in the Balkans: Macedonian, Bulgarian, and Albanian'. *Evidentiality: The Linguistic Coding of Epistemology*, (Advances in Discourse Processes, Vol. 20), ed. by Johanna Nichols and Wallace Chafe, 168–87. Norwood, NJ: Ablex.

—— 1989. 'Macedonian: codification and lexicon'. *Language Reform, Volume IV*, ed. by I. Fodor and C. Hagège. Hamburg: Helmut Buske. 1989. 299–34.

—— 1993a. 'Language policy and language behavior in Macedonia: background and current events'. *Language Contact, Language Conflict*, ed. by Eran Fraenkel and Christina Kramer, 73–99. New York: Peter Lang.

—— 1993b. 'The loss of the imperfective aorist in Macedonian: structural significance and Balkan context'. *American Contributions to the Eleventh International Congress of Slavists*, ed. by Robert A. Maguire and Alan Timberlake, 285–302. Columbus: Slavica.

—— 1993c. 'The first philological conference for the establishment of the Macedonian alphabet and the Macedonian literary language: its precedents and consequences'. *The Earliest Stage of Language Planning: The 'First Congress' Phenomenon*, ed. by Joshua Fishman, 159–80. Berlin: Mouton de Gruyter.

——1995. 'The differentiation of Macedonian and Bulgarian in a Balkan context'. *Balkan Forum* 3(3): 291–305.

——1996. 'Observing the observers: language, ethnicity, and power in the 1994 Macedonian census and beyond'. *Toward Comprehensive Peace in Southeastern Europe: Conflict Prevention in the South Balkans*, ed. by Barnett Rubin, 81–105 & 119–26. New York: Council on Foreign Relations/Twentieth Century Fund.

—— 1998. 'The implementation of standard Macedonian: problems and results'. *International Journal of the Sociology of Language* 131: 31–57.

—— 1999. 'Macedonian language and identity: recent history and recent historiography'. *Guard the Word Well Bound: Proceedings of the Third North American-Macedonian Conference on Macedonian Studies*, (Indiana Slavic Studies 10), ed. by Christina Kramer and Brian Cook, 71–86. Bloomington, IN: Slavica.

—— 2000a. 'The emergence of literary languages in Southeastern Europe'. *Language, Blacks and Gypsies: Languages without a Written Tradition and their Role in Education*, ed. by Thomas Acton and Morgan Dalphinis, 37–51. London: Whiting and Birch.

—— 2000b. 'The modern Macedonian standard language and its relation to modern Macedonian identity'. *The Macedonian Question: Culture, Historiography,*

Politics, ed. by Victor Roudometoff, 173–206. Boulder, CO: East European Monographs.

—— 2002. *Macedonian*. (Languages of the World/Materials 117). Munich: LinCom Europa.

—— 2003a. 'Language in Macedonia as an identity construction site'. *When Languages Collide: Perspectives on Language Conflict, Language Competition, and Language Coexistence*, ed. by Brian Joseph, Johanna DeStafano, Neil Jacobs, and Ilse Lehiste, 257–95. Columbus: Ohio State University.

—— 2003b. ' "One" as an indefinite marker in Balkan and Non-Balkan Slavic'. *American Contributions to the Thirteenth International Congress of Slavists*. ed. by Alan Timberlake and Michael Flier. Bloomington, IN: Slavica. 2003b. 93–112.

—— 2003c. 'Evidentiality in the Balkans'. *Studies in Evidentiality* ed. by Alexandra Aikhenvald and Robert Dixon, 189–218. Amsterdam: Benjamins.

—— 2004. 'Language planning and status in the Republic of Macedonia and in Kosovo'. *Language in the Former Yugoslav Lands*. ed. by Ranko Bugarski and Celia Hawkesworth, 197–231. Bloomington, IN: Slavica.

—— 2005. 'From Orientalism to democracy and back again'. *Developing Cultural Identity in the Balkans: Convergence vs. Divergence*, ed. by Raymond Detrez and Pieter Plas, 25–43. Berlin: Peter Lang.

—— 2007. 'Balkanizing the Balkan sprachbund: a closer look at grammatical permeability and feature distribution'. *Grammars in Contact: A Cross Linguistic Typology*, ed. by A. Aikhenvald and R.F.W. Dixon, 201–19. Oxford: Oxford University Press.

—— 2008a. 'Balkan Slavic dialectology and Balkan linguistics: periphery as center'. *American Contributions to the Fourteenth International Congress of Slavists*. ed. by Christina Bethin, 131–48. Bloomington, IN: Slavica.

—— 2008b. 'The Konikovo Evangelarium and Macedonian identity in the late eighteenth and early nineteenth centuries'. *The Konikovo Gospel*, ed. by J. Lindstedt, Lj. Spasov, and J. Nuorluoto, 385–91. Helsinki: Societas Scientiarum Fennica.

—— 2008c. 'Macedonian dialectology and eurology: areal and typological perspectives'. *Sprachtypologie und Universalienforschung* 61(2): 139–46.

—— 2009. Review article. 'Evangelia Adamou' (ed.) *Le Patrimonie plurilingue de la Grèce. (Le nom des langues II)*. Balkanistika 22: 215–26.

—— 2010. Introduction: 'Challenging crossroads: Macedonia in global perspective,' *Slavic Review* 69(4): 811–15.

Friedman, Victor A., Masha Belyavski-Frank, Mark Pisaro and David Testen (eds) 1997. *Da Mu E Veśna Slavata: Studies Dedicated to the Memory of Zbigniew Golab* (= Balkanistica 10).

Gal, Susan and Judith Irvine 1995. 'The boundaries of languages and disciplines: how ideologies construct difference'. *Social Research* 64: 967–1001.

Herzfeld, Michael 1986. *Ours Once More: Folklore, Ideology, and the Making of Modern Greece*, Austin: University of Texas Press.

Human Rights Watch/Helsinki 1994. *Denying Ethnic Identity: The Macedonians of Greece.* New York: Human Rights Watch.

Karadča, Vasko 2009. *Grčko-Makedonski rečnik.* ['Greek Macedonian Dictionary'] Salonica: Zora.

Karakasidou, Anastasia 1997. *Fields of Wheat, Hills of Blood: Passages to Nationhood in Greek Macedonia 1870–1990.* Chicago: University of Chicago Press.

Kočev, Ivan (ed.) 2001. *Bălgarski dialekten Atlas. Obobštavašt tom: I–III Fonetika, Akcentologija, Leksika.* [Bulgarian dialectal atlas. General volume. Phonetics, Accentology, Lexicon'] Sofia: Trud.

Kōstopoulos, Tasos 2000. *Ē Apogogeumenē Glōssa* ['The forbidden language']. Athens: Maurē lista.

Lekov, I. (1968). *Kratka sravnitelno-istoričeska i tipologičeska gramatika na slavjanskite ezici* ['A short comparative-historical and typological grammar of the Slavic languages']. Sofia: Bulgarian Academy of Sciences.

Lithoksoou, Dēmētrēs 1998. Ellēnikos antimakedonikos agōnas [≈The Greek anti-Macedonian struggle≈]. Athens: Megalē Poreia.

Misirkov, Krste P. 1903. *Za makedonickite raboti.* ['On Macedonian matters'] Sofia: Liberalni klub. (Reprinted 1974, Skopje: Institut za makedonski jazik, Posebni izdanija 8.)

Nastovski, Katherine. Forthcoming. 'Between nationalism and solidarity: assessing the KKE's post civil war positioning of the Macedonian Question'. Proceedings of the Seventh Macedonian-North American Conference on Macedonian Studies, ed. by Victor A. Friedman and Donald L. Dyer, *Balkanistika* 25(2).

Pulevski, Ǵorǵi 1875. *Rečnik od tri jezika.* Belgrade: Drčavna ätamparija.

Rossos, Andrew 1991. 'The Macedonians of Aegean Macedonia: a British officer's report, 1944'. *Slavic and East European Review* 69(2): 282–309.

—— 1994. 'The British Foreign Office and Macedonian national identity 1918-41'. *Slavic Review* 53: 369–94.

—— 1997. 'Incompatible allies: Greek communism and Macedonian nationalism in the civil war in Greece, 1943–49'. *Journal of Modern History* 69: 42–76.

—— 2008. *Macedonia and the Macedonians.* Stanford: Hoover Institution.

Rougheri, Christina 1998. Traditional Greek Nationalism Breeds New Display of Intolerance. Greek Helsinki Monitor and Minority Rights Group – Greece (24/6/1998, AIM Athens) http://www.greekhelsinki.gr/english/articles/AIM24-6-98.html (accessed 5 May 2011).

Šmiger (=Schmieger), Roland 1998. *Nestramski govor.* Munich: Otto Sagner.

Sterjovski, Vasil 2008. Parahodite nosea Makedonci vo Amerika [Ships Brought Macedonians to America]., *Prespa: Vestnik na Zaednica na Makedoncite vo Albanija* 10.56: 1–2.

Troebst, Stefan 1994. 'Yugoslav Macedonia, 1944–53: building the party, the state and the nation'. *Berliner Jahrbuch für osteuropäische Geschichte* 1994/2: 103–39.

Van Boeschoeten, Riki 2006. 'Code-switching, linguistic jokes and ethnic identity: reading hidden transcripts in a cross-cultural context'. *Journal of Modern Greek Studies* 24: 247–377.
Vinočito 2006. *Bukvar anagnōstiko* ['Unknown primer']. Thessaloniki: Batavia.
Upward, Allen 1908. *The East End of Europe*. London: John Murray.
Wace, A.J.B. and M.S. Thompson 1913. *The Nomads of the Balkans*. New York: Dutton.
Weber, Eugene 1976. *Peasants into Frenchmen: The Modernization of Rural France, 1870–1914*. Stanford: Stanford.

2

'EU AS FUTURE?': FROM A MACEDONIAN VIEWPOINT – THE MULTIPLE WAYS OF BEING EUROPEAN IN MACEDONIA AND NOT BEING IN EUROPE

Ilka Thiessen

In this chapter I discuss the issue of European borders and how those borders are supposed to define specific identities. My case study follows a group of young female electrical engineers in the city of Skopje between 1988 and 2007, and derives from 27 months of intensive fieldwork in the crucial times from 1991 to 1995 (the height of the Yugoslav war). My research examines 'identity-in-the-making' from a micro perspective and how this group of informants had to deal with superimposed changes to their personal identity: from Yugoslav/European/Modern to Macedonian/Balkan/Traditional (Thiessen 2007).

The following examines the details of these superimposed groups and personal identities and how my group of informants construct their identities in ways quite unexpected by international organizations and political leaders. In contrast to my earlier claims taken from my research in the 1990s, today my informants oppose the European identity they were seeking to emulate then in order to be accepted to a United Europe. I argue today that they react to Europe's refusal to recognize Macedonia as European by creating their private and public world in Skopje as what I call 'Hyper-European', meaning in their translation: 'better than European'.

I will demonstrate that the European border construction project, initiated after the fall of the Berlin Wall and after the supposed demise of socialism in the former Eastern European Block, is being challenged by the individual identity creation of my informants in Skopje. Yugoslavia was identified as belonging to this Eastern European Block; furthermore, it was identified as more 'hinterland', being Balkan according to nineteenth-century definitions (Rebecca West 1994 [1942]; see also the film *Ulysses' Gaze* 1995, directed by Théo Angelopoulos). I suggest that this explains the refusal of the European Union to include Macedonia into the EU, despite the fact that Bulgaria and Romania have been included.

This should turn our eyes towards the issue of 'borders' itself and how borders are represented by governments as physical entities, when in fact they are metaphors of inclusion and exclusion. Giroux points out that at the centre of the European territorial border definition lies the idea of 'European High Culture' as the centre of civilization in which the overlap from the metaphorical use of borders implies 'a transgress of the borders sealed by modernism' (Giroux 1992: 55). Gupta and Ferguson (1992: 6) also address the hegemonic topography of borders:

> For example, the representation of the world as [a] collection of 'countries,' as in most world maps, sees it as an inherently fragmented space divided by different colors into diverse national societies, each 'rooted' in its proper place.

For my informants this 'incarceration' is imposed on them by the European Union through visa regulations, specifically the Schengen visa.[1] Malki (1992: 25) argues:

> Often, the concern with boundaries and their transgression reflects not so much corporeal movements of specific groups of

people, but, rather, a broad concern with the 'cultural displacement' of people, things and cultural products (Clifford 1988; Goytisolo 1987; Hannerz 1987; Torgovnick 1990).

As Malkki points out, the boundaries created by the Schengen zone have very specific concerns with the purity of 'cultural identity'. The question that my informants are now asking is, how is it that Macedonia is threatening this 'Western' cultural purity?

Appadurai (1988: 37) also offers great insight into how the issue of the exclusion of Macedonia from the current European Project is currently being used by international organizations and governments, pointing out the assigned immobility of drawn borders that can only be crossed from the West to the rest and not the other way around:

> The slightly more subtle assumption behind the attribution of immobility is not so much physical as ecological. Natives [read: Balkan] are those who are somehow confined to places by their connection to what the place permits. Thus all the language of niches [read: Non-Western], of foraging [read: Balkan mentality of ancient hatred], of material skill [read: Balkan peasants], of slowly evolved technologies [read: slow development of liberal market economy], is actually also a language of incarceration.

So, while international organizations and government leaders define the territorial borders of sovereignty and membership, the borders of individual and group identity may be quite different and certainly are formed by very different processes.

Borders and Tangentiality

Renato Rosaldo's work is useful in understanding the metaphorical extension of border images and how identities are negotiated around borders: 'Social borders frequently become salient around such lines as sexual orientation, gender, class, race, ethnicity, nationality, age, dress, politics, food, or taste' (1989: 208). What Rosaldo points out is that the examining of borders is a useful model for determining how people negotiate multiple identities, but my question is how do these processes actually work? The EU enlargement, borders, nation-states and independent statehood illustrates that borders seem to be far more visceral, far more fleeting than the issues that are represented by governments and international agencies. It is interesting that the definition of borders comes at a time when people are discussing the fluidity of border crossings. Given this extension of how identity and borders are created, it is appropriate to introduce into the discussion the term 'tangentiality'. When we think of borders, we think of lines and cultural fields that are separated from each other. However, if we look at the power fields surrounding borders we can start to understand how my informants in the Republic of Macedonia currently feel, think, reflect and oppose the borders that 'incarcerate' them as personified through the Schengen visa.

I will demonstrate how the borders of group and personal identities in Macedonia stand in tension with the idea of borders as created by the '"Western" idea of the nation-state'.[2] If we look at the issue of the name 'Macedonia' it becomes apparent that there are three competing definitions of how to define, encompass and draw lines around the entity known as Macedonia: (1) Macedonia as a geographical area that includes parts of northern Greece, Bulgaria and Albania, and some argue Serbia; (2) Macedonia as a historical entity 'created' by Philip II and his son Alexander the Great – claimed as being part of a 2,000-, 3,000- or 4,000-year history by Greece (the stickers all over Greece do claim very different time frames for the historical Macedonia); (3) the political entity of the Republic of Macedonia that has not come to an agreement with Greece over the right to carry that name and is officially referred to as FYROM (Former Yugoslavian Republic of Macedonia) or, as some newspapers called it in the 1990s: 'the country that cannot be named'.[3] Each citizen of the Republic of Macedonia has to deal with these personal analytical problems in their daily lives. Added to the mix is, of course, their proud identification as Yugoslavian that nearly overnight was overturned, leaving a lacuna in their identity. As a result, informants had to create their own style of tangibility through discourse. Discourse during the 1990s drew borders between the Macedonian and Albanian populations,[4] between the village and the city, between rich and poor, between Balkan and European (this identification is very much linked to religiosity, Balkan standing for religion, European for a rejection of religion[5]) and between European women's bodies and Albanian women's bodies.

The medical term 'tangentiality' is very fitting to explain my informants' daily struggle to identify themselves – to actually know who they are. I will go further and suggest that we should look at the definition of borders in the same manner. Tangentiality leads to different meanings that all seem to apply to the sense of identity that has been experienced throughout Macedonia's recent past.

In the first sense, tangentiality refers to all things that are perpendicular to unity. Perpendicularity creates a 90° angle to a given plane. People understood very early on that they were not in 'direct alignment' with the West. The Greek blockade cut any ties with the European Union and to travelling freely. However, during the blockade from February 1994 to September 1995 there was a tremendous influx of European (versus socialist) goods such as Ariel© washing power, Always© pads, Muesli and other imports from Greek companies. Surprisingly, even though my informants were cut off from Europe, they became more European through this inundation of consumer goods.

Informants were watching the horrors of Srebrenica on CNN and were told that the Balkan War was caused by ancient hatred that could explode at any time, especially in Macedonia where 'two religions' were living in close proximity. I took part in many discussions at that time about whether this could really happen in Macedonia. Other people felt that such discussions would, in effect, lead to such conflict. I will go so far as to argue that the conflict of 2001 was partly caused by this 'outside view' of Macedonia – by its tangentiality to Europe. This outside view of Macedonia can be directly linked to the discussion of the Schengen visa:

> The opening of east-west borders has coincided with a burgeoning internal security agenda within the EU. A policy area that could be called 'micro-security' is growing fast as policy-makers respond to myriad threats to the security of their citizens by

developing new instruments at both national and EU levels. Unlike the 'macro-security' concerns of the Cold War – which primarily involved state-controlled and politically driven threats from national militaries – the new micro-level risks are from private individuals. This privatization of security threats from the east presents a complex dilemma because the movements of autonomous citizens are much more difficult to deal with in the international security framework [...] (Grabbe 2000: 520).

Grabbe goes on to define the new security risks that are behind the Schengen visa first and foremost as instability caused by refugees, crime, and the breakdown of law and order (2000: 520). What those in Skopje are, of course, very well aware of is that the European Union links their individual travelling to cross-border crime and the breakdown of civilization. It is not difficult to see that this is quite insulting to informants who regard themselves as professionals and good citizens of a United Europe. In fact, many of them have claimed greater morality and less crime within Macedonia because of its socialist past and the compassion that has made Southern Europe a 'Europe with a heart'.

The question that both Macedonia as a state and individual actors within Macedonia are faced with is: what are the conditions that Europe demands from Macedonia to be included in Europe? According to Grabbe (2002: 252), these conditions are general, vague and mostly centred on an economic agenda:

> The thrust of the EU's economic agenda [...] is neoliberal, emphasizing privatization of the means of production [and] a reduction in state involvement in the economy [...]. The socio-economic system they implicitly promote has a more 'Anglo-Saxon' flavor than [...] [of the] social market economies of France or Germany.

This presents a core problem to those in Skopje who might not have identified themselves with dictatorial socialism but who, in many conversations over the years, have identified the social democracy of Sweden as their ultimate political system, a system that they had hoped to establish with independence. In this light I question if the term 'post-socialist' can be used as freely as it is in a lot of the literature of Eastern Europe and the former Soviet Union. My informants all do subscribe to democracy, but they also do not want to give up on the 'socialist idea'. Here, I am talking about the core of my informants; I do know people who would not subscribe to such politics by choosing to vote for the Nationalists rather than the Social Democrats. I argue that such a vote is made in part with the wish to expel 'the Muslim-Albanian' population – not at all in discrepancy with the EU's position on Turkey's acceptance to the EU.

However, such policies and decisions have real-life implications for the daily life of my informants. They do not define the European Union spatially. It is not a place they would like to enter, such would be defined as 'exile', but they define Europe mostly metaphorically. Their metaphorical definition of their personal identity enacted in personal life choices on gender issues, consumer choices, and living the economic reality of Macedonia through their workplace choices, is based on a similarity to Europe rather than an emulation of the only identity that is given to them by Europe as a pariah identity. Many Macedonians I know are rejecting the idea of a liberal market economy. Their daily life choices are based on such rejection. In this way, I argue tangentiality enacts itself again in defining Macedonia not as being part of but rather separately connected in a lateral way to Europe and 'the West'. In many conversations it was pointed out to me that Macedonia was very much able to give something to Europe, if you will, to improve Europe. Such discussions usually came up when discussing abortion or childcare.

There is a different sense of tangentiality used in psychiatry in relation to schizophrenia. There it describes a pattern of speech characterized by oblique, digressive, or irrelevant replies to questions and where the responses never approach the point of the questions. It is also described as a disturbance in the associative thought process in which one tends to digress readily from one topic under discussion to other topics that arise through association. I argue that my friends see the relationship of their country to the EU in a very similar way, and that they are starting to reject this relationship:

> Europe does not care for us. They wish we would not exist, swallowed up by Serbia (so they could hate us), or just, for convenience sake, be part of Greece. Hah! The Greeks would like that, wouldn't they? Can you imagine? (Informant 2006)

And:

> I cannot understand what Europe wants from us, they talk to us, but not really. All the foreigners here – I do not know what they do here. If I look at them they look lost to me. You love Macedonia, you have been here for such a long time, but why do they come? Just to make money, that's all. We are just another Bangladesh to them. I am sure when they come home they cannot even point out on a map where Macedonia is, especially the Americans. Just this place within Europe that is not Europe – do you get this? (Informant 2007)

So what creates Macedonia's identity for those from outside of Macedonia? I do not think that these questions have ever been seriously considered by European policymakers or other international organizations that have come to Macedonia to ease its transitions from socialism to post-socialism to a liberal market economy. However, from conversations with foreigners in Macedonia I gathered the lack of a vision for Macedonia. Most foreigners that I spoke to were only temporarily in Macedonia. They expressed concern and pity for Macedonia. But when I asked them why, they could not explain. The best explanation I got was: 'Look at their garbage everywhere – it stinks.'

Rather than take the existence of borders and their recent political transformations for granted, I intend to explore what borders are for my friends. It is important to recognize where they appear in their daily lives, how sometimes borders merge into each other, and how sometimes borders change significantly in their meaning, depending on who is using the term. To do this, I will look at the process of 'border crossings' that my group of informants are involved in today.

Border Crossings/ Crossing Borders

Today, crossing borders differs in meaning from when my informants travelled as Yugoslav citizens, and also differs from when they were not able to travel at all due to an unrecognized passport.[6] Now it is not about crossing borders, but about how borders are crossed. In this respect in 2006 and 2007, the Macedonians I know have taken an active role in reshaping the Western borders that exclude Macedonia from Europe. This 'boundary-shaping' is reshaping the meaning of the Balkans and Europe in a surprising manner. What if boundaries do not exclude, but merge, creating mutual interdependence? What if there is a 'border identity' of Macedonia as the borderland between the Balkans and Europe, as Macedonia the first real 'post post-socialist' country of Europe?

I do argue that such 'border identity' can be found everywhere in Skopje today. This 'border identity' is based on the fact that my informants feel that the place and its history has formed their identity,[7] but also that they have the right to participate in and profit from 'transborder' activities, specifically international organizations working in Macedonia.[8] These negotiations call forth new social processes of identity formation.

Identity: the 'Us' and the 'Them'

In the time of my first research the identity borders, fuelled by the 'ethnic conflict' in the former Yugoslavia and by Western European and North American News reporting on 'ancient hatreds' and religious wars, were formulated as 'us' (Orthodox Macedonians) and 'them' (Muslim Albanians). I argue that this was a European or North American superimposed population identification. The 1994 census, designed by a French organization, asked the citizens of Macedonia to declare themselves as either Orthodox or Muslim. I helped an informant with the census taking, and also asked my informants how they had identified themselves, which they answered with 'Orthodox'. When I asked how this could be, since most of my informants were staunch atheists, they told me: 'We did this so they (the Albanians) would not outnumber us.' Interestingly, in the same census many Romani citizens of Macedonia, based on their Muslim belief, identified themselves as 'Albanian'. So what role does religion play in identifying 'Europe' or 'Balkan' within and outside of Macedonia?

The Cross on Vodno

The Millennium Cross on the top of Mount Vodno should exemplify this type of 'religious identity formation'.[9] However, I argue that the Cross should be read as a signal to Europe as a process of 'exclusion' of the Albanian population rather than as forming or confirming the Christian identity of Madedonia. It suggests Macedonia as a Christian country ready to be included into the 'Christian Club' of the European Union.[10]

I have not talked to Albanians in Macedonia about the Millennium Cross, but in most of my discussions with Macedonians the Cross has not had many fans and some of my informants have compared it with a Ku Klux Klan cross.[11] The exceptions were interviews with the architect Jovan Stefanovski-Zan in July 2006, who nearly made me fall in love with the Cross in the way he described it, Oliver Petrovski (his co-architect) and members of Ljubčo Georgievski's[12] VMRO-DPMNE party. What the Cross on Vodno signifies though, is that from a political and personal sense Macedonia is a borderland of identity. Macedonia is formed by the specific political circumstances of a United Europe, with its border drawings and its exclusion of the Balkans in the European Project. This affects individual reactions to the alteration of the landscape of Skopje, with religious markers whose first intent seems to be to divide the Macedonian and Albanian population.

What does this mean? I argue that the Cross on Vodno and a new religiosity has nothing to do with religion in and for itself, but is based on a discourse on inclusion and exclusion. A discourse that expands on difference and boundaries, between 'the West' and the 'Balkans' and between Macedonians and Albanians. All these different identities intersect at the Cross. An article in Macedonia asked, "Cross on Vodno or on [our] Shoulders?" and continued to explain:

On the Balkans, the religion is still used as an instrument to benefit nationalism and politics, stated Erhard Busek, special Coordinator of the Stability Pact for Southeast Europe. He gave as an example the installation of the 'largest cross on the Balkans, on Vodno, in Skopje [...]'. The cross was set up four years ago by the Macedonian Orthodox Church (MOC). With all lights on it can be seen from a distance of 80 kilometers. It is set up as 'a political signal towards the Albanian community who are mostly Muslims', Busek pointed out in Vienna. In response Father Timotej, spokesman of MOC13, says: Who could be provoked by such cross when 80% of the citizens in Skopje are orthodox as are the inhabitants living on the other side of Vodno?

However, I do not agree with Busek that the Cross was built to antagonize the Albanian population. Nor does it 'prove' there is a Balkan attitude of intolerance of other religions as many argued was the case in Bosnia.[14] The Cross does not tower over Skopje to call people to a deeper religiosity nor is it to be read by the Albanian minority as a symbol of their exclusion from the Macedonian state. It initiates another discourse: religion as a political tool declaring Macedonia to be part of the 'Western Club' of Christianity and, by that, denying the 500 years of Ottoman rule.

When I asked my informants this year what they thought about the exclusion of Turkey from the EU membership discussions, they felt that Turkey did not belong to Europe because it was an Islamic nation. With some cheekiness I asked my Macedonian atheistic friends whether Macedonia belonged to Europe if it was Christianity that defined Europe; however, I was refused an answer. As such, I would like to argue that religion in Macedonia has little to do with belief but rather more with a political discourse on metaphorical borders.

When representatives of the Islamic Religious Community (IRC) were asked what they thought about the Millennium Cross, they stated that from today's perspective the Cross is a reality, and the Islamic community is not bothered by it as long as there is no political message. IRC has nothing against the Christian symbols that have always existed together with the Muslim ones. But it is unacceptable if the construction has a political background. The Muslims didn't react to the building of the Cross. At the moment they do not consider it as a message against Islam (Jakub Selimovski, IRC).

I argue that in today's Macedonia the boundaries drawn between the Macedonian and Albanian population are seen as safe, giving rest to each other, whereas the boundaries between Macedonia and Europe are being seen as a threat to Macedonia's modern identity. I see the Cross as an icon for so many boundaries, symbolizing the daily struggle of people in Macedonia: 'to be' and 'what to be'. However, does this mean that Macedonians feel that they need to be of Christian denomination and exclude the Muslim Albanians in their midst, Albanians who have lived as long in Macedonia as the Slav-Macedonians themselves? One of the demands by the EU is to approve constitutional changes, improving the position of ethnic Albanians in the country.[16]

What can my informants conclude from these two expectations? That their connection with Europe is through Christianity and acceptance of their Albanian Muslim population in a post-9/11 world, where Muslims in any European city are regarded with suspicion. The personal conclusion that my informants drew when I talked to them in Skopje in 2006 is not that Macedonians want to be part of Europe, but rather that Macedonia should be part of Europe. This changes the dynamic of the EU demands quite dramatically. The Macedonia in the mind of my informants has the full right to demand something from Europe and not the other way around, thereby switching at least the metaphorical border drawing.

Interestingly enough, today, none of my informants said that Albanians were keeping Macedonia away from Europe – a statement that was common in the mid-1990s. Instead it was Europe's exclusion policy, favouring Bulgaria and Romania over the far more civilized Macedonia that kept it apart by promoting Europe as a beneficial father-figure not interested in a confident Macedonia. This discourse is a very complex one. Boundaries shift their meanings and their significance. In the 1990s the discourse on the boundaries between Europe and Macedonia was internally expressed by my informants through the contrast between Macedonians and Albanians. Macedonians portrayed themselves as modern Europeans and with the hyper-modernity of the sculptured bodies of Macedonian women contrasted against the 'traditional', 'peasant', 'oppressed' bodies of Albanian women. For my informants in 2006 and 2007, the Albanian population has become a silent partner in the conversation on exclusion and inclusion. Many NGOs have concentrated their efforts on improving the situation of the Albanian and Roma population, in effect becoming the receivers of modernity just as in Yugoslav times,[17] but in turn becoming co-conspirators in the 'resistance against Europe', at least in the eyes of many of my informants.

I argue that the effect of this is that what and who defines Macedonian and Albanian 'identity' has been taken out of the hands of the Europeans, and my Macedonian friends have reinvented it. It would be of great interest to find out how Albanians feel about this redefinition of boundaries. For the moment it appears that despite some skirmishes between Macedonians and Albanians, the 'aggression' between Macedonian and Albanians, deriving from the struggle of who defines the outside perspective of Macedonia being within the borders of Europe (Macedonian) or Balkan (Albanian), is redirected towards Europe itself.

Border Drawings on Bodies

Today in Macedonia my women friends enjoy great freedoms. Most of them have high-paid jobs, they have a partner who shares the housework and childcare, or they live on their own. However, these achievements did not arise from supra-political changes, they were not born out of the resistance to communism, nor given by a free market economy and democracy as 'introduced' by the West in redrawing the boundaries of Europe into 'Europe' and 'Eastern Europe'.

I argue that they were 'taken' by my informants in resistance to democracy and a liberal market economy. My friends have re-created their lives as an act of defiance against the 'outside', fully endorsing their socialist past. 'We are proud of our past, it was what made us superior to you Western Europeans' (2006 personal communication). This defiance has to be read in respect to some of the policies that had been suggested by outside agencies: the suggested change of the working time from 7–3 to 9–5 (which would make it necessary for one parent to be at home when schoolchildren were coming home for lunch at 3), changes in the abortion law (now abortions are mostly only possible in private clinics and they cost money), changes in the closing time of cafés from indefinite to 11 p.m., changes in advertising and television (pornography) and changes in workplace regulations (women in several organizations were asked to wear skirts, especially if they would come into contact with foreigners), and last but not least the extreme rise in childcare costs that today cost as much as one parent most likely earns (most of my friends today enlist their retiring mothers to help them with childcare).

During my research in the 1990s, my friends became more and more beautiful, slimmer, starved. They bought designer clothes they could not afford, had unprotected sex with their boyfriends, got pregnant, had abortions and got angry. The anger, however, in their interpretation, did not direct itself against their bodies (through starvation – they did not see their hunger as deprivation but as surplus – being able to afford a luxurious body like Linda Evangelista), but against the West. I argue that it is then that their defiance was born. 'Why can we not travel any more? Do they think we are some little Balkan people that come begging on their doors?' 'When I went to Slovenia tourists were surprised I was not wearing a veil – they are so stupid.' 'There they [the West] think they are so superior – but German women cannot even have an abortion you told us – who is Balkan, them or us?' 'I saw some German news and the women they showed were all drab.' Added to such comments more and more stories started to circulate of women who came back from the States, Canada and Australia complaining how badly dressed women were 'in the West' and how they did not know 'how to have fun'.

Especially in the area of sexuality and reproductive rights, my friends felt empowered, and I suggest this is why they often agreed to having unprotected sex. It was in their power to give life or to decide to abort. It was their decision when they got pregnant if they should get married or get rid of the baby, and in the unlikely event of a divorce (since it was not approved of by society) the children nevertheless would go with the mother. It is one of the major topics on which my informants see themselves as superior to Europe, especially Germany.

How does the world look through the eyes of my informants today? Where are the borders drawn that define who they are and who they belong to? In recent years, things have changed dramatically. I have just been back to Macedonia this year and Skopje was buzzing. My informants still look stunning, consumer goods are available in abundance, and abortion is still legal and practised regularly. However, there are a lot of misgivings, especially towards foreigners (US and European government agencies, military personnel and NGOs).

The free market economy has fully exploded in Skopje, and my informants moan for the socialist past. However, with so many foreigners in the country there have been advantages for my friends, especially economically. As such, the fully empowered women that my informants have created themselves to be has been useful to them. They have also boosted the image of Macedonia to the Western world by engaging with foreigners in the country (professionally and otherwise), and by looking European and having foreign-financed jobs. They are able to obtain visas to travel (though with difficulties) to better the image of Macedonia to the outside world. Macedonia seems less and less a hinterland. In that way, I have argued the beautified bodies of my friends have become very much politicized.[18]

Nevertheless, today, the liberal market economy claims these bodies as its product by painting the peasant and socialist past in Macedonia as an oppression of women (hard labour as peasant, and the double burden idea of socialism), creating borders around a peasant, post-socialist Macedonia. I suggest that if we are looking at borders we need not only look at topography but at bodies as metaphors of boundaries, as suggested already by Mary Douglas (1966). The notion of 'liberation' that comes with drawing borders between the 'liberators' and those 'to be liberated' has created major pitfalls for many, which they have circumvented with a lot of innovation and imagination. In today's power structure of Macedonia's dependency on foreign development and military aid, their bodies are becoming exploited through precisely this discourse of liberation. Abortions are less and less respected, beautiful bodies serve the country's economic interests, and the idea that my informants have to be liberated (being put into this specific border realm) has taken away the little freedom they had.

My informants were computer and electrical turbine engineers, which are not needed in a country with little industry, and with whatever jobs available being taken up by men. Today women engineers are valued for their translation and secretarial skills working with foreign agencies. The common sexual division of labour from the West has moved into Macedonia on the border drawing of 'liberation-economy' and 'post-socialism'.

Border Shifting

My argument so far is that the boundary between Europe and Macedonia has shifted in its meaning. Real borders do mark significant differences between one side and the other far more than a benign piece of earth would ever suggest. I always wondered, looking at borders, how they can be so powerful even though they are so artificial and not ingrained into the soil (but then I am from Berlin and for me, borders were marked in concrete). If there would be a wall between Macedonia and Europe the question would be, where would it start physically? Would it be between Macedonia and Greece? The continuous cross-border travel and cross-border shopping excursions by my Macedonian informants to Ikea and Zara would question this. It is them who determine the borders that define their belonging. Is there a border between Bulgaria and Macedonia? As with Ljubčo Georgievski (see endnote 2), Macedonians start to declare themselves as Bulgarian in order to receive a Bulgarian (European Union) passport. What about the border between Serbia and Macedonia? Macedonians only feel pity for Serbia, the black sheep of Europe (or the Balkans).

Is Albania bordering Europe? Is Italy more European than Macedonia? Macedonians feel a close affinity to Italy, especially women with a fashion sense. Maybe we have to look to other factors defining borders such as religion. My Macedonian friends define themselves paradoxically as atheist Christians and, in their mind, this makes them true Europeans. Isn't it true that the Polish requested to include God in the European Constitution and was declined? Where are the borders of Europe? There are differences that are marked by these borders that are not identified; however, these differences are always contingent on who is the other that one defines oneself for; Macedonians versus Albanians/Roma, Macedonian women versus Albanian women, Macedonia versus Europe. Essentially the Balkans is a myth perpetuated by Europe and there should be a new discussion in anthropology on borders being far more fluid than even the term 'culture' would suggest. What is the EU – is it based on self-definition, military, customs officials – how does one live an EU life? That I believe, is the next question to ask.

When I recently asked people what they most wished in that moment to possess, they answered they would like to have a Schengen visa. Not only would they like to have a Schengen visa, but to receive a Schengen visa without harassment from the issuing embassy (referring mostly to the expressed suspicion that Macedonians who are given a Schengen visa would run away from Macedonia to live illegally in Europe and follow a life of crime). They stress that they are seeking the Schengen visa in order to travel to see the Eiffel Tower or to see the Museumsinsel. Macedonia's total ignorance of such normality becomes apparent in the example of a Macedonian friend of mine applying for a Canadian tourist visa. She was told that Macedonians, Iranians and North Koreans are the most unlikely to receive a visa for Canada.

Today, the Schengen visa is seen as Europe's attempt to keep Macedonia outside of Europe. As an additional source of aggravation, individuals pointed out that the price of the Schengen visa was being raised to 65 euros in order to finance the biometric European passport. The irony of this was not lost on my Macedonian friends: 'Europe obviously cannot afford its unity without countries like Macedonia, outside its borders, which are made to pay for it.' Further, 'it seems that Macedonia cannot become part of the EU because otherwise Europe could not afford its own unity. Where would all the development workers find employment and still be able to go home for the weekend?'

Europe's argument against Macedonia's acceptance in the EU that 'it could not afford to support millions of immigrants', was countered by pointing out that 2 million Macedonians would hardly bring Europe to such a critical point. And when wondering about the threat that Macedonia would pose to Europe, many feel that the American fashion sense is a greater threat: shorts and white socks on men, and big women in pink with water bottles and baseball caps are seen today in the city of Skopje in abundance. These contrast drastically against the modern chic of the European-Macedonian bodies. This summer I was amazed at how many smartly dressed people could withstand the temperature of 45°C, while I was dissolving into a puddle, asking myself if I was ready to live in European Macedonia.

Conclusion

My central argument is that Macedonians are redefining the image of Europe, rather than Europe defining Macedonia or the Balkans. This pattern points to the de facto instability of borders:

> ...once hallowed as fixed and monolithic boundaries of disparate national and cultural identities. [This] increasingly reveals processes of cross-border cultural negotiation and raises new and provocative questions about the relationship between local and global (Tsing 1994), space and place (Gupta and Ferguson 1992), and nation and state (Donnan and Wilson 1994a). [...] [Borders are multivocal and] are sites where political, cultural, and social identities converge, coexist and sometimes conflict. Because they are meeting areas of diverse political, economic and cultural systems, they provide unique insights into the ways in which identities are constructed (e.g. Donnan and Wilson 1994). (Flynn 1997: 312).

The essential question then is: are Macedonians Europeans, or are Europeans Macedonians? Macedonians are aware of the imagery of the Balkans, and their design of themselves responds to this imagery. Macedonians in the Republic of Macedonia are in constant process of redefinition of themselves along the lines of the Balkan image given to them by external forces. However, this redefinition makes them create themselves as modern Europeans. This creation happens in my informants' daily lives, their daily actions becoming political ones that challenge the definitions of territorial borders misunderstood by Europe. International organizations and government leaders are not 'cultural' leaders, 'political' borders are not based on sovereignty, and 'social' definitions shouldn't be based on Europe's definition of Eastern Europe and post-socialism. Borders today should be looked at, as Grabbe suggests (Grabbe 2000: 520), as continuously formed by individual's daily lives and not by the nation-state.

Notes

1. The 15 Schengen countries are: Austria, Belgium, Denmark, Finland, France, Germany, Iceland, Italy, Greece, Luxembourg, Netherlands, Norway, Portugal, Spain and Sweden. All these countries except Norway and Iceland are European Union members. With a Schengen visa, one can enter one country and travel freely throughout the Schengen zone. Internal border controls do not exist within the Schengen zone. However, not having a Schengen visa disallows travel within the whole of the Schengen zone. Since there are so many countries involved it makes it extremely difficult to obtain a Schengen visa. In effect, the Schengen visa is the metaphorical and physical exclusion for 'border transgressors' – people outside the 'West'. People that are allowed to travel within the Schengen zone are: Andorra, Argentina, Australia, Austria, Belgium, Brazil, Brunei, Bulgaria, Canada, Chile, Croatia, Costa Rica, Cyprus, Czech Republic, Denmark, El Salvador, Estonia, Finland, France, Germany, Great Britain, Greece, Guatemala, Honduras, Hong Kong, Hungary, Ireland, Israel, Italy, Japan, Latvia, Liechtenstein, Lithuania, Luxembourg, Macao, Malaysia, Malta, Mexico, Monaco, Netherlands, New Zealand, Nicaragua, Norway, Panama, Paraguay, Poland, Portugal, Romania, San Marino, Singapore, Slovakia, Slovenia, South Korea, Spain, Sweden, Switzerland, United States of America, Uruguay, Vatican, Venezuela.
2. I am using the term my informants are using. To know who they see as 'West' one has to look at the countries in footnote 1 that do not need a visa to enter the 'Schengen-Europe'.
3. Voldemort (*Harry Potter*, J.K. Rowling) comes into mind.
4. I hesitate to identify these groups based on their religious affiliation: that is, Christian Orthodox for the Macedonians, and Muslim for the Albanians, since most people from both groups in Skopje rather identify themselves as socialist.

5. See the rejection of the European Parliament of Poland's request to include God in the EU constitution.
6. To make the reader understand what that means I am choosing a very current situation concerning Kosovo. For example, Canadian citizens officially require a Serbian visa if they book a flight from Pristina. However, Serbia today (July 2007) is not controlling the borders of Kosovo. In the same sense, my informants in the early 1990s had a Yugoslav passport, but only Serbia was recognized to be 'Rump-Serbia'. New Macedonia passports were issued but not recognized by Greece.
7. For most of my informants in Skopje 'history' means the history of Yugoslavia, not 'ancient' history.
8. There are 4,000 NGOs registered in Macedonia, a country of 2 million inhabitants.
9. The Millennium Cross is one of the newest symbols of Skopje. It was built during 2002, and finished in August 2002. This Cross was built by the Macedonian Orthodox Church, and partially financed by the prime minister at the time (and VMRO founder) Ljubčo Georgievski, in order to 'celebrate 2000 years of Christianity in the World and on Macedonian soil'. It was constructed and placed on the highest point on Vodno mountain, a place that held a small cross for most of the Ottoman's rule in Macedonia (fourteenth to twentieth century), so Turkish and local Macedonians called it 'Krstovar' (place where there is a cross).
10. I make this argument based on two facts: the resistance of including Turkey in the EU and Poland's request to include God in the European constitution.
11. I argue that this reference is seen as direct criticism of the racism that exists in what my friends define as 'the West' and with which they do not like to be identified with.
12. Of interest is that on July 14 2006 it was announced that Ljubčo Georgievski, former leader of the strong nationalist party in Macedonia, applied for and was granted Bulgarian citizenship on the basis that his parents are Bulgarians.
13. Macedonian Orthodox Church.
14. I do not believe that the war in Bosnia had anything to do with 'religion'.
16. NATO brokered the peace agreement with the KLA (Kosovo Liberation Army) infiltrated NLA (National Liberation Army) led by Ali Ahmeti in the 2001 conflict in Macedonia. Ethnic Albanians in Macedonia were given greater rights by the constitutional reforms made as part of the NATO brokered peace agreement.
17. Aleksander Krzalovski, personal communication, 2006.

18. Thiessen, *Waiting for Macedonia*, 2007.

References

Angelopoulos, Théo (director) (1995) *Ulysses' Gaze*.
Appadurai, Arjun 1988. 'Putting hierarchy in its place'. *Cultural Anthropology* 3 (1): 36–46.
Clifford, James 1988. *The Predicament of Culture: Twentieth-Century Ethnography, Literature, and Art*. Cambridge, MA; London: Harvard University Press.
Donnan, Hastings and Thomas M. Wilson 1994. 'An anthropology of frontiers'. *Border Approaches: Anthropological Perspectives on Frontiers*. Hastings Donnan and Thomas M. Wilson (eds) 1–14. Lanham, MD: University Press of America.
Douglas, Mary 1966.*Purity and Danger: an Analysis of the Concepts of Pollution and Taboo*. London: Ark.
Ewing, Katherine Pratt 1998. 'Crossing borders and transgressing boundaries: metaphors for negotiating multiple identities'. *Ethos*, 26:2: 262–67.
Flynn, Donna K. (1997) '"We are the border": identity, exchange, and the state along the Bénin-Nigeria border'. *American Ethnologist* 24:2: 311–30.
Giroux, Henry 1992. *Border Crossings: Cultural Workers and the Politics of Education*. New York, London: Routledge.
Goytisolo, Juan 1987. *Landscapes After the Battle*. New York: Seaver Books.
Grabbe, Heather 2000. 'The sharp edges of Europe: extending Schengen Eastwards'. *International Affairs* 76: 3: 519–36.
—— 2002. 'European Union conditionality and the "Acquis Communautaire"'. *International Political Science Review / Revue internationale de science poliique* 23: 3.
Gupta, Akhil, and James Ferguson 1992. 'Beyond "Culture": space, identity, and the politics of difference'. *Cultural Anthropology* 7: 6–23.
Hannerz, Ulf 1987. 'The world in creolisation'. *Africa* 57 (4): 546–59.
Malki, L. 1992. National Geographic: The Rooting of Peoples and the Territorialization of National Identity among Scholars and Refugees. *Cultural Anthropology* 7:24–44.
Rosaldo, Renato 1989. *Culture and Truth: The Remaking of Social Analysis*. Boston: Beacon Press.
Thiessen, Ilká 2007. *Waiting for Macedonia*. Toronto Boradview Press.
Torgovnick, Marianna 1990. *Gone Primitive: Savage Intellects, Modern Lives*. Chicago, Ill.: University of Chicago Press.
Tsing, Anna Lowenhaupt 1994. 'From the margins'. *Cultural Anthropology* 9: 279–97.
West, Rebecca (1942) *Black Lamb and Grey Falcon: the Record of a Journey Through Yugoslavia in 1937*. London: Macmillan.

3

'MY FAITH, MY NATION': EXPLORING THE 'NATURAL' AFFINITY BETWEEN ORTHODOX CHRISTIANITY AND NATIONAL IDENTITY IN MACEDONIA

Violeta Duklevska Schubert

Introduction

For Macedonians, as with many others in the Balkans, *'vera'* (faith) plays a significant role in collective identity and structuring everyday ritual practices. To be sure, the religiosity of Macedonians is not based on a distinction in beliefs, ethics or religious practices but as Borowik notes, in a 'subjective sense of belonging to the Orthodox tradition' (2006: 275). As one priest said, everyone performs or attends rituals and everyone calls themselves *'Pravoslavni'* (Orthodox), but no one knows what *'vera'* really is. That is, the Macedonian Orthodox Church is symbolically a 'cultural guardian' of sorts, to borrow Ramet's (1984) phrase. Much to the chagrin of priests, Macedonians attend ritual practices and call on them where necessary but generally such occasions are not 'religious'. They are instead vital opportunities to mobilize extended family and social networks that reaffirm their 'strength' as people of social substance. As such, there is a fundamental difference between the symbolic or cultural place of Orthodoxy and everyday beliefs and practices. In many villages, as with cities, orthodox belief is utilized with much eclecticism in what Hann refers to as 'orthopraxy' (2007: 397). No single set or body of doctrine regulates engagement with Orthodox Christianity, and even the most nominal adherence is perceived as indicative of having faith. The interpretiveness that is inherent in ritual participation speaks to the overwhelming concern with the social context of performing Orthodoxy.

The enormous number of churches, *'monastiri'* (pl. monasteries) and gigantic crosses visible in villages, towns, and littered along forest tracks and major highways also attests this performativity of Orthodoxy. In the case of Ohrid, for example, the town boasts a church or *monastir* for every day of the year! Moreover, the rejuvenation of existing churches and the building of further *monastiri* is facilitated by remittances from the Macedonian diaspora. These are often accompanied by plaques in honour of ancestors or absent kin, even as home villages are rapidly disappearing due to depopulation. Likewise, the presence of the Orthodox Church in the public arena and the privileged time it is allowed in the media, especially on government television stations during Christmas, Easter and significant saints' days is symbolically important in so far as it reinforces the 'national' character of collective ethnic/cultural identity. As with Perica's observation that the 'cult of ethnic [native] saints' is one of the hallmarks of Serbian Orthodoxy and Serbian national identity (2002: 8), church and state celebrations today pay particular attention to 'native' saints such as 'Kiril and Metodija' (Cyril and Methodius), 'Kliment Ohridski' (Clement of Ohrid) and Naum.

The visibility and performativity entailed in being *'Pravoslavni'* (Orthodox) reinforces the inherently social (collective) and local nature of the belief. Orthodox belief is, by and large, the background noise of everyday practices in which the household and *familija* is reaffirmed as a central unit of society and, in this, a detailed understanding of Christian doctrine is irrelevant and indeed most often absent. In what is arguably a strong legacy of early Orthodox Christianity in which non-proselytism was canonically enshrined, identity as '*Pravoslavni*' is taken for granted as 'natural' – i.e. reproduced via birth/ kinship rather than the act of concerted individual will or agency to adopt the faith. Thus, though ritual attentions are varied and may wane among individuals, the fundamental identity of being 'born' *Pravoslavni* remains. Indeed, as a condition of 'being', identity as *Pravoslavni Makedonci* (Orthodox Macedonians) is difficult to shake off even, for example, in the case of individual proclamations of non-belief and mistrust of the politics and corruption of 'churches'.

In short, the very character of Orthodox Christianity as understood by Macedonian's *vera* is a social or collective identity. Influence by priests and the Church, therefore, is generally not due to a particularly strong religiosity as much as it is useful in reaffirming one's social place and status. The utilitarianism and pragmatism with which people engage with Orthodox Christianity suggest that this *vera* is an accompaniment to social practices and rarely transcends the social or profane context. Ironically, it is deeply internalized (naturalized) and yet objectified. This may be an outcome of the lack of influence of the Reformation, which did not reach this region, and the reconstituting of religion as an individual relationship between self and God, or a means to define and regulate either individual or collective. The ongoing need to position the institutions of the state and church as complementary systems of meaning today requires a determined collective gaze on the '*minatoto*' ('the past') as providing 'proof' of the collective struggle for survival in the national and religious sense. Beyond the discourses of Macedonians, however, the historical context of contestation and dissidence speaks to the unique way that the people of this region engage with both church and state. The Macedonian worldview is grounded in collective experiences of survival and through navigating volatile and chaotic civic and political contexts that extend from conversion to Christianity, Ottoman rule, and Yugoslav communism through to the contemporary context of ongoing national and religious struggles. Orthodox identity today may be synonymous with national identity (to ethnic Macedonians), but for this fusion to have developed it requires that there is a homogenization and symbolic reduction of complex processes that condenses collective experience into a single and unitary rhetoric of belonging.

Heathens, Heretics and Believers: Conversion to Christianity by Slavs of Macedonia

Rendered symbolically central to notions of distinction, Orthodoxy has also produced a peculiar worldview among the Macedonians that has been shaped by a body of collective experiences that continue to resonate in contemporary society. Indeed, identity as *Pravoslavni* (i.e. orthodoxy) is so deeply embedded today among the *Makedonci* that it is difficult for many to perceive a time in which they were anything but that. However, conversion to Christianity and Orthodox identity has proven to be a significant point of contestation and dissidence across the history of Macedonia.

Dimevski (1989) provides an extensive account of the spread of Christianity in the Balkan region, and I draw on his work to highlight the nature of engagement with Christian Orthodoxy by the Slavs of Macedonia. Briefly, the spread of Christianity in the region is attributed to St Paul who visited Thessaloniki (Solun), an administrative outpost of the Roman Empire in the first century. By the fifth century, the Christian Church in the Macedonia region was relatively well organized. Nonetheless, as Dimevski notes, despite having two administrative units of the church in Thessaloniki and Skopje, the Byzantium Empire could not make inroads with the Slavs of the Balkans (1989: 21–22). Concern with consolidation of power by the Byzantium Empire over the Balkans meant that the integration of Slavs via Christianity was a vital strategy for domesticating unruly tribes who remained beyond the reach of the empire (Dimevski 1989: 24–26).[1]

There is much debate about the ethnicity of Kiril and Metodija and whether they were of Slavic (Bulgarian or Macedonian) or Greek[2] origin and there is undoubtedly an 'entangled history' and 'transnational' significance of these saints (Rohdewald 2008: 289). However, their role in establishing the means for conversions of Slavs to Christianity and the development of Old Church Slavonic (based on dialects of the Slavs in the geographic region of Macedonia) is indisputable. Old Church Slavonic became the basis of Slavic Orthodoxy across the Balkans, Moldavia and Russia. This was greatly facilitated by the work of Kiril and Metodija in devising an alphabet to translate the Bible into Slavic and later the recruitment of a local priestly class from among the Slavs. Kliment Ohridski (ca. 840–916), a student of Kiril and Metodija, played a fundamental role in establishing the city as a centre of faith and the development of what was to become a literary Macedonian language, albeit geared towards religious instruction. The very notion of *'peenje'* (chanting) by priests in Old Church Slavonic carries a deeply sensed historicity of a language[3] and form that was created by 'holy' people, and according to Dimevski, was already present in the period following the death of Kiril and Metodija (1989: 62).

Christianity, compounded by myths of resistance and persecution, set in motion aggressive reactions by Byzantium authorities towards 'heretic' or dissident Christian cults and the eventual denouncement of Kiril and Metodija and their followers (Dimevski 1989: 40). The process of conversion to Christianity also reinforced a process of cultural distinction and political mobilization resulting from the development of a literary Slavic language. The establishment of Ohrid as a site of faith for Slav locals, for example, was facilitated by a local priestly class who conducted liturgies in local Slav dialects. Certainly, as Roudometof notes, 'at least until the conversion of Slavs to Orthodox Christianity and the creation of the Cyrillic script' what had become established as of the Great Schism of 1054 was that the Greek language became synonymous with 'Eastern' Christianity (2008: 70).

This does not necessarily mean that there was a particularly 'Macedonian' consciousness or ethnic identity, but the uniqueness of the Slav tribes relative to others of the region was clear. By the end of the tenth century, conversion as a strategy to enfold unruly Slavs into existent Byzantium power structures appeared to be successful. There continued to be ongoing discrimination and marginality; however, that produced a refashioning of a particular kind of engagement with Christianity. The close affinity between language of instruction and local communities was thus strongly utilized to capture concerns relating to discrimination and was reaffirmed by priests who were proactive in becoming involved in political and social dissidence. By the twelfth century, and despite extensive conversion to Christianity, recurrent wars and an agrarian crisis provided the grounds for emergent social and religious movements that were labelled 'heretical'. Among the most significant was *Bogomilism,* emerging in Macedonia during the first Bulgarian Empire under Tsar Peter I, and spreading to Bosnia, Italy, France and Russia.[4] The charismatic priest, Bogomil, advocated an austere life and the rejection of materialism and religious symbolisms. Bogomil's teachings were based on eclectic ideologies and beliefs[5] that easily incorporated disparate and socially powerless people. Importantly, he dictated to his followers that they withdraw their services to the state. As most of Bogomil's followers were from the servant class, his vehement opposition to the clergy and strong critique of the Orthodox Church as well as his expressed hatred for the king and the ruling class meant that his instructions to followers to withdraw services did not go unpunished by authorities.

The close affinity between language of instruction and local communities was strongly reaffirmed by priests such as Bogomil in the process of political and social dissidence. For example, the removal of a local (Slavic) archbishop of Ohrid in order to re-establish central church governance over the diocese at the time the Bogomili movement was gathering strength was in no small measure indicative of the perceived threat. The new Archbishop of Ohrid, a Greek priest named Teofilakt, called on the empire to eradicate the 'heretics' out of fear that dissidence was spreading among local Slavs.[6] According to Dimevski, denouncements of the followers of Bogomilism only served to make it more appealing to local Slavs influenced by other renegade local Slav priests.

In short, charismatic priests played a significant role in mobilising disparate and marginalized Slavs, in establishing the basis of a literary Slavic language and reinforcing a peculiar relationship between Slav locals and Orthodox Christianity and church governance. The emergence of a local priestly class able to have an affect on local issues was also made possible because of the mode of church governance. The canonical principle of 'one city–one bishop', which emphasizes the unity of the Christian Church and all Christians, makes significant claims not only of people but political and geographic territory by rendering a territory Orthodox. Unity between church and state is thus a critical strategy of governance. This canonical principle is certainly evident today as reflected in the constitutional privileging of the Orthodox Church in Greece and Serbia (Henkel 2009: 53–54). In other words, early Orthodox Christianity cemented a mode of thinking and governance that has complex ramifications in constructing nationalist territorial claims today.

Another important outcome of this period was the establishment of Ohrid as a centre of learning and faith. In particular, during the brief rule of Simeon I (893–927), Ohrid became the epicentre of religious instruction. Here Clement and Naum, along with their disciples, succeeded in founding an independent Orthodox patriarchate of Ohrid. However, in 1767, fearing a local uprising, the Ohrid patriarchate was abolished by the Ottomans and was only re-established in 1967 as part of Yugoslavia. Nonetheless, the imagery of Ohrid as the heart of Macedonian Orthodox culture and faith, and the country as the birthplace of Slavic Christianity due to the efforts of Kiril, Metodija, Kliment and Naum, remains powerful and is drawn upon in contemporary discourse on national identity. Just as importantly, after this period of conversion and recruitment into Orthodox Christianity, non-proselytism links membership almost entirely to the idea of 'natural' reproduction.

Ottoman Rule, Christian Identity and Competing Nationalist Orthodox Churches

Various aspects of engagement with Orthodoxy and church governance structures established during the Byzantium period and throughout the Middle Ages continued throughout the Ottoman period between the mid-fifteenth and early twentieth century. During Ottoman rule, one's identity as 'Christian' governed daily life under the *millet villayet* system. It constituted the key mode of civic engagement and formal status, rights and duties within the state. As Payton notes, although formal authority lay with the patriarch in Constantinople and he was 'responsible to the sultan for the conduct of the people of his millet and for their manifestation of loyalty to or rebellion against the Ottoman state', it seems clear that such a mode of governance was weak in regulating local dioceses and dissidence given that 'archbishops and priests in dioceses had much freedom in how they administered over their followers' (2006: 13).

Though rule via millets appears tolerant, the system of control of ordinary people was complex and multilayered. The formal authority of the Orthodox Church contrasted sharply with the linguistic and cultural diversity of the members of Christian villayets and the privilege and distinction awarded to some. Further, as Roudometof notes:

> In the *millet* system, collective rights were tied to particularistic rather than universalistic criteria (the latter being the case in Western democracies). As a result, Balkan nation-states claimed the loyalty of prospective nationals living within the Ottoman Empire on a similar basis, since this was the only way that prospective nationals could be legally identified. Membership in a state came to be viewed as the natural consequence of membership in a nation (defined in terms of an ethnic or religious group) (1996: 257).

Thus, the territorial claims that emerged in the late nineteenth and early twentieth centuries as Ottoman rule began to crumble in the region of Macedonia relied heavily on the presence of churches and a priestly class that could further the ambitions of neighbouring ethnonational states such as Greece, Serbia and Bulgaria. The holding of church services in a particular 'national' language cemented nationalist projects; it also created significant resentment, marginality and discrimination among the Slavs and various other non-dominant groups of Ottoman Macedonia. In short, the legacies of both the Byzantium and Ottoman periods in solidifying civic and community identity along the lines of religion continue to influence people's perceptions and indeed political actions.

For example, in the mid-1990s when I commenced doctoral research in Macedonia, there were many old people in a village I visited who used the term '*Rim*' or '*Rimi*' (literally 'Romans') to refer to a Christian identity to distinguish themselves from that of Muslims. Even younger generations of Vlachs insisted that they were Macedonian, 'no different than other Macedonians', on the basis that they held to the same *'vera'*. That is, insisting on an Orthodox Christian identity was not only a marker of critical distinction from rulers and the privileged Islamic communities during the Ottoman period, but today serves as a model to counter claims of an authentic Macedonian civic or national identity among minority ethnicities such as the Vlachs.

The eventual fusion of church, state, ethno-national and Orthodox identities among the Macedonians is in many ways a product of interaction with the neighbouring states. The initial autonomous Macedonia movement of the late nineteenth century was civic and liberal in ideology and endeavoured to separate religion and state as attested by the original 1880 draft Constitution. However, in the ongoing process of negotiation across volatile social, economic and political fields, the model for independence eventually adopted became far more influenced by the 'enemy' states of Greece, Serbia and Bulgaria than by civic ideology. As Rossos wrote, 'Macedonian nationalism was belated, grew slowly and, at times, manifested confusing tendencies and orientations that were, for the most part, consequences of its protracted illegitimate status' Andrew–Rossos (1994: 369). It was more than a simple matter of illegitimacy. Locals of the region, accustomed to continually navigating their way across a multitude of coexistent civic identities in an overwhelmingly complex and violent political and social arena, found it difficult to follow or wholeheartedly reject the endeavours of the competing Bulgarian, Serbian and Greek churches. In their endeavours to 're-educate' locals about who they really belonged with, the success of the three neighbouring states was that they instilled an ideology of fusion between church and state.

In the face of the ideologies of the nationalist movements in the nineteenth century and the importance of constructing bounded, territorial and homogenous identities, coexistent identities became competing and aggressive fields. Likewise, though Christianity had for centuries been a crucial civic identity marker within competing Church institutions and their affiliations with nationalist political movements, locals of the Macedonia region were, yet again, caught in a tug of war between internal processes and external power structures. In this sense, while membership in a particular national Church might or might not signal changing faith, it certainly compelled a declaration of 'nationalist' loyalties. Flipping to and fro from one national and church identity to another, as a common strategy for surviving invasion and political domination, gradually became a central point of contestation of the authenticity of Macedonians and their claims to a specific national identity. This theme resonated greatly within anthropological scholarship in the post-Yugoslav independence. It wasn't merely that identities were fluid and the character of the region an 'ethnic chessboard'. Rather it was the fact that historically Macedonians lacked consistency in how they identified themselves, and this was viewed as indicative of a lack of authenticity that shaped international relations and policies – a characteristic feature of international diplomacy that was indeed present in the emergence of the autonomous Macedonia movement at the San Stefano/Berlin Congress.

In short, a similar kind of fusion between ethno-national and religious identity that began in the nineteenth century among the neighbouring societies of Bulgaria, Greece and Serbia also emerged relatively late among the Macedonians. The experiences of living through the competing and enforced enculturation processes by the 'nationalist' churches of these neighbouring societies also significantly reshaped the nature of Macedonia identity. Moreover, in this formative period from the late nineteenth to early twentieth century there was an emergence of notions of a Macedonian nation-state. Albeit sporadic and weak in political success, the struggles over national state and church affiliations provided the impetus for the cementing of an ideological frame for the construction of a uniquely 'Macedonian' worldview that is readily drawn upon today. The simultaneous distinction and unity between the sacred and profane is, to a great extent, based on a sense of historicity coloured by continual conflict and struggle (or what some refer to as *'robstvo'* – literally, 'enslavement'). The struggle to maintain identity as *'Pravoslavni'*, especially during the Ottoman period, and more recently under communism, is proof in itself for many individuals of the existence of the Macedonian ethno-nation.

'Tito's' Macedonia

I'll give you one example about my uncle who was a General and for my wedding he was supposed to be the *starosvat*[7] that was in the 70s. He didn't want to enter the church. What I want to say is that the propaganda that the communists had about the church was severe and if anyone of them went inside a church they got punished... (Anonymous, excerpt from interview)

Post-communism was undoubtedly a significant period of ethno-national and religious revival.[8] The failure of the Socialist Federative Republic of Yugoslavia (SFRY) in uniting complex national, ethnic and religious differences along the lines of '*bratsvo i edinstvo*' (brotherhood and unity) suggests that communism was unable to become embedded in the hearts and minds of disparate people. Indeed, in Macedonia communism, as in previous periods of political rule, was unable to shake the hold that Orthodox Christianity had over people's lives. As the previous quote suggests, for ordinary Macedonians communism disrupted the place of religious practice and split kin loyalties and relationships, but it did not produce the eradication of either church or religious practices in everyday life.

A recurrent theme in the study of Macedonian national identity, state and church formation is the idea that they are products of Yugoslavia[9] and the presumably strategic forethought of Tito. The subordinating subtext of such accounts requires critical exploration, but it is beyond the scope of this chapter. Suffice it to say that there is an element of presumed naivety and passivity on the part of Macedonian politicians and clerics alike, and yet a simultaneous recognition of the rampant nationalist sentiment and activism during the Yugoslav period. With a few exceptions, notably among Macedonian scholars, there has been little attention paid to the ongoing activism of both politically and religiously motivated people within the region of Macedonia between the post-Balkan Wars 1912–13 and the formation of the Yugoslav federation after World War II. This neglect has been in terms of both negotiations with ruling states of which they were a part of and in international forums. This is not to say that there was continuity or consistency to either nationalist or religious activism. However, from local Macedonian perspectives and oral accounts of those who had lived through not only the Yugoslav period but also prior to it, it is clear that there has been a strong sentiment of an ongoing church or religious struggle. This sentiment resonates easily with and is symbolically attached to the perceived continuity of the struggle for national expression and political autonomy.

The Yugoslav period was undoubtedly significant in the consolidation of Macedonian national and religious identity. However, it is far removed from what most accounts have suggested of it being a gift or creation that is ahistorical and based on a tenuous or shallow cultural, religious presence preceding the federation. Macedonian activism and lobbying in the 1950s and 1960s leading to the establishment of semi-autonomous church status was but one of these expressions. In 1967 the Macedonian Orthodox Church split from the Serbian Church and unilaterally declared itself autocephalous. This status was eventually acknowledged by the Yugoslav socialist government but not without protests, and it was not legitimized or sanctioned by the Ecumenical Patriarch of Istanbul, the World Council of Churches or the Serbian Orthodox Church.[10] In establishing itself as a 'de facto' independent entity, the synod of the Macedonian Church resurrected Ohrid as the key loci of faith with the archbishop-metropolitan of Ohrid being the head, even though administration was in both Skopje and Ohrid. The argument of Macedonian clerics and political leaders alike was centred on the historical significance of the Ohrid diocese. Moreover, in a similar vein as the plea for international recognition of the Republic by the name 'Macedonia' today, the endeavours to gain external legitimacy by the Macedonian Orthodox Church after the 1967 schism with the Serbian Orthodox Church were problematic. Nonetheless, after Macedonian independence in 1991, the claim for its Church to be recognized became even stronger (Ramet 2005: 268–71). Thus, though it holds a privileged position vis-à-vis other churches and religious institutions in the Republic today, it continues to face ongoing internal and external challenges to its legitimacy.

Ageing Bachelors and the Threat to the 'Natural' Reproduction of *Pravoslavni Makedonci*

It is perhaps a truism that men are engaged in politics and in the defence of the nation, and *vera* comes more easily to them than women. However, in the case of ageing *stari bekjari* (bachelors), who cannot resolve the lack of a socially acceptable status and legitimate identity as adult men because they remain unmarried past the socially acceptable age (i.e. roughly speaking after 25–27 years of age), turning to politics is a significant endeavour. Moreover, it is not only that *stari bekjari* are prolifically engaged in politics, but they are also involved with the Church. As a result, both church and state are concerned with them and their place in the nation.

Their identity as *Pravoslavni Makedonci* (Macedonians) is important to *stari bekjari* and is often an alternative to the complex and competing systems of identity formation, counter-discourses of personhood, and changing kinship and individual contexts. It is a stable marker of identity and the primary mode of facilitating political activism and civic identity that enables the men to engage socially beyond that of being 'family men'. Ironically, as the *stari bekjari* seek to refashion society to suit their changed circumstance of being adult, despite being unmarried and of having a sense of civic responsibility for their country, both church and state position themselves as arbitrators of familial and social morality and endeavour to compel the men to marry. That is, state and church seek to reconstitute individuals, kinship and the essence of the fusion between ethno-national and Orthodox identity demands that the men marry and produce children. Despite this, the number of men who remain past the socially acceptable age of bachelorhood is large and growing

The import of reproduction in the social production of church and state is highlighted by several Malthusian measures of the state. These actions (which can only be seen as a response to the perceived fear of being overrun by Albanians) are seen in state incentives for Macedonian women to bear more children and in the determined activism on the part of the church to 'find' women for single men. At the local level too, such fears were on occasion voiced. For example, one school teacher, fearing that the village school would soon be closed because there were not enough *'Makedončina'* (Macedonian children) and taking for granted that the Albanian children would be redirected to neighbouring villages where Albanians were a majority (and thus where the language of instruction would be also in Albanian) proclaimed that all that was needed was to compel the men to marry, and if all did so and had one or two children each, the school would be saved!

The saving of a family, school, village, church or state being somehow or another reduced to men and their contribution to reproduction speaks to the co-opting of kinship in the 'natural' reproduction of national and religious identity. Because membership, status and recruitment to both Macedonian ethno-national identity and the Macedonian Orthodox Church is presumed to be based on notions of 'being' from birth, natural reproduction is of critical importance to social reproduction. This 'naturalization' means that this formulation of birth equals national and religious identity is rarely questioned. Further, perhaps grounded in the experiences of economic and political chaos, drawing on kinship networks and obligations is seen by most Macedonians as vital for navigating the often hostile socio-political world and corrupt civic institutions.

Since the early to mid-twentieth century, the predominantly agnatic kinship system (Schubert 2005) has provided the basis for the *familija* to remain a relatively cohesive economic, social and political unit. This is mainly a consequence of the well-structured system of authority based on seniority and the concept of what is proper or *'po red'* (in order). The notion of the fortress *familija* has persisted to a great extent in rural Macedonian communities, particularly in relation to the role of men in perpetuating the *familija* and the agnatic house. But it also points to the weakness of such a pervasive agnatic ideology – it requires that men marry and produce legitimate heirs to support the symbolic ascendance of agnatic kinship and a supposedly 'natural' order of ascendance of men over women. But, caught up in a process of modernization that began with the Yugoslav federation, most *'mladi'* (i.e. the category of 'youth' or unmarried) have been particularly determined to pursue change that will enable them if not to leave the village, at least be acknowledged as individuals who are the 'same' as those of the city. During Yugoslavia, the rejection of rural identity was crucial to a construction of a 'modern' identity. In particular, the *mladi* had become, as Scheper-Hughes noted for rural Ireland, 'thoroughly romantic about life's meaning' (2001: 50) and sought not simply to marry 'just anyone' but someone whom they loved, who could be a reflection of their image of self as a modern being. That is, the issue of marriage has become a key site of contestation and the disclaiming of existent identity, or assertion of 'modernity'. For many men this has been particularly synonymous with a rejection or questioning of one's familial identity and obligation. However, refusing to marry until they could find the 'right' woman, and given the absence or reluctance of women to be associated with villages and village men, has meant that there is today an exorbitant and disproportionate number of ageing bachelors relative to unmarried women in villages. The *stari bekjari*, therefore, are caught in an ongoing struggle with self and others in which they must challenge the very foundations of what is taken for granted as the essence of continuity of family, state and *vera*. But familial kinship identity is *a priori* and as such the individual first and foremost 'belongs' to the family, and personhood and individuality are by-products of meeting one's social (familial) responsibilities. In this, the family is the nexus of change and conflict for *stari bekjari* – a microcosm of the political and social chaos in the broader society that they are powerless to avoid as they struggle to redefine themselves as individuals (adults) beyond marriage.

By contesting their place within kinship defined as their place within the family, the meaning or purpose of marriage and whether to have children, individuals are reconstructing their relationship with both state and church. Qualities such as 'freedom' and 'choice' are presumed to be the essence of 'modern' people. To be sure, neither the state nor church can accommodate the full range of expectations and desires of individuals seeking personal identities associated with these qualities. So too, the incursion of aid and development in post-independent Macedonia has brought with it an increasing presence of world churches (or, prophetic ones), and these too are challenging the stability and sustainability of the ethno-nationalist state and the Orthodox Christian Church.[11] Moreover, given the 'ethnic chessboard' of the country (Cowan & Brown 2000), and competition with other groups – especially with the rising demographic (and political) significance of Albanians – strategies to consolidate and protect the Macedonians from pending numerical decline are perceived as critical. In the endeavour to consolidate or construct the model ethno-nation, the state has encouraged a rise in birth rates of Macedonians and marriage, as evident for example in a proposal by a parliamentarian to tax unmarried individuals past the social age of marriage (Schubert 2009).[12] Hence independence, the family and the individual are being reconstituted and harnessed as a subject of the emergent state. State loyalty, in order to supersede other loyalties, demands that the individual become first and foremost a familial subject (i.e. a citizen) and simultaneously co-opts kinship in the service of the state and church. Likewise, the Macedonian Orthodox Church has begun to assume a more prominent public role as a moderator of moral life. Coinciding with the state's campaigns in relation to birth rates and marriage, the Church too has begun to take a firmer position with regards to private life such as voicing concern with the lack of sanctity in marriage (i.e. high divorce rates) and abortion. As church and state are concerned with harnessing kinship for the greater good, so too parents of *stari bekjari* are concerned with harnessing the wayward individuals for the good of the family.

The presumption that the perpetuation of the state and the Orthodox Church rests on the perpetuation of the *familija* and that loyalty to family and identity is primarily tied to kinship relations is being challenged. *Stari bekjari*, as the instruments and agents of its perpetuation, are expected to be conscious of their duty and to become resolved to 'find' a woman and marry her. Women, because they are presumed to 'wait' for men to offer marriage are pitied (not accused or harassed) for remaining unmarried, although once married they face pressures to reproduce. It is beyond the scope of this chapter to do justice to the issue of the extent to which this kind of familial ideology mirrors that of the state and church. In their quest to assert their place within modernity, individuals in Macedonia, as I suspect in other Balkan states, are unconsciously changing the fabric of the society in step with the increasing fervour and political discourses of ethno-national and religious sentiments.

Nonetheless, for *stari bekjari* today there is no denying that the issue of individualism is particularly important, and yet complex. They are both the *mladi* of the new state and precede it. As 'youth' of 40 or 50 years of age, they perceive their role in the state-building project privileges them and imposes a duty to see it through the tumultuous period because 'they' fought for it. There is an emotional attachment to the state even when it too is criticizing or rejecting them. In particular, the state as the new symbolic foci of identification is not living up to its promise to make things better for all individuals. Nonetheless, the sense that things will be better in the future compels many *stari bekjari* to continue to be involved in politics as a necessary, if not critical strategy, for setting the foundations of their own personal liberation – even when it also isolates them as a 'problem'.

Stari bekjari are generally more complicit with state objectives to transform them into subjects of the nation, precisely because it suggests an avenue for asserting individualism via the category of citizen. At loggerheads with family and engaged in relations of conflict, stress and confrontation with 'others', they invariably return their attention to politics precisely because there is at least the hope of it being more accepting of them and their endeavours to reconstitute themselves. Yet, the symbiotic enmeshing of political, religious and kinship identity into a homogenous collective identity as '*Makedonci*' is only possible through a functioning *familija*. Kinship, the *familija*, is the nexus upon which faith and nation survive, which brings us full circle back to the need for men and women to marry and women to bear children – the very antithesis of the *stari bekjari's* identity. It is not only that a symbolic kinship of sorts is presumed between all members of the nation, it is the material and concrete forms of kinship that structures and perpetuates the legitimacy to claims of both collective and individual identities.

Despite their own discontents, *stari bekjari* continue to focus on both church and state as symbolic containers of their personhood. In the overall struggle to adjust to being the majority ethnicity in postindependent Macedonia, and given the multitude of competing identities and individual aspirations, there continues to be a saliency to being 'Macedonian'. For the *stari bekjari*, the fact that both church and state continue to be contested by others today reinforces the idea that there is a 'truth' to being Macedonian. As one man said, 'Why would they want to destroy us, deny who we are as a nation? Why do they reject our Church as if we do not exist, as if we do not have our own faith, our own *sila* [force]?'

A uniquely Macedonian cosmological order has emerged in which *sila* is perceived to reside in the simultaneous distinction and unity of the sacred and profane, in the belief that there is a higher, non-material world order. The 'truth' of being Macedonian is conjoined with a need to be resilient, resourceful and determined to fight (struggle) for both '*vera*' and '*država*' (country). This order serves as a powerful rhetoric for social mobilization. Yet, this is also indicative of the success of the co-option of kinship and natural reproduction into an instrument of the state which requires, as Abu-Lughod notes for the Bedouins, '[s]eparating kin groups and regulating individuals' (1990: 52). Similarly, the relationship between the Byzantium state and the Orthodox Church plays a front-line role in this process by priests in constructing the domesticated, 'ruled' people whereby there is a 'sacredness' attached to non-contestation, fatalism or being in the hands of God (and thus state).

Kinship is in the service of both church and state today only because of the depth of internalization of the rhetoric and ideology of Orthodox Christianity. In this context, a functioning, depoliticized and servile kinship system in which the role of the *familija* becomes a primary vehicle for reproducing faith and nation rather than contestation of the order of things is critical. Thus, in not living up to their expected role in reproduction, *stari bekjari* are now more often than not pitted against the collective, against church and state and their own families and yet, simultaneously, deeply embedded within them.

Concluding Remarks

The rhetoric and strategies of states and churches through time and across different civic and political contexts have been geared towards the construction of identity as 'naturally' reproduced. As such, ethnonational and religious identities have been grounded in and valorized via a fertile kinship order. Both in terms of reproducing the faithful within communities as well as the priestly class, kinship is of fundamental importance. The greater 'truth' for Macedonians has become a cosmological order in which the realization of statehood is their reward for sacrifice – having a country of their own and a moment of historical exaltation in the face of *robstvo*, rejection and denial by others that provides credence and ongoing salience to a purveying view of the collective, suffering Self. In what is arguably one of the most contentious regions of the Balkans– where there is perpetual crisis, contestation and interference by powerful others survival and validation of 'truth' and meaning has become grounded in notions of perseverance, resourcefulness and clever navigation through complex socio-political minefields – like 'a snake manoeuvring between the cracks' as one priest said. There is a self-perceived uniqueness to Macedonians as people, as a nation, because of the liturgy of external powers that have invaded, vied or interfered in the region, and also because of their own resilience and resourcefulness developed in the face of such *'haus'* ('chaos').

The chaos, invasions and conflicts synonymous with the geographic region is a felt experience, embodied and transmitted through kinship. As such, the claim that 'We are *Macedonians*' is in essence a call for others to understand the history of the region itself, 'We *are* Macedonia'. Holding firm to the name 'Macedonia' in the face of protests by Greece and various international pressures serves to reaffirm the validity or 'truth' that *being* Macedonians and *of* Macedonia are one and the same thing. The *Makedonci* generally have the view that they are the people who carry the history of the region on their bodies (the sacrifices of the collective body), in their shared memories and collective experiences and their *'vera'* (faith). The place of the Orthodox Church is a vital component of their perceived success. A worldview coloured by mythologies, folksongs and stories of 'grandmothers and grandfathers', of harsh treatment, stolen children, women enslaved into the harems of Turkish *begs* and *pashas*, Orthodox churches destroyed or forced to be built in ditches or unattractive or invisible places, alongside very low rates of intermarriage between Christians and Muslims has shaped and continues to shape Macedonian perceptions as well as relations within and across different ethnic and religious groups today.

Even while gaining independence where the *Makedonci* were the ethnic majority and their church was in a privileged position, the idea of a collective, suffering Self and of 'wolves at the door' is of paramount importance to mobilization and identity because one cannot be 'Macedonian' if there is no enemy, no struggle for recognition or sacrifice. Indeed, to be Macedonian means to be engaged in a constant and ongoing battle for survival in which vigilance is critical and it is thus the duty of each and every Macedonian to maintain a steadfast loyalty to reproduction. The discourse of 'enslavement' may have a unifying purpose, but it is also proving to be embarrassing for some, a discomfort given that in the Republic they are the privileged within the state, as is their church. That privilege, however, is tenuous and requires that individuals are harnessed to the greater, collective good.

The fusion between church and nation and the construction of what is both 'natural' and 'sacred' is perpetuated by a myth of a perceived unbroken link with the past that 'marks the centre as centre', to borrow *Clifford Geertz's phrase*. This is nothing new in the Balkans. But, there are a multitude of collective and personal struggles faced by the *Makedonci* in the Republic today. For example, adjusting to independence and having more 'freedom' does not come easy because, as one interviewee says:

> You know for a very long time with the enslavement we had, and then with communism, I mean the atheists who put so much pressure on the people, it came to the edge [of tolerance] for people and now there is a little more freedom. Fine, but we are not used to it, it's hard for people to adjust to this kind of [mode] of living and everything annoys them. But with time all will come into its own.

Adjusting to freedom is perhaps a new kind of struggle to the more familiar forms experienced by *Makedonci*. The 'cultural intimacy' (Herzfeld 2005) of mistrust of both politicians and priests who are often assumed to be part of 'corrupt' systems does not deflect the seemingly steadfast loyalty to both church and nation. The perceived, imminent threat that comes with 'wolves' (Judah 2007) at the door (both within and without), the protests over the use of the name, and the persistent lack of recognition of the Macedonian Church by the synod of the Orthodox Christian Church, serves to transform state and church, politicians and priests into symbols of shared unity and, indeed, shared salvation (*'spas'*). As one man said, 'The only salvation for us is to fight for Macedonia, for our country, our Church' despite the fact that, in the words of another man, 'Politicians are more powerful on the tongue and always dictate how the system goes.' In the epic battle to save the nation and church, this unity has a powerful, mobilizing potential. Indeed, in a mass show of unity, slogans such as *'Verata ne si ja smenuvam'* ('I don't change my belief') and *'Državata ne si ja napuštam'* ('I don't give up on my country') have proliferated.

The name 'Macedonia' is a symbol that, as one informant said, 'stems from memories of those who have gone in the past' (*'doaga od spomenite na onie koi pominale vo minatoto'*). Oral histories and family myths of the experiences of kin members fuse past into present, symbolic into actual kin relations. In this sense, kinship continues to play a fundamental role in structuring social, political and religious identity and engagement. Just as it is 'natural' that one marries and has children, so too the presumed 'naturalness' of being *'Makedonci'* and *'Pravoslavni'* ('Orthodox Christian') relies primarily on a mode of social production facilitated by folk myths, stories and lived experiences of generations of kinfolk that reaffirms the 'struggle for life' (*'Borba za život'*), country and faith into an emotive '*our* faith, *our* Church', which no challenge to the Church as institution can address. Faith in nation and church appears unshakable for many – all it needs is more *Makedonci* for it to continue to be so!

Notes

1. Conversion to Christianity was also an important strategy for Slav and Bulgar unification in the ninth century in the case of Bulgaria. See Crampton 1987: 2–3.
2. See Karakasidou 1993; Danforth 1993; Rohdewald 2008; Soulis 1965 for significance of Cyril and Methodius to Slavs.
3. See Friedman (2000) for an account of the development of Macedonian literary language and its place in national and religious identity.

4. According to Dimevski, though mention of the Bogomili is typically under the name 'Bulgarians' it is sometimes referred to as 'Dragovitckata Crkva' ('Dragovi Church'), i.e. the Dragovi Slav tribe prominent in the region of Macedonia (1989: 72).
5. For example, it was also influenced by Sufism and is perhaps one of the reasons for the appeal of Bogomilism even among Bosnian converts to Islam in the period following Ottoman rule, if not today.
6. In some places authorities responded violently to such dissidence with the eradication of whole towns believed to be sympathizers such as in the Pelagonia region (see Dimevski 1989: 110–11).
7. The term *'starosvat'* refers to an agnatic kinsman who stands on the side of the groom at a wedding.
8. See Stan & Turcescu 2000; Zubrzycki 2001; Herbert & Fras 2009; Hann & Pelkmans 2009.
9. See, for example, Perica 2002: 12; Pettifer 1992: 483–84; Adamson & Jovic 2004: 294; Henkel 2009.
10. For more detailed account of the 1967 split and the Serbian Orthodox reaction see, for example, See Perica 2002: 46; Ivekovic 1997: 28; Ilic 2004: 33.
11. I refer here to the broad modernization strategies that are compelling demands for changing the constitution to accommodate religious freedom as part entry to the European Union or international development aid conditionalities set for ex-communist states. For a complementary analysis see also Herbert & Fras (2009) re EU integration of Poland, Hungary and Romania who illustrate that despite the endeavours to impose a kind of secularism there is a strengthening of religious sentiments post EU integration conditionalities.
12. Low birth rates, a proposal to tax the unmarried at higher rate, and the generally increased interference by state and church into private lives is suggestive of a similar process of enculturation and domestication noted by Karakasidou (1993) of the 'Slavo-Macedonian' minority in northern Greece.

References

Abu-Lughod, L. 1990. 'Romance of resistance: tracing transformations of power through Bedouin women'. *American Ethnologist*, vol. 17, no.1, pp. 41–55.

Adamson, K & D, Jovic 2004. 'The Macedonian-Albanian political frontier: the re-articulation of post-Yugoslav political identities'. *Nations and Nationalism* 10 (3), 2004, pp. 293–311.

Brown, K.S. 1994. 'Seeing stars: character and identity in the landscapes of modern Macedonia', *Antiquity*, Dec, vol. 68, pp. 784–97.

Cowan, Jane K., & K.S. Brown 2000. 'Introduction: Macedonian inflections', in Jane K. Cowan (ed.), *Macedonia: The Politics of Identity and Difference*, Pluto Press, London, pp. 1–27.

Crampton, R.J. 1987. *A Short History of Modern Bulgaria*, Cambridge University Press; Cambridge.

Danforth, Loring 1993. 'Claims to Macedonian identity: the Macedonian question and the breakup of Yugoslavia', *Anthropology Today*, vol. 9. no. 4, pp. 3–10.

Dimevski, S. 1989. *History of the Macedonian Orthodox Church*, Makedonska Kniga: Skopje.

Friedman, V. 2000. 'Modern Macedonian standard language and its relation to modern Macedonian identity' in V. Roudometof (ed.) *The Macedonian Question: Culture, Histiography, and Politics*, Eastern European Monographs, Boulder, Columbia University Press: New York.

Hann, C. 2007. 'The anthropology of Christianity per se', *European Journal of Sociology*, vol. 48, pp. 383–410.

Hann, C & M. Pelkmans 2009, 'Realigning religion and power in Central Asia: Islam, nation-state and (post)socialism'. *Europe- Asia Studies*, vol. 61, no. 9, November, pp. 1517–41.

Henkel, R. 2009. 'Religions and religious institutions in the post-Yugoslav states between secularization and resurgence'. *Geographica*, nos. 1–2, pp. 81–97.

Herbert, D & M. Fras 2009. 'European enlargement, secularisation and religious re-publicisation in Central and Eastern Europe'. *Religion, State & Society*, vol. 37, nos. 1/2, March/June, pp. 81–97.

Ilic, 2004. Religion in Eastern Europe, vol. 24, no. 6, Dec., pp. 26–37.

Ivekovic, 1997. 'Political use and abuse of religion in Transcaucasia and Yugoslavia'. *Comparative Studies of South Asia, Africa and the Middle East*, vol.17, no.1, pp. 26–31.

Judah, T. 2007. 'Wolves and Bears'. *The World Today*, vol. 63, no. 11, Nov., pp. 23–25.

Kaplan, R.D. 1991. 'History's Cauldron', *The Atlantic;* Jun., vol. 267, 6, p. 92.

Karakasidou, A, 1993, 'Politicizing culture: negating ethnic identity in Greek Macedonia', *Journal of Modern Greek Studies*, vol. 11, No. 1, May pp. 1–28.

Payton 2006. 'Ottoman millet, religious nationalism, and civil society: focus on Kosovo'. *Religion in Eastern Europe*, vol. 26, no. Feb., pp. 11–23.

Pettifer, J. 1992, 'The new Macedonia Question'. *International Affairs*, vol. 68, no. 3, pp. 475. 485.

Perica, V. 2002. *Balkan Idols: Religion and Nationalism in Yugoslav States*, Oxford University Press: New York.

Ramet, S. P. 1984. *Nationalism and Federalism in Yugoslavia, 1963–1983*, Indiana University Press: Bloomington.

——— 2005. *Thinking about Yugoslavia: Scholarly Debates about the Yugoslav Breakup and the Wars in Bosnia and Kosovo*. Cambridge University Press: Cambridge.

Rohdewald, S. 2008. Figures Of (Trans-) National Religious Memory of the Orthodox Southern Slavs Before 1945: An Outline on the Examples of Ss. Cyril and Methodius. *Trames* 12(3): 287–298.

Rossos A. 'The British Foreign Office and Macedonian National Identity, 1918–41'. *Slavic Review*, vol. 53, no. 2, Summer.

Rossos, A. 1994. Macedonia and the Macedonians: a History. Stanford: Hoover Institution Press.

Roudometof, V. 1996. 'Nationalism and identity politics in the Balkans: Greece and the Macedonian question'. *Journal of Modern Greek Studies* 14.2.

—— 1998. 'From rum millet to Greek nation: enlightenment, secularization, and national identity in Ottoman Balkan Society, 1453–1821'. *Journal of Modern Greek Studies,* vol. 16, no. 1, May, pp. 11–48.

—— 2008. 'Greek Orthodoxy, territoriality, and globality: religious responses and institutional disputes'. *Sociology of Religion*, vol. 69, no. 1, pp. 67–91.

Scheper-Hughes N. 2001. *Saints, Scholars and Schizophrenics: Mental Illness in Ireland*, University of California Press: Berkley.

Schubert, V. 2005. 'Dynamics of Macedonian kinship in a Mediterranean perspective: Contextualizing ideologies and pragmatics of agnation'. *Journal of Mediterranean Studies*, Vol. 15, no. 1 pp. 25–50.

Schubert 2009, 'Out of turn, out of sync: waiting for marriage in Macedonia', Chap. 9 in *Waiting,* Ghassan Hage (ed.), Melbourne University Press: Melbourne.

Soulis, G.C. 1965. 'The legacy of Cyril and Methodius to the Southern Slavs'. *Dumbarton Oaks Papers*, vol. 19, pp. 19–43.

Southern Slavs before 1945: An outline of the examples of SS Cyril and Methodius'. *Trames*, 12(62/57), 3, pp. 287–98.

Stan, L & L. Turcescu 2000. 'The Romanian Orthodox Church and post-communist democratisation'. *Europe-Asia Studies,* vol. 52, no. 8, pp. 1467–88.

Zubrzycki, G. 2001. '"We, the Polish nation": ethnic and civic visions of nationhood in post-communist constitutional debates'. *Theory and Society*, vol. 30, pp. 629–68.

4

NATIONALISM AND THE USE OF CULTURAL HERITAGE: A FEW POST-SOCIALIST MACEDONIAN EXAMPLES

Davorin Trpeski

According to the contemporary idea of the nation, nationalism is the creator of national identity. For Ernest Gellner (Eriksen 2004: 169), nationalism does not merely awaken the self-consciousness of the nation as an entity: it also invents nations, a sense of homogeneous community where they didn't exist. Historically, the nations on the Balkan Peninsula emerged relatively late compared to those of Western Europe. Macedonia, a Balkan nation, was one of the youngest to appear. According to Gellner's theory, with the establishment of the new independent Macedonian state, political elites with nationalistic tendencies emerged and worked to 'strengthen' the idea of a Macedonian national identity. The concept of profiling the newly formed Macedonian state was completely different from the concept utilized by the former Republic of Yugoslavia, within which Macedonia and the Macedonian ethnic community once existed. Through nationalistic elements used by some of the political centres of power, Macedonian political leaders aimed at mobilizing part of the civil society which demonstrated power and, in certain circumstances, gave legitimacy to power and political control of the country. Simultaneously, it is important to note that conditions for Albanians were similar to that of Macedonians during the time of the Yugoslavian state. Both groups felt threatened and inferior to the dominant, Serbian group. The Albanian community soon became a target for the development of myths regarding the famous historical past of Albanian political authorities. Also, both Macedonian and Albanian political centres of power were, in the years before the fall of Yugoslavia, active mainly among the Western European and overseas diasporas.

Nationalism is primarily an identity where political and national entities overlap. As a movement, it can be best defined as a feeling of anger caused by disruption of the political principle of the nation, or as a feeling of satisfaction when this principle is respected. Hence, a nationalistic movement is one based on these feelings (Gellner 1983: 1). Gellner also considers that as a nation is being built, the notion of a 'national entity' is expressed as a synonym for 'ethnic community'. He explains, 'nationalism is a theory of political legitimacy, according to which the ethnic borders should be harmonized with the political' (Gellner 1997: 56). Nationalism thus becomes an ethnic ideology that determines which particular group should dominate in the state. As a consequence, the national state is one in which one ethnic community is supreme, and the basic features of its identity (such as language or religion) are usually already integrated into official state symbols and national legislation. In these states, the tendency to integrate and assimilate all citizens is evident, although Gellner recognizes that nations sometimes encompass people and communities that could not be assimilated, or as he says, groups that are resistant to entropy (Eriksen 2004: 173).

Benedict Anderson (1991: 6) says that nationalism is an imaginary political community, and is thought to be both fundamentally limited and essentially sovereign. By 'imaginary community' Anderson doesn't necessarily consider it 'invented', but rather that people who define themselves as members of one nation 'will never know the majority of other members of their nation, they will never meet them, but anyhow they possess [the] representation of a collective unity in their heads' (Anderson 1991: 6). Despite the differences in focus, Anderson's perspective is largely compatible with that of Gellner. Both highlight that nations are ideological constructs that need to establish a fictitious link with the cultural group, and that the state and nation are at the same time abstract communities, fundamentally different from the former communities that were mainly based on kinship relations (Eriksen 2004: 173).

In theory, nationalism is neither exclusively a 'leftist' nor a 'rightist' ideology. It often emphasizes the equality of all citizens, so it can be regarded as 'leftist'. On the other hand, since it often insists on vertical solidarity and exclusion of foreigners (sometimes of minorities as well), it could also be interpreted as a right-wing ideology (Eriksen 2004: 185). Despite this, Anderson suggests that nationalism and all other ethnic ideologies are placed on the same level with kinship and religion and not with fascism and liberalism (Anderson 1991: 15).

One of the central tenets of contemporary nationalist ideology is the claim that the community, which is threatened by a global society, can only be saved if it returns to its roots. This rhetoric often includes claims of cultural continuity. Also nationalism often relies on the symbolism of religion and myth, while at the same time it is often rife with violence.[1] Nationalist ideology can fully possess the individual, perhaps in a way that he or she would experience as *primordial*. When eventually passions burst, people 'burnout'. Just like other ethnic ideologies, nationalism appropriates symbols that are important to people of the relevant group and then argues that these symbols represent the nation-state. Also, death is a very important element in nationalist ideologies; the public displays of people who have died in war or as martyrs, who gave their lives defending the nation, is evidence of this (Eriksen 2004: 187).

Key terms often used in nationalist rhetoric are ones related to kinship (e.g. country – mother, father of the nation, brothers and sisters, etc.), and the abstract community from which nationalists originate *a priori*. Paradoxically, nationalism has emerged and continues to emerge in periods of decline of the social significance of family ties. It may satisfy some of the needs usually met by kinship. It offers security and a sense of continuity and an opportunity to make a career following a unique educational system and labour market. Metaphorically as *pater familias*, according to nationalism, all members of the nation are essentially one big family, and in the national courts it punishes its disobedient children. It is an abstract version of something specific that arouses strong feelings in every individual, and it tries to transfer this emotional charge to the state. Thus, nationalism appears as an ideology of metaphorical kinship tailored to large modern societies. Simply put, this metaphor is the foundational ideology of the nation-state (Eriksen 2004: 187–88). Like other ideologies, nationalism has to justify the specified structure of power (real or potential) and meet the legitimate needs of the population. From this perspective, nationalism has to strive to link ethnic ideology with the actual state apparatus. But unlike other political systems, the nation-state relies on an ideology that argues that political boundaries have to overlap with cultural boundaries (Eriksen 2004: 187–88).

The notion that protection of cultural heritage is the prerogative of nation-states is based on the idea that national boundaries are firmly fixed, control of their territory is absolute and established only with the formation of the modern nation-state (Bilig 2009: 51–64). These boundaries are perceived as eternal (except when there is a tendency to expand the boundaries of the 'natural' / 'real' nation-state) and equated with ethnic boundaries, also regarded as eternal and immutable. Ironically the boundaries of nation-states in fact do change relatively often. Therefore, Maria Todorova does not speak only for the Balkans, but also for Europe, in noting that a nation-state is a palimpsest composed of different units (Gavrilović 2009: 37).

In the world of nations, each is unique and each one is 'chosen'. Unlike historically when each community was a world unto itself, modern-day cultural heritage and cultural values are selected from the treasury of the same community in order to be reinterpreted to take part in the creation of a new national identity. Nationalism as ideology and symbolism legitimizes every cultural configuration, calling for intellectuals everywhere to transform 'low' culture into 'high' culture, the spoken literary tradition into written in order to retain it for future generations (Smit 1998: 134–35). The 'chosen' people once chose their gods; today the gods are chosen by the ideology and symbols that praise both the unique and universal, transforming it into reality. However, in such conditions of statelessness and lack of opportunity for establishing an ethnic community, the newly established Macedonian state led by the right-wing party with nationalist inclinations (VMRO-DPMNE) shortly began intense activities related to developing the national identity of Macedonians. In fact, using their position of power and populism, weak opposition and the numerous media outlets placed under its influence, the political party in power started changing Macedonian identity by changing the history of hitherto known historical facts. Although the government of VMRO-DPMNE usually denies this, it subtly places itself in a position to support and stimulate the newly formed thesis on Macedonian history. Among many examples that relate to this 'new' understanding of history and the new meanings and interpretations of cultural heritage sites and artefacts, I note the so-called *Makedonska molitva* (Macedonian prayer), *Rozetski kamen* (Stone of Rozeta) and *Burushaski jazik* (Burushi language).

Macedonian Prayer

One of the more significant examples of the Macedonians as the oldest people and as a nation that is close to God is called the 'Macedonian prayer'. It was a nine-minute TV commercial broadcast on the Macedonian Radio and Television (MRTV) in 2008, featuring a Macedonian addressing God with prayer and questions. The central questions were related to Macedonian national identity, Macedonian existence and the denial of Macedonians by neighbours. Moreover, Christianity was presented as an 'all Macedonian' religious belief. In this context the 'prayer' revealed that before addressing God, the Macedonian in his dream came into contact with St. Nicholas who also identified himself as Macedonian. Particularly impressive were the two histories arising from the 'prayer', one true and one considered false. In fact, it was argued that the false history was promoted by Macedonian neighbours and traitors. The existence of 'true' and 'false' readings of history is a generally accepted thesis. The truth is determined as what is seen by 'our' current discourse and considered 'objective', while all other possible and alternative views are false, regardless of whether such readings are created by some 'other' or we have shaped it in another time and another context (Gavrilović 2009: 41). The prayer mentioned the address of the Macedonian to Apostle Paul, who was required to come to Macedonia and help the Macedonians. The most probable purpose for mentioning this scene is the need to confirm 'Christian attributes' of Macedonians and to show that, as a nation, they were among the first to accept Christianity and are mentioned in the Bible. In the Macedonian's prayer to God, Govrlevo, a village in the vicinity of Skopje, was mentioned. The village is associated with a male figurine discovered in its vicinity which, according to archaeologists, dates from the neolithic period. Researchers call it 'Adam of Govrlevo'[2] or 'Adam of Macedonia' and this is, not coincidentally, reminiscent of the first biblical man and is considered part of ancient Macedonian history. Particularly impressive is that the 'prayer' mentioed that Adam of Macedonia 'prayed' before the world's largest cross (probably thought to be the Millennium Cross on the Vodno Mountain). According to the narrator in the video, Macedonia is a country that will play an important role in the final battle between God and Satan (Armageddon). Macedonians are on the side of God, and seek help from him to deal with the servants of Satan, i.e. those who oppose the existence of the Macedonians and Macedonia.

National identities, like ethnic identities, are formed in relation to 'the other'. The very idea of a nation derives from the existence of other nations or other people who do not belong to the particular nation (Eriksen 2004: 191). In fact, many national myths pronounce that the nation was born or created during conflicts with either an external or internal enemy (Eriksen 2004: 193). The 'other' has great significance in shaping ethnic identity and plays a mediating role in the selection of symbols that the ethnic ideology will have. At the same time, the 'other' is used to justify the current structure of the government and attribute deeper meaning to citizens' lived experience in giving them a motive to personally sacrifice for the nation. Also, the potential effect of identification on an ethnic basis grows exponentially when ethnic identity is associated with the modern state via nationalism (Eriksen 2004: 193).

Finally, it is 'clear' that God and the Macedonians will win over evil and Satan, so in the prayer, the Macedonian asked God to present the Macedonians to the world and to tell the truth about them and Macedonia:

> Lord, dearest God, who art in heaven, do you see the plight of our Macedonian? Do you hear the cries of our mothers, fathers, brothers, sisters and our children for the children who died for Macedonia? Thousands of years we bleed, wounds alive to our unborn we leave. God, you're the only one in the sky, it's only you that sees our mother, crucified on four sides, just as the Son of God. Wherever you go, you step over grave and stumble of the bones. Lord, tell us now, tell the truth, to us and to the world, why St. Nicholas came in my dream and told me: 'I'm from the land of love and kindness, and I am Macedonian and I shed bloody tear in the boiler of our pain. But the truth is with the Almighty, ask him and he'll say, because our time, Macedonian time has come.' Lord, only you know that there are two truths, but only one is the right one. Thousands of books around the world our neighbor's shared, with false history and distorted truth about Macedonia. Lord, only you know our real truth, who we are, where are we from and why are we Macedonians? The Macedonian appeared in the dream of Apostle Paul and said: 'Come to Macedonia and help us'. And St. Apostle Paul listened to the prayer and came straight to us, Macedonians. And now for two thousand years we believe in you only and in two thousand churches and monasteries we pray and wait for you from the eternity. No longer I remember, but I know, I Macedon of Govrlevo, eight thousand years I'm alone with God and pray in front of the world's largest cross. You, the only Lord, dearest God, who art in heaven, listen to our prayer and come to Armageddon, give us your hand and tell the truth about evil and goodness, to us and to the whole world, because no blood remained in us for the Great Mother – Macedonia (Македонска молитва, website).

It is particularly important to note that the prayer of the Macedonians had been heard and that God addressed the Macedonians in the

Macedonian language. In fact, the words God told them revealed that the Macedonians are the chosen people and God had eagerly awaited their prayer, so he would be able to address them. Moreover, in his speech, God emphasized that when creating the nations He created the white race as well, and called it 'Macedonoids'. This term was strongly disputed in public, because of the racist rhetoric of those who participated in the creation of the video, as well as those who ordered and allowed its broadcast on the state television. In his address, God emphasized that all white men are brothers of Macedonians, because they have the Macedonian gene, and departing from Macedonia they migrated north, and formed other nations and states. God recognized that the Macedonians have suffered for thousands of years, and that they have lived a life full of troubles, but that it is due to these temptations that He is prepared to see how faithful they are. This motif originates from the Old Testament (Свето писмо 1998), i.e. the story of Job and his temptations. Among the many Macedonian kings God sent, the most significant was Alexander of Macedon whose grave, according to God, was located in Macedonia. Once God shows the exact location of his grave and the Macedonians unearthed it, they were to expect the world to come to worship, and thus God would present to the world the Macedonians – 'the first among the first and the worthiest among the worthy'. After all, the Macedonian time had already come and the world would soon find out that it was an honour and a blessing to be a Macedonian, a descendant of Macedon, son of the God of the Universe:

> God's blessings to you my Macedonians. Thousands of years I'm waiting for your call. Always with you, from eternity now I come. I'm with you already, because neither time nor space exists here. The time stands still for me here, but to you, down, now the time has come. Let me explain you, I populated your mother Earth with three races: white – macedonoids, yellow – mongoloids and black – negroids, the remaining – all mulatto. From you Macedonians, descendants of Macedon, I concieved the white race and everything started here to the Japan Sea. All white people are your brothers because they carry the Macedonian gene and all migrations from your land to the north began. Kokino, Porodin,

Radobor, Angelci, Barutnica, Govrlevo, wherever you dig, you will find the truth, who you are, why are you here and where are you from. Evil shadows of the Devil for thousand years hided the truth and lied to the world. How much you suffered and how many pains you went through? I gave you temptations, but you still remained faithful. My children, children of sun and flowers, blessed with joy, love and kindness, thousands of years kings I sent and now again I'm giving you one. You give them all away, and don't keep any for yourself. How many kings are here with me and how many Macedonians, as the stars of the sky and the sand in the sea. Let all the angels sing, for all that are with me, who changed their life for eternity, for the love of Macedonia, and shared with me my kingdom. And all the angels already sing for you, who understand God's glory, for all of you whom part of the heaven I gave, for all you whom love and peace I gave, for all you who waited for me and celebrated. So, now I come to Macedonia, I am among you now, to tell you the real truth, which you have under your ground. The tomb of Alexander, the Macedonian king, I open for you and the whole world to worship I bring. How many Macedonian tombs there are yet to be opened, because their souls for the truth yearn. Love your biggest enemies, because I have them send you to help you the most, the truth about Macedonia and you, the Macedonians, the world to know, because you were the first among the first, and the worthiest among the worthy. Now the Macedonian time has come, the whole world the truth to know, that it is an honor and blessing to be a Macedonian, a descendant of Macedon, son of the God of the Universe. My children, be blessed and eternal, here where the sun and flowers reign, so shall the joy, love and goodness be eternal. Among yourselves now I'm noble, in the eternal Macedonia blissfully. Amen (Македонска молитва, website).

This broadcast lasted for a few days and provoked strong reactions from the Macedonian public. Certain non-governmental organizations and individuals demanded accountability from the responsible person that allowed a commercial with nationalist and racist content to be broadcast on Macedonian state television. One of the authors of the commercial, Niche Dimovski, the general secretary of the World Macedonian Congress, appeared in front of the public and said that he made the video for patriotic reasons (A1 TVa, website). In public debate the 'Macedonian prayer' produced both 'pro' and 'contra' arguments. The host of the TV show *Voice of the People*, Slobodan Tomic, said in its defence that without prayer Macedonians would have no success: 'If we have a prayer, our Macedonian, it is the holiest thing, because without a prayer we have no success, wherever we go. I believe you will agree with me, that before starting something, we always pray for its succeess' (A1 TVb, website). On the other hand, a bit later one columnist wrote a column with arguments against the prayer. The column presented the prayer, especially the part explaining the origins of the first humanoid, macedonoid, as a parody (Utrinski vesnik, 2009).

Through the so-called prayer of the Macedonians and the address of God to the Macedonians, the authors intended for the public to discover new 'known facts' which, supposedly, are part of Macedonia's existence. It was also intended to change the already 'known' history by alluding to the fact that Macedonians are the chosen people, far ahead of other nations in the world and a nation that is in direct communication with the supernatural, with God. The basis of the story of the creation of the Macedonians lies in what Eleazar M. Meletinsky called Jewish-Christian mythology, found in the Bible. But in this case, things are really scrambled. Promoting the prayer through public media in Macedonia was not just an attempt to historicize the myth concerning the origin of the Macedonians, but also to mythologize history. In fact, it is known that mythology does not oppose history, but often complements it (Мелетински 2002: 8). Furthermore, in the video, the Macedonians called on God to solve problems, to make order from the chaos in the Balkans. Macedonians have 'suffered' mysteriously for centuries and are innocent, but at the same time, their suffering has been a necessary sacrifice, just as Christ the Saviour, humble to the father, willingly suffered and died. Here it is also about political ethno-myth making, which, according to Roland Barthes (Мелетински 2002: 8), has the power to turn history into ideology. Basically, the myth has two main functions. The first is to answer some fundamental questions like those posed by children, such as: Who created the world? How will the world end? Who was the first man? Where do souls go after death? The second function of the myth is to justify the existing social system and to confirm traditional rules and customs (Graves 1987: 5). Myths are, in fact, a significant factor in shaping the boundaries of the possible in the establishment of the cognitive field for political and cultural understanding and in highlighting the rules which allow politics to funcion (Schöpflin 1997: 24).

It is interesting that the story of the Macedonians and God was not told by an individual but by the Macedonian Radio Television, which transmitted their conversation directly and was a direct witness to the event, transferring it to the audience, the Macedonian public. In fact, the veracity of their dialogue was not questioned here. It was accepted that the narrator (the direct witness), or the Macedonian Television was omniscient and transmitted the absolute truth without, thereby, having to offer evidence and various arguments to show the authenticity of the event that it broadcast.

Myth is an insufficiently specific category. Some use this term to mean 'fictional history', or as a display of the past that is known to be wrong; therefore, to call an event mythic is the same as claiming it did not happen (Lič 1982: 65). The definition implies that prior to the demythologization of the myth, as a misreading of the past, it previously existed as truth for humans. The time distance helps, but is not essential for demythologizing stories. This task seems difficult, primarily because much of our human predicament always centres on our own unawareness of the generative power of myths and the limit of their mental concepts of tailored shape (Douglas 1975: xiv). The quest for the 'truth' is always present as an opponent of the fact that most of human existence is expressed through the 'truth' of the invented. The basic question for the study of current myths is: what parameters can be used to label a narrative as myth? Whether it is about archaic cultures or modern society, past or present, the boundary between myth and history remains unclear. The example of the 'Macedonian prayer' perfectly fits into the thinking of Iveković (Iveković 2002: 523) that 'religion is a historical force in Balkan societies, defines social identities and is used as a basis for national myths'.[3]

Rosetta Stone and Burushi Language

People still understand identity as something that is 'inherent' and therefore unchangeable. This indicates that the anthropological deconstruction of the different, particularly national or ethnic, identities persists with the 'new historians' and the other deconstructionists of societal myths and practices. The public and a significant number of the experts remain stuck to the undeconstructed, idealized concept, which puts an inherent and always defined closeness between 'us' and 'them' (Gavrilović 2010: 42) either synchronically or diachronically against, at times, mythical ancestors. Researchers, regardless of whether they are individuals or groups, call the past 'domestication' (Simandiraki 2006: 43) as the distant past is appropriated and interpreted as recent past. Despite the great time distance, certain individuals or institutionalized processes create conditions for this distant past to become close in an attempt to enlist it in contributing to community cohesion.

In that respect, a relevant example that has attracted the attention of the Macedonian public is the emergence of a new theory about the ancient Macedonian language. It has been launched by two professors from the University of Ss. Cyril and Methodius University in Skopje – the Academician.[4] Tome Boshevski, and Professor Aristotel Tentov at the Faculty of Electrical Engineering. Their theory began as a project of the Macedonian Academy of Sciences and Arts, entitled 'Tracing the alphabet and the language of ancient Macedonians' (Бошевски и Тентов 2005). Their claim is that the central text of the document written in three languages on the Rosetta Stone is ancient Macedonian, similar to today's Macedonian language, primarily the Bitola dialect. They argue that the Ptolemaida dynasty (which ruled Egypt at that time) originated from a region south of Bitola (Utrinski vesnik 2007). The theory of Professor Boshevski and Professor Tentov was covered by the media and reached its ultimate target audience who were eager for confirmation that today's Macedonians are direct descendants of Alexander the Great and, as a result, more than 2,000 years ago, the world 'knelt' at their feet.

Vojislav Sarakinski (Саракински 2006: 168–69), a doctoral student of ancient history in Skopje, has tried to explain why Boshevski and Tentov chose exactly the inscription of the Rosetta Stone:

> If there is truth in what they say – that they wanted to search for 'old Macedonian' language reading the demotic, why did they choose the document with the least demotic text (thirty-two rows, versus forty-two appearing on the Pitom Stele and even seventy-four lines on Stele of Canopus)? From a scientific, methodological standpoint, it would be logical to choose the longest record, one that gives the most opportunities for identification – and not one that has the most striking name. It seems that our professors have not seen the other decrees of the Ptolemaic dynasty, except the most famous one – the Rosetta Stone! All inscriptions are readily available, and their translations are available even in the most basic scientific literature. (Саракински 2006: 168–69).

What Sarakinski indicates as 'most striking' is an answer to the above question. The Rosetta Stone is famous not only in academic circles but among the wider public as well because one young French adventurer and explorer, Jean-Francois Champollion, managed to decipher the old Egyptian hieroglyphs written on it. It is exactly the popularity of the Rosetta Stone that triggers the interest among novice researchers of ancient cultural heritage who yearn for sensational publicity. The popularity would have been much less if it was about any other script or document less known to the public. What is particularly important is the fact that the two professors gained notoriety in numerous media outlets.

Boshevski and Tentov's theory was launched in 2006. As it gained importance, the two professors started to participate as guests on television talk shows in Macedonia (*Jadi Burek*; *Late Night Show*; *Milenko Nedelkovski Show*, *Glasot na narodot* etc.). Keep in mind that these were politically determined as being close to the ruling party that was trying to promote a change in the interpretation of Macedonian history and, simultaneously, influence the public through television broadcasts. Moreover, it is critically important that the theory of these two researchers was promoted in the reception hall of the Macedonian Academy of Sciences and Arts (MANU) in Skopje in front of a wide audience, personally, by the head of the Center for Strategic Research in MANU, the Academician Nikola Kljusev (Makedonko sonce, 2006), who was also the first President of the Macedonian government after independence.

After presenting the results related to the ancient Macedonian language in their home country, the two Macedonian researchers began an international presentation of their findings. Their first destination was the international conference in Slovenia, 'The Origin of the Europeans' (Vecer 2007). In 2008 they attended an International Congress in Russia offering a tendentious title: 'Pre-Cyrillic Literacy and Pre-Christian Culture among Slavs' (Utrinski vesnik 2008, Global dialogue, website) to present their latest findings for the script on the Rosetta Stone. After their three-day stay in Russia, the two researchers were greeted with cheers and the enthusiasm of hundreds of people and media at the airport 'Alexander the Great', while accompanied by performers of Macedonian folk music (Trn blog 2008).

Despite the timely reaction of the Department of Linguistics and Literary Theory at MANU and its Academician Peter Hr. Ilievski, a researcher in classical languages, the project of Boshevski and Tentov was approved in 2003 as an official project of the Department of Mathematical and Technical Sciences at MANU. The results were published in 2005 (Илиевски 2006: 24). As a result, in 2006, the Academician Ilievski was requested to scientifically comment on the results of the project of his colleagues, so he published the paper 'Two opposite approaches to the interpretation of ancient texts with *anthroponomic* content'. However, according to Ilievski, 'the release of that text was in very scarce quantity, so it mysteriously disappeared'. About three months after its publication, Ilievski was informed that there were no samples to send even to the collaborating institutions of MANU (Илиевски 2006: 5–6). In November 2007, there was a request by the Office for Book Exchange of the Library of MANU to reprint the edition where his text was published. In his article, Ilievski provided an argument against the results of Boshevski and Tentov.

Among other things, Ilievski said that 'the authors, undeniably, invested enormous effort to re-decipher the middle text of the Rosetta Stone, but their approach is wrong and the results have quasi-scientific value'. According to Ilievski, the authors tried to identify the ancient Macedonian language with dialects of the contemporary Macedonian language without taking into account the language development processes and the historical facts, ignored all previous extensive studies of the ancient Macedonian language and wrote without any real foundation (Илиевски 2006: 25). Particularly impressive was the self-confidence of these two researchers of the ancient Macedonian language in their claims that today's Macedonian pronunciation fully complies with the script of the Rosetta Stone: 'We defined the alphabet, and what surprises and delights us is that the alphabet completely coincides with the pronunciation of the Macedonian language. And now the Cyrillic writing of the middle text of the Rosetta Stone will be released for the first time, and we showed that it is a text of the ancient Macedonians' (A1 TVc, website). The two researchers defended themselves from these criticisms by claiming that these attacks were from academics who had not 'performed their job professionally'.

However, despite the harsh criticism of their theory, they also had supporters within academic circles. Support for their theory was given by Macedonian linguists and historians through a workshop dedicated to the results of the deciphering of the middle text of the Rosetta Stone. The conclusion was that the methodology of Boshevski and Tentov should be applied to other scripts found within Macedonia as well. According to the supporters of Boshevski and Tentov, some of these scripts are believed to be almost 6,000 years old, and some 50,000 years old.

Another similar example is the 'research' of Professor Ilija Casule, who tried to trace the 'roots' of the Bryges language, spoken about 3,000 years ago in Macedonia and in Central Asia, by the Hunza people in Pakistan. The language of the Hunza people, known as Burushi, has achieved worldwide publicity for being a linguistic isolate (Munshi 2006: 7), meaning a language that is not related to any of the currently existing languages such as the Basque language in Spain and France. Professor Casule (at the University of Ss. Cyril and Methodius, engaged in the Macedonian language departments in Australia), explored a completely different idea by suggesting that the Burushi language of the Hunza people of Pakistan is the direct successor of the language spoken by the Balkan Bryges who lived on the territory of Macedonia until the eighth century AD. In looking to show the similarities of today's Burushi language and the contemporary Macedonian language,[5] he also suggested a connection with the language of the Bryges:

> Their language is the direct successor of the language spoken on the territory of Macedonia. This discovery opens tremendous opportunities in scientific research. The links between the Bryges language spoken here and the one spoken in Asia Minor and Burushi language, according to the research I made, are proven and solid. The links are so fascinating, so when I went to Hunza I sometimes thought I was in Macedonia... The feeling was like finding a lost relative. (Makedonsko sonce 2004)

Casule's thesis, which claimed the alleged closeness of today's Macedonians or the Macedonian language and the Hunza people of Pakistan, or the Burishi language, appeared among the Macedonian public in 2001 with the release of Casule's book *Basic Burushi Etymologies*. Essentially, one can find certain common features between the Rosetta Stone and the Burushi language:

- Both are based on world renowned examples and are of great importance to science.
- Both examples have been used and popularized in Macedonia by people from academic circles who bear scientific titles.
- They are particularly interesting for the public, attracting lots of attention by the media as sensational discoveries of the century.
- The two favour euphoria about the possible ancient origin of modern Macedonians.
- They are completely divergent from, and are in conflict with, already accepted Macedonian history.

Conclusion

After the fall of the Socialist Federal Republic of Yugoslavia, social conditions in Macedonia changed drastically. The representatives of the so-called anti-socialist parties and centres of power gained an increasingly important place in society aimed at rebuilding the national identity, claiming that it was inevitable in order for the nation to survive. It is in this context in which the Macedonian prayer, the central letter of the Rosetta Stone and the Burushi language can be understood to make claims of great age, and hence, legitimize the authenticity of the Macedonian people and language. They are actually part of the ideological framework for provoking national fervour, patriotism and optimism for the future of the country. A country, it should be recalled, where Macedonians are denied the name 'Macedonia' as a legitimate and accepted name, as well as their identity and statehood, by neighbouring nation-states. Consequently, Macedonia is unable to join international political, economic and military structures. Attempts to revive the national consciousness of the people are deliberate. The goal is to arouse nationalistic passions by creating a new, seemingly homogenous, culture which is adapted to contemporary conditions. As a consequence, we see that nationalism in its very essence is political because its goal is to take control over a mythopoeic cultural space. Eriksen (2004) observed that this is a common feature of nation-states during the period of nation building, in order to prove that they are old and have a historically legitimate claim to nationhood. Alleged authenticity and continuity with the past can be a very strong tool for political legitimization.

Notes

1. A good example is the attack on a group of young people who, in 2009, protested peacefully in the main square, 'Macedonia' in Skopje, against the idea of the central and local government to build a church on the main square. (Илиевски 2006: 5–6)
2. 'Adam of Macedonia' is the name of a small ceramic figurine of a sitting male torso, discovered in 2000 at one archaeological excavation of the site Govrlevo (near Skopje). The research was led by Milos Bilbija, an archaeologist from

the Museum of Skopje. The artefact was excavated on the border between the cultural layers belonging to the Neolithic and Eneolithic period. The figurine, which dates between the fourth and third millennium AD, is one of the ten unique archaeological findings in the world. Immediately after its discovery, it was regarded as a millennial discovery. Initially it was named 'Adam of Govrlevo', but the name was later changed to 'Adam of Macedonia'. Adam has an unusual artistic processing. It is a fully preserved attempt to represent the man in a moment of physical or spiritual activity. The male body has a sitting position, accentuated anatomy, deeply indented belly, prominent belly-button, well-defined muscles, visible spine and broken phallus (Корени, website). (Илиевски 2006: 5–6).
3. Also, Loring M. Denfort talking about the creation of national identities in the Balkans, writes that 'One of the most important steps in building the nation in the Balkans is the establishment of an autocephalous national church...' (Денфорт 1996: 95; Ристески 2009: 144–88).
4. A reference to a member of an academy promoting science, art or literature or an adherent of a particular artistic or philosophical tradition.
5. The idea of connecting today's Macedonian language with the Burushi language, and the contemporary Macedonians with the Hunza people, originated at the end of the 1980s (Risteski 2009).

References

Anderson, Benedict 1991. *Imagined communities. Reflections on the origins and spread of nationalism,* 2nd edition, London: Verso.

A1 TVa (website). Авторот на молитвата во одбрана на својот текст, http://www.a1.com.mk/vesti/default.aspx?vestID=105104, Accessed on 14.06.2010.

A1 TVb (website). Господ на МТВ, http://www.a1.com.mk/vesti/default.aspx?VestID=103341, Accessed on 14.06.2010.

A1 TVc (web site) Писмото на древните Македонци откриено на каменот од Розета, А1 Телевизија, 17.12.2008, http://www.a1.com.mk/vesti/default.aspx?VestI D=1 01855, Accessed on 14.06.2010.

Bilig, Majkl 2009. *Banalni nacionalizam,* Biblioteka XX vek, Beograd.

Бошевски, Томе и Тентов, Аристотел (2005) „По трагите на писмото и на јазикот на античките Македонци', Прилози 26.2, Одделение за математичко - технички науки, МАНУ, Скопје, 2005.

Саракински, Војислав 2006. Дискретна смрт на методологијата', Историја, 42.1–2, Филозофски факултет, Институт за историја, Скопје, pp. 165–177.

Свето писмо 1998. Свето писмо (Библија), „Книга Јов', Скопје, pp. 764–93.
Douglas, Mary 1975. *Implicit meanings,* London: Routledge.
Денфорт, М. Лоринг 1996. Македонскиот конфликт: Етничкиот национализам во транснационалниот свет, Македонска книга, Скопје.
Eriksen, Tomas Hilan 2004. *Etnicitet i nacionalizam.* Biblioteka XX vek, Beograd.
Ethnologue (website). *Ethnologue: Languages in the world,* http://www.ethnologue.com/ show_ language.asp?code=bsk, Accessed on 06.06.2010.
Gavrilović, Liljana 2009. 'Kulturno nasleđe u inostranstvu', Етноантрополошки проблеми, н.с. год. 4. св.3, Београд, pp. 31–45.
Gavrilović, Liljana 2010. 'Nomen est omen: baština ili nasleđe – (ne samo) terminološka dilemma', Етноантрополошки проблеми, н.с. год. 5, св. 2, Београд, pp. 41–45.
Gellner, Ernest 1983. *Nations and nationalis.,* Oxford: Blackwell.
—— 1997. *Nationalism.* London: Weidenfeld and Nicolson.
Global dialogue (website) *The first international Congress Pre-Cyrillic Slavic Written Language and Pre-Christian Slavic Culture,* http://www.globaldialoguefoundation. org/files/precyrillic.pdf, Accessed on 14.06.2010.
Graves, Robert 1987. *New Larousse Encyclopedia of Mythology.* New York: Crescent books.
Iveković Ivan 2002. 'Nationalism and the political use and abuse of religion: the politicization of Orthodoxy, Catholicism and Islam in Yugoslav successor states', *Social Compas* 49(4), pp. 523–36.
Илиевски, Петар Хр. 2006. Два спротивни приода кон интерпретацијата на антички текстови со антропонимиска содржина', Прилози, XXXI 1, МАНУ – Одделение за лингвистика и литературна наука, Скопје, 2006 (2008), http://www.manu.edu.mk/Prilozi_MANU_OLLN_XXXI_1.pdf.
Kanal 5 (website). Хунзите, кои за себе велат дека се потомци на Александар Македонски, утре доаѓаат во Македонија, ТВ Канал 5, 10.07.2008, http://www.kanal5. com.mk/default.aspx?mId=37&eventId=36320&egId=1 3, Accessed on 06.06.2010.
Корени, (website). Адам од Македонија, http://www.koreni-macedonia.org/ chuda /adam-od-makedonija.html, Accessed on 09.06.2010.
Lič, Edmund, (1982) *Klod Levi Stros.* Prosveta, Beograd.
Makedonsko sonce 2004. Историјата на Македонија под дебели слоеви на лага, Македонско сонце, бр. 495–496, 26.12.2003–02.01.2004, Скопје, http://www.makedonskosonce.com/broevis/2004/sonce495.pdf/10_17_ intervju.pdf, Последен пат посетена на 06.06.2010.
Makedonsko sonce 2006. Идентификувани писмо и јазик на античките Македонци, Македонско сонце, бр. 627, 07.07.2006, http://www.makedonskosonce.com/broevis/ 2006/sonce627.pdf/36_38_manu.pdf, Accessed on 14.06.2010.

Македонска молитва, (website). http://www.youtube.com/watch?v=PZJ62MG F7xI, Accessed on 06.06.2010.

Мелетински, М. Елеазар 2002. *Поетика на митот*, Табернакул, Скопје.

Munshi, Sadaf, 2006. *'Jammu and Kashmir Burushaski: language, language contact and change'*, Dissertation, Austin: The University of Texas at Austin.

Nova Makedonija 2009. Лингвистите го поздравија обидот за читање на Каменот од Розета, Нова Македонија, бр. 21734, 10.07.2009, http://www.novamakedonija.com. mk/NewsDetal.asp?vest=71091029473&id=16&setIzdanie=21734, Accessed on 14.06.2010.

Ристески, С. Љупчо 2009. Признавање автокефалност на Македонската православна црква (МПЦ) како прашање на македонскиот национален идентитет', ЕтноАнтропоЗум, бр.6. Списание на Институтот за етнологија и антропологија, ПМФ – Скопје, pp. 144–88.

Risteski, S. Ljupco 2009. 'Himalayan, yet ours. A postsocijalistic saga of the Macedonian kingdom in the Himalayas', Konferencija: *Horor – porno – ennui: kulturne prakse post – socijalizma*, Institut za etnologiju I folkloristiku, Šubićeva 42, Zagreb, (in print).

Schöpflin, George 1997. 'The functions of myth and a taxonomy of myths', во: Hosking, Geoffrey (ed.), and Schöpflin, George (ed.). *Myths and nationhood*, Routledge, New York, pp. 19–35.

Simandiraki, Anna 2006. 'International education and cultural heritage: alliance or antagonism?', *Journal of research in international education*, vol. 5 (1), pp. 35–56.

Smit, D. Antoni 1998. *Nacionalni identitet*, Biblioteka XX vek, Beograd.

Trn blog 2008. Пречек на Аристотел Тентов и Томе Бошевски на скопскиот аеродром!, http://trn.blog.mk/2008/05/17/prechek-na-aristotel-tentov-i-tome-boshevski-na-skopskiot-aerodrom/, Accessed on 14.06.2010.

Utrinski vesnik 2009. За потеклото на првиот хуманоид – македоноид, Утрински весник, 9.02.2009, http://www.utrinski.com.mk/default.asp?ItemID=F2038953287BAA4 AA610B129 DEAF03C7, Accessed on 14.06.2010.

Utrinski vesnik 2007. *На Каменот од Розета карактеристики на битолскиот говор*, Утрински весник, бр. 2378, 09.05.2007, http://www.utrinski.com.mk/ ?ItemID=9C2514D8D1862545B6980618A4830FF8, Accessed on 06.06.2010.

Utrinski vesnik 2008. *Томе Бошевски и Аристотел Тентов на меѓународен конгрес во Русија*, Утрински весник, бр. 2685, 14.05.2008, http://www.utrinski.com.mk/ ?ItemID=0DF812425C709C4EB1A96E4B1AC817A7, Accessed on 14.06.2010.

Vecer 2007. *Во странство има реакции за Каменот од Розета*, Вечер, бр. 13655, 21.11.2007, http://www.vecer.com.mk/default.asp?ItemID=AE4400 4B00407049B3E6C B28E5990670, Accessed on 14.06.2010.

Vlada 2008. Средба на премиерот Никола Груевски со делегација од земјата на Хунзите, Влада на Р. Македонија, http://www.vlada.mk/?q=book/export /html/699, Accessed on 06.06.2010.

5

CONCEPTUALIZING GENDER IN MACEDONIA

Victor C. de Munck and Davorin Trpeski

How do Macedonians conceptualize gender? Do Macedonians have patriarchal or egalitarian conceptions of gender? Is there consensus or divergence in the way Macedonian males and females conceptualize male and female personality characteristics and engendered abilities? In this study we seek to answer these questions and also reflect on the socio-cultural consequences of our findings. Using a published cross-cultural survey on gender, our results provide a clue as to how Macedonian conceptions of gender relate to those of Western culture. Our work will also be useful to policymakers and NGOs who are working on gender issues in Macedonia.

The social-science literature on Macedonian gender roles has been confusing – ranging from patriarchal conceptions (the most typical) to gender equality (less typical). For instance, in 1987 David Gilmore wrote that one of the defining characteristics of Mediterranean cultural unity was 'patterns of intersex relations' (Gilmore 1987: 174), implying a complementary division of labour between the sexes. However, he fails to be very specific about the content of these patterns. More typical views are presented by Rheubottom (1996), Denich (1974) and Ramet (1996) who have argued that the agnatic social organization of southern Slavic has led to the gender norms of these societies being pronouncedly patriarchal relative to their non-Slavic (and non-Muslim) neighbours. Denich writes that, 'the formal [social] structure, consisting of agnatically related males, does not include women at all, and would operate more neatly if women did not exist' (1974: 259). Schubert points out that, 'Denich's influence has continued unabated to the present (2005: 66),' adding that '...even Simic, who noted the "authoritative and influential positions [are] occupied by older women [i.e. mothers]" in Serbia, felt compelled to comment that this was "anomalous" (Schubert 2005: 66).' Indeed, Rozita Dimova (2006; 2003) has used the concept of private and public spaces as 'a model' for examining not only Macedonian and Albanian nationalism but also gendered spaces and relations. Dimova's point was not complementarity but rather division on the basis of patriarchal tenets.[1]

Violeta Schubert has questioned this patriarchal/agnatic 'pattern' by noting that 'approximately one third of marriages are uxorilocal' and that the 'incoming *domazet*' (son-in-law) does not inherit the wife's father's estate but rather the couple's children do' (Schubert 2005: 66). In a subsequent ethnographic monograph on a rural Macedonian village, Schubert notes that the family life cycle is organized through the association of the concepts of *red* (order) and *vreme* (time) (Schubert 2011: 117, unpublished ms). She demonstrates that while patriarchy is part of the normative discourse of everyday life, it is 'negotiated' by mothers, sisters and wives who seek to impose their conceptions of *red* onto family life. Further, she writes about the tremendous disparity between unmarried men and women in rural Macedonia; in the southwest village where she worked 64 men were unmarried compared to only 9 women (2011: 124). She found that in Capari (the pseudonym of the village she worked in) women were successful in moving to urban areas (or abroad) and finding both jobs and grooms, while men lacked such opportunities and tended to remain in their natal homes (2011: 125).

Ilka Thiessen (2006) has written about unmarried young adult females who are mostly engineering students looking for jobs abroad because there are no jobs (at least no well-paying jobs) in Macedonia. These women are depicted as having Western European sensibilities and while quite different from the rural women described by Schubert, they also are mobile and opportunistic. Based on extensive and solid ethnographic work, Schubert and Thiessen suggest that patriarchy is not a monolithic ethos or structure and that for different reasons (economic and marital opportunities in the case of Schubert's informants and educational qualifications in Thiessen's case) Macedonian women have access to opportunities that men don't have. Their work suggests a modern rise in female status and economic opportunities. On the other hand, in a more recent paper presented to the Human Rights Committee, Jasminika Frisick and Mariana Duarte state that in Macedonia, '[t]here is a persistent presence of a traditional model in the division of roles in the family, where the man is expected to be the bread winner and the woman must raise the children' Frisick and Duarte (2007: 4, article 23).

In short, depictions of gender seem to range from those that conform to a Western European model of, more or less, gender equality to one of patriarchy, with women in the kitchen and garden and men in the fields or factories and bars. Schubert's analysis modifies the patriarchal nature of such traditional depictions by noting that women do have space within the larger patriarchal field to manoeuvre and make claims, but patriarchy itself remains a default ideology for shaping gender relations. Thiessen's evocative depiction of Macedonian female engineering students seeking careers presents an alternative model to patriarchy but it must be noted that many, if not most, of her informants are looking to leave Macedonia. As the title of her book *Waiting for Macedonia*, implies, modernity is not yet there.

The aim of this chapter is to help set the record straight by using a survey and explanations of the survey by participants to present a description of Macedonian conceptions of gender in 2009. We note, with Schubert (2005, 2011), that conceptions of gender are associated with, and therefore cannot be discussed independent of patriarchy. We hasten to note the obvious, that patriarchy is probably a cultural universal. Indeed, Donald Brown (1991), in his book *Cultural Universals*, wrote that all societies practise patriarchy, which he defines as 'male dominance' expressed in 'control over public and political' arenas of life (Brown 1991: 186). The condition of patriarchy is not unique to Macedonia but, in order to examine gender relations, patriarchy needs to be taken into account. Consequently, we adopted a cross-cultural survey that had previously been used for cross-cultural research on gender and patriarchy (de Munck, Cardinale and Dudley 2002).

This chapter is organized as follows: (1) a discussion on methods, (2) a presentation of the survey findings; (3) an analysis of the findings; (4) a conclusion summarizing our findings. Our goal is to provide a baseline description of Macedonian conceptions of a range of common gendered traits and tasks obtained from a published cross-cultural survey. The study is pertinent not only to describing gender conceptions of Macedonians but also, because we used a cross-cultural survey, how Macedonians compare with other cultures.

Methods

We employed a cross-cultural survey on gender published in 2002 (de Munck, Cardinale and Dudley). In that study cross-cultural comparisons were made across gender, nations and ethno-religious groups in order to: (1) find out which of those three identities – gender, nationality and ethnicity – were most important in shaping conceptions of gender; (2) develop a cross-cultural index of patriarchy which could be used for comparative purposes; (3) discover and describe possible cultural universal and culturally specific models of gender; (4) examine the methodological problem of whether informants from different ethnic and cultural groups understood the questions in the same way. For the latter reason, informants were asked to provide explanations for their answers and we followed this methodology.

Using a form of factor analysis, the authors discovered that conceptualizations of gender were most influenced by national identity and least by gender.[2] The survey had been derived from colloquial statements about gender among different people and seems to be the only cross-cultural survey on this subject so constructed. Such a bottom-up survey, based on what ordinary rural and urban people from different gender ethnic and national statuses said about gender, seemed to us to be a better fit for our use than either constructing a new survey or using a 'top down' survey constructed by experts to test a particular theory or for diagnostic purposes. The gender survey is presented in Figure 5.1 in English; it was translated into Macedonian and Albanian

Gender: F___ M___ ;   Age:___ ;   Ethnicity/Nationality_____ ;
Level of Education_____ ;   Marital Status_____

Please compare males and females on the traits below; circle 'M' for male, 'F' for female, or 'E' for equal. This is part of a cross-cultural study on gender. We recognize that there will be a tendency to put 'equal' for most answers, but please try to avoid that, if in your opinion you think there is a tendency, in your society, for one gender to possess one of the traits listed below more than the other gender. Please provide a brief explanation for your answer.

1. In general, who is physically stronger? M F E
explanation:

2. In general, who works harder? M F E
explanation:

3. In general, who has the greater sexual drive? M F E
explanation:

4. In general, who tends to be the most honest? M F E
explanation:

5. In general, which is the more physically attractive sex? M F E
explanation:

6. In general, who tends to be more jealous? M F E
explanation:

7. In general, who gossips more? M F E
explanation:

8. In general, who tends to cheat more on their partner? M F E
explanation:

9. In general, who is more intelligent? M F E
explanation:

10. In general, who tends to manage money better? M F E
explanation:

11. In general, who tends to be happier? M F E
explanation:

12. In general, is it better to be born a male or a female? M F E
explanation:

13. In general, who loves their children more, males or females? M F E
explanation:

14. In general, who takes better care of their children, males or females? M F E
explanation:

15. In general, who tends to be more religious? M F E
explanation:

16. In general, who tends to be friendlier? M F E
explanation:

17. In general, who tends to be more sympathetic? M F E
explanation:

18. In general, who tends to be more argumentative? M F E
explanation:

19. In general, who tends to be more foolish? M F E
explanation:

Figure 5.1: Nineteen Item Cross-Cultural Survey on Gender

(though only the Macedonian results are presented here) and back translated by an independent translator to check their accuracy.

For each survey question, informants were asked to explain their answer. The purpose for this was twofold: first, to determine if they understood the question in the same way; second, to provide culturally relevant explanations for each concept. The survey was distributed to 22 females and 22 males, all of them between 18 and 30 years old. We wanted to sample a young adult educated population from Skopje in order to obtain as modern and Westernized a view of gender relations as possible. We did this because we assumed that this group would harbinger a cultural profile of gender that will become part of the normative model of gender for Macedonians.

Presentation and Analysis of the Survey Findings

The results of the survey were put through consensus analysis. Briefly, consensus analysis is a method akin to factor analysis but measures the degree of agreement between respondents' answers to see if there is enough agreement to fit a 'one culture assumption'. That is, one assumes that if the sample respondents were all members of the same culture there would be greater agreement across the spectrum of answers than if the respondents were from different cultures. For there to be consensus, the eigen value ratio (a measure of agreement across the case profiles) should be above 3.0 (Table 5.1).[3]

Table 5.1: Eigen Value Ratios of Gender Conceptions Among Macedonian Males and Females

Eigen Values Factor	Value	Per cent	CUM %	Eigen Value Ratio
1:	4.400	47.7	47.7	1.637
2:	2.688	29.2	76.9	1.263
3:	2.128	23.1	100.0	
	9.217	100.0		

WARNING: Your data are not well-explained by a single factor. This condition violates the One Culture assumption of the Consensus Model.

In the Macedonian sample (N=44), the ratio of the first factor to the second is 1.637 and does not meet the 'one culture' requirement of having an eigen value ratio of 3.0 or higher. For all other national and ethnic samples that had been tested using this survey a *within cultural* eigen value of 3.0 or higher was always obtained. Thus, the Macedonian sample is quite unique; this is possible because of the ambiguous cultural history and geocultural placement of the Balkans between East and West, North and South. Even when we massaged the data with a heavy hand – i.e. eliminating outliers (people who answered significantly different from the norm), testing for consensus within gender, or eliminating questions for which answers were highly dispersed – we could not obtain an eigen value of 3.0! Thus we had to conclude that within this relatively homogenous sample there was no agreement across enough questions to infer that there is a Macedonian cultural model or shared understanding of gender.[4] Macedonian males and females disagreed on 10 of the 19 questions (53 per cent).

We considered that we might discern a gender difference if we compared the profiles of the respondents' answers on a multidimensional scale (MDS). An MDS provides a visual representation of the proximate relationship between respondents. Those who were most similar in their responses are closer to each other in non-geometric (i.e. conceptual) multidimensional space.[5] Figure 5.2 does indicate a difference in gender responses but we would emphasize that the difference was not enough to distinguish males and females as holding different conceptions of gender.

The individuals are coded by gender (F or M), age and ethnicity (here all are MAK for Macedonian). For readability, females are italicized and males underlined. It is clear that there is a distinction between males and females, with females along the left side and men along the right side of the MDS. Later, we examine in more detail why the MDS shows apparent agreement among females while the statistical results from consensus analysis indicate no consensus within female or male genders. We suggest that some women tended to mark gender as 'equal' while others would favour

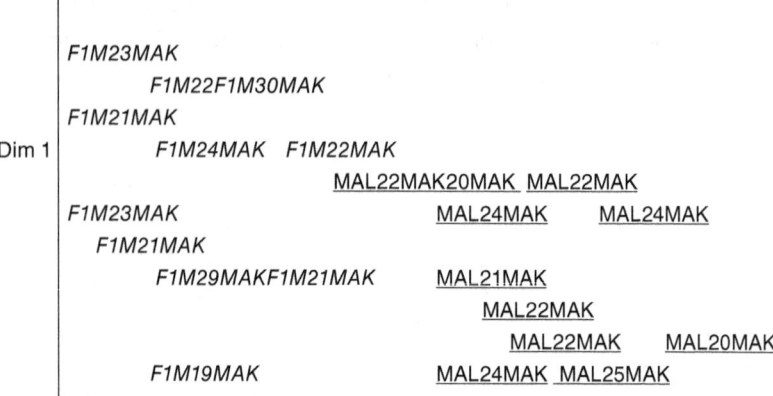

Figure 5.2: MDS of Macedonian Female and Male Respondents of the Gender Survey

marking 'female' over 'equal' on many of the questions. Conversely, while males do not appear as politically encumbered by favouring 'equal', they were split between less and more patriarchal conceptions of gender.

To further examine gender differences, we compared the answers for both on each of the questions. The results are presented in Table 5.2. The answers for each group are presented side by side with males on the left and females on the right. We expected that if Macedonia fit the patriarchal model presented by most researchers on gender in Macedonia, then both Macedonian males and females should agree on prototypical male characteristics of dominance, especially as related to power and public life. Conversely, they should also agree on the most prototypical characteristics of females associated with the roles of mother or wife and with traits identified with the domestic arena of life. We also expect that gender concepts influence gender practices and these should be borne out in the second and third sections of this chapter when we focus on social practices.

The pattern of answers is provided in Table 5.3 (split into two segments).

Table 5.2: Comparison of Macedonian Male and Female Answers to Gender Survey
Code: Equal = 1 Female = 2 and Male = 3.

	Male Responses				Female Responses		
QUESTION 1: STRENGTH				**QUESTION 1: STRENGTH**			
Response	Frequency	Wtd.	Freq. Prob. Correct	Response	Frequency	Wtd.	Freq. Prob. Correct
1.0000	2	0.59	0.000	1.0000	2	0.34	0.000
2.0000	0	0.00	0.000	2.0000	0	0.00	0.000
3.0000	20	10.41	1.000	3.0000	20	10.66	1.000
QUESTION 2: WORK				**QUESTION 2: WORK**			
Response	Frequency	Wtd.	Freq. Prob. Correct	Response	Frequency	Wtd.	Freq. Prob. Correct
1.0000	6	3.13	0.107	1.0000	20	10.41	1.000
2.0000	8	3.75	0.306	2.0000	2	0.59	0.000
3.0000	8	4.13	0.587	3.0000	0	0.00	0.000
QUESTION 3: SEX				**QUESTION 3: SEX**			
Response	Frequency	Wtd.	Freq. Prob. Correct	Response	Frequency	Wtd.	Freq. Prob. Correct
1.0000	10	4.29	0.082	1.0000	12	6.14	0.870
2.0000	2	0.95	0.000	2.0000	0	0.00	0.000
3.0000	10	5.77	0.918	3.0000	10	4.86	0.130

Table 5.2: Comparison of Macedonian Male and Female Answers to Gender Survey (Continued)
Code: Equal = 1 Female = 2 and Male = 3.

Male Responses

QUESTION 4: HONESTY

Response	Frequency	Wtd.	Freq. Prob. Correct
1.0000	4	1.85	0.005
2.0000	8	4.22	0.266
3.0000	10	4.93	0.728

QUESTION 5: ATTRACTIVE

Response	Frequency	Wtd.	Freq. Prob. Correct
1.0000	0	0.00	0.000
2.0000	20	9.97	1.000
3.0000	0	1.03	0.000

QUESTION 6: JEALOUS

Response	Frequency	Wtd.	Freq. Prob. Correct
1.0000	6	3.20	0.012
2.0000	12	5.99	0.987
3.0000	4	1.81	0.001

Female Responses

QUESTION 4: HONESTY

Response	Frequency	Wtd.	Freq. Prob. Correct
1.0000	4	2.66	0.002
2.0000	14	7.44	0.998
3.0000	2	0.90	0.000

QUESTION 5: ATTRACTIVE

Response	Frequency	Wtd.	Freq. Prob. Correct
1.0000	4	0.93	0.000
2.0000	14	8.38	1.000
3.0000	4	1.69	0.000

QUESTION 6: JEALOUS

Response	Frequency	Wtd.	Freq. Prob. Correct
1.0000	8	3.53	0.248
2.0000	8	4.10	0.568
3.0000	6	3.37	0.184

QUESTION 7: GOSSIPS

Response	Frequency	Wtd.	Freq. Prob. Correct
1.0000	0	0.00	0.000
2.0000	22	11.00	1.000
3.0000	0	0.00	0.000

QUESTION 8: CHEAT

Response	Frequency	Wtd.	Freq. Prob. Correct
1.0000	10	4.71	0.555
2.0000	4	1.72	0.004
3.0000	8	4.57	0.440

QUESTION 9: INTELLIGENT

Response	Frequency	Wtd.	Freq. Prob. Correct
1.0000	8	3.69	0.003
2.0000	0	0.00	0.000
3.0000	14	7.31	0.997

QUESTION 10: MONEY

Response	Frequency	Wtd.	Freq. Prob. Correct
1.0000	2	0.74	0.000
2.0000	4	1.45	0.000
3.0000	16	8.81	1.000

QUESTION 7: GOSSIPS

Response	Frequency	Wtd.	Freq. Prob. Correct
1.0000	10	4.52	0.792
2.0000	6	3.10	0.083
3.0000	6	3.38	0.126

QUESTION 8: CHEAT

Response	Frequency	Wtd.	Freq. Prob. Correct
1.0000	10	4.67	0.250
2.0000	2	0.91	0.001
3.0000	10	5.42	0.749

QUESTION 9: INTELLIGENT

Response	Frequency	Wtd.	Freq. Prob. Correct
1.0000	10	4.30	0.102
2.0000	10	5.80	0.897
3.0000	2	0.90	0.001

QUESTION 10: MONEY

Response	Frequency	Wtd.	Freq. Prob. Correct
1.0000	4	1.12	0.000
2.0000	12	6.56	0.992
3.0000	6	3.32	0.007

Table 5.2: Comparison of Macedonian Male and Female Answers to Gender Survey (Continued)
Code: Equal = 1 Female = 2 and Male = 3.

	Male Responses				Female Responses		
QUESTION 11: HAPPY				**QUESTION 11: HAPPY**			
Response	Frequency	Wtd.	Freq. Prob. Correct	Response	Frequency	Wtd.	Freq. Prob. Correct
1.0000	16	8.17	1.000	1.0000	12	5.58	0.972
2.0000	4	1.97	0.000	2.0000	6	2.95	0.019
3.0000	2	0.86	0.000	3.0000	4	2.48	0.009
QUESTION 12: BETTER BORN				**QUESTION 12: BETTER BORN**			
Response	Frequency	Wtd.	Freq. Prob. Correct	Response	Frequency	Wtd.	Freq. Prob. Correct
1.0000	2	0.95	0.000	1.0000	10	5.08	0.831
2.0000	0	0.00	0.000	2.0000	4	1.91	0.007
3.0000	20	10.05	1.000	3.0000	8	4.01	0.162
QUESTION 13: LOVE CHLD				**QUESTION 13: LOVE CHLD**			
Response	Frequency	Wtd.	Freq. Prob. Correct	Response	Frequency	Wtd.	Freq. Prob. Correct
1.0000	16	8.00	1.000	1.0000	14	6.47	0.948
2.0000	2	1.11	0.000	2.0000	8	4.53	0.052
3.0000	4	1.89	0.000	3.0000	0	0.00	0.000

CONCEPTUALIZING GENDER IN MACEDONIA   121

QUESTION 14: CARE CHLD

Response	Frequency	Wtd.	Freq. Prob. Correct
1.0000	8	3.48	0.002
2.0000	14	7.52	0.998
3.0000	0	0.00	0.000

QUESTION 15: RELIGIOUS

Response	Frequency	Wtd.	Freq. Prob. Correct
1.0000	12	6.51	0.956
2.0000	10	4.49	0.044
3.0000	0	0.00	0.000

QUESTION 16: FRIENDLY

Response	Frequency	Wtd.	Freq. Prob. Correct
1.0000	10	5.13	0.862
2.0000	4	2.01	0.005
3.0000	8	3.86	0.103

QUESTION 17: SYMPATHETIC

Response	Frequency	Wtd.	Freq. Prob. Correct
1.0000	6	2.74	0.044
2.0000	8	4.52	0.751
3.0000	8	3.74	0.206

QUESTION 14: CARE CHLD

Response	Frequency	Wtd.	Freq. Prob. Correct
1.0000	4	1.25	0.000
2.0000	18	9.75	1.000
3.0000	0	0.00	0.000

QUESTION 15: RELIGIOUS

Response	Frequency	Wtd.	Freq. Prob. Correct
1.0000	10	5.08	0.898
2.0000	4	2.18	0.008
3.0000	8	3.74	0.094

QUESTION 16: FRIENDLY

Response	Frequency	Wtd.	Freq. Prob. Correct
1.0000	16	8.01	0.99
2.0000	6	2.99	0.001
3.0000	0	0.00	0.000

QUESTION 17: SYMPATHETIC

Response	Frequency	Wtd.	Freq. Prob. Correct
1.0000	4	0.93	0.000
2.0000	18	10.07	1.000
3.0000	0	0.00	0.000

Table 5.2: Comparison of Macedonian Male and Female Answers to Gender Survey (Continued)
Code: Equal = 1 Female = 2 and Male = 3.

	Male Responses				Female Responses		
QUESTION 18: ARGUES				**QUESTION 18: ARGUES**			
Response	Frequency	Wtd.	Freq. Prob. Correct	Response	Frequency	Wtd.	Freq. Prob. Correct
1.0000	6	2.44	0.000	1.0000	6	2.38	0.001
2.0000	16	8.56	1.000	2.0000	4	1.84	0.001
3.0000	0	0.00	0.000	3.0000	12	6.78	0.998
QUESTION 19: FOOLISH				**QUESTION 19: FOOLISH**			
Response	Frequency	Wtd.	Freq. Prob. Correct	Response	Frequency	Wtd.	Freq. Prob. Correct
1.0000	6	2.52	0.004	1.0000	12	5.83	0.725
2.0000	4	2.51	0.004	2.0000	0	0.00	0.000
3.0000	12	5.98	0.992	3.0000	10	5.17	0.275

Table 5.3: Comparison of Male and Female Aggregate Responses to the Gender Survey

	Strength	Work	Sex	Honesty	Attractive	Jealous	Gossip	Cheat	Intelligent	Money
male	Male	Male	Male	Male	Female	Female	Female	Equal	Male	Male
female	Male	Equal	Equal	Female	Female	Female	Equal	Male	Female	Female

	Happy	Better Born	Love Child	Care Child	Religious	Friendly	Sympathetic	Argues	Foolish
male	Equal	Male	Equal	Female	Equal	Equal	Female	Female	Male
female	Equal	Equal	Equal	Female	Equal	Equal	Female	Male	Equal

Analysis of Our Findings

The data illuminates how males and females have quite different conceptions of gender on 10 of 19 questions (53 per cent). Females were twice as likely to respond with 'equal' to a question as males, doing so eight times compared to four for males. We can confidently conclude that Macedonian females have a much more egalitarian view of gender than Macedonian men. We suggest that the egalitarian view held by women reflects a generalized claim to equality while many men may be more reluctant to let go of the real and perceived entitlements associated with a more patriarchal construction of gender. Below, we begin by discussing where both genders agreed that a trait was a male trait, followed by where both agreed it was a female trait, and then discussing some traits where they disagreed.

Agreement on male traits: The only question where both genders agreed that 'male' would be the generally most agreed on answer was 'strength', This is hardly surprising given that 'strength' was mostly interpreted in terms of mass and muscle. In the explanations for this some of the comments written by males were: 'this is natural, normal'; 'we should be like that'; 'strength is nature's gift' [to males]; 'naturally'. These answers show that strength is seen as a natural attribute of males. Females often conceded that males were 'strong' but some would add as a counterpoint that females are *zenstvena* or *nezna* (soft). However, most females also saw 'strength' as 'god's gift' or 'natural' to men.

Agreement on female traits: Both male and female informants agreed that 'attractive', 'jealous', 'care for children' and 'sympathetic' were typically female traits. For 'attractive', males were united in agreeing that women were more attractive than males. Typical male comments were: 'it's natural'; 'I think like that'; 'for me – women; I don't care about men'; 'for me, females; for females, males'. Thus, 'attractive' is largely sexualized, identified with women and seen as both an adjective (attractive) and as a verb (attracting a male). 'Attractive' is sexualized and perceived as a 'natural' or 'biological' attractor by Macedonian men. For females, the 'naturally hetero-sexualized' sort of explanation was only mentioned once. More typical answers were: 'for me, women [are more attractive]'; 'women labour hard at being attractive'; 'they take care of their looks' and 'they have their beauties'. In other words, for women, 'attractive' is either not natural but a project they work on or, if natural, it is viewed as an intrinsic quality that is appreciated without being sexualized.

While both Macedonian men and women 'agree' that 'jealous' is associated with 'females', 12 (55 per cent) males agreed that women were more jealous and women were split with eight marking 'equal', eight marking 'females' and six marking 'males'. The reason consensus analysis shows 'females' as the answer for the female informants is that those eight had higher rates of agreement with the majority on other questions; therefore, their responses are weighed more than the other male respondents.

Those males who said that females were 'more jealous' than males explained either that women were irrational – 'women are jealous without reason'; 'they just do so, without thinking' – or that jealousy was a rational response to male promiscuity – 'they like sex more'; 'they think about it 1,000 times in a day'. However, females more typically saw jealousy as a matter of personal 'character' or as a consequence of relationship problems – 'because there are no arguments [in a relationship], we get jealous wondering why there are no arguments'. 'Care for children' was marked by both male and female informants as a 'female' trait. However, males saw it as slightly more 'equal' than females, with eight males indicating that both are 'equal', but only four females thought that 'care for children' was 'equal'. No informant saw this as a male trait. Males saw this as 'normal' and part of 'mother love' but also some noted that males 'don't have time for that'. Females, more so than men, saw this as a deep part of their 'nature' stating that it was 'instinct'; 'men are not able to do that'; 'women only know this'; 'we are more emotionally connected to children'.

'Sympathetic' was the last attribute that both male and female informants agreed was a female trait. However, while eighteen females agreed that females were more sympathetic and four said it was 'equal', males (like females for jealousy) were much more divided – eight males indicated males, eight females, and six that they were 'equal'. Sympathy when it was associated with women was seen as 'natural' and semiotically interpreted as 'soft' versus male *cvrst* or *mazestven* (hardness). A poetic but typical answer by a male was 'they are the soft gender, even if they jump on eggs they won't break them'.

Agreement that males and females equally shared these traits: On the questions 'who is happier', 'who loves children more' and 'who is friendlier' the normative answer for both male and female informants was 'equal'. Most of the informants seemed confused by the question about 'happiness' and responded that 'happy is happy' and saw happy not so much as a quality of life but as contingent on the type of person or situation and hence not a quality that could be attributed to a gender or, for that matter, members of a social category. Some identified happiness with money, 'no work means no happiness for everyone'. Interestingly, females who did not mark 'equal' for this question appeared biased towards their own gender as happier, with six females indicating females as 'happier'. Only two males indicated 'males' as 'happier', while four marked 'females' as 'happier'. Both males and females who answered that females were 'happier' indicated that this was due to stress on men from the high unemployment rate (around 40 per cent) and low wages chronic to Macedonia. This interpretation stems from answers by males such as 'men don't [find] work'; 'everyone wants big cars, house, money'.

For 'love of children' there was strong agreement among males and females that both 'equally' loved their children. This answer was linked to the role of parents and the presumably culturally dominant value that both parents should love their children equally. This was evident in succinct remarks such as 'its parent love'; 'parents should give in the same way equally'; 'if the child is made with love then it's normal for both to love the kid equally'.

The question 'Who is friendlier' was marked 'equal' by both genders, but there was a notable gender bias in favor of one's own gender. Thus eight males marked males as friendlier while six women marked females as friendlier and no woman marked males as friendlier. Those who marked both genders as 'equal' saw 'friendly' as a non-gendered personality trait – 'it depends on character'; 'individual'; 'it depends on character and education'; 'everyone wants to be friendly'.

Disagreement on traits: There was disagreement between the genders for the remaining ten traits (53 per cent). For eight of those ten traits the difference was that one gender (usually females) marked the trait as equal and the other as gendered. Below we will present the analysis for only those traits for which there was the strongest disagreement: 'honesty', 'gossip', 'intelligence', 'money', and 'argues'. These traits are particularly focused on the functional aspects of trust and 'equality in cognitive abilities'. Regardless of commitment or love for another person, intimate relationships cannot function well without trust. Trust requires that one perceives the other as honest and that they won't gossip about you. Further, 'argues' typically implies that one party perceives the other as malfeasant; frequent or chronic arguments suggest that one or both partners perceive the other as lacking in some personal virtues that are important for a functional relationship. Hence, 'honesty', 'gossip' and 'argues' all refer to some absence of virtues or weakness of character that affect the quality of relationships. While 'honesty', 'gossip' and 'argue' are associated with trust, 'intelligence' and 'money' with regards to this survey refer to a perceived gender difference in inherent cognitive abilities. Members of a gender may be honest, not gossip and not argue, but they may still be considered less intelligent and less rational or less able to manage money than a member of the other gender. As a result, the gender diminished in these capacities is perceived as inferior.

In two different cross-cultural studies, de Munck and Korotayev (1999, 2007) showed that a rise in female status is significantly correlated with, and the main predictor of, romantic love as the primary criterion for marriage and for male–female intimacy. Mutuality, or the perception of each other as equals, appears to be a necessary precondition for romantic love because it is hard to imagine loving someone romantically who one perceives as inferior to oneself. Lindholm (1995, 1998) also makes this point when he writes that lovers among the Mari Baluch, a tribe in northeast Pakistan, construct a sort of anti-hierarchical bubble in which they perceive each other as equals despite being members of a highly patriarchal society. Thus, trust and equality are preconditions for intimate relations, and if males or females are perceived to be inherently incapable of either, then it seems unlikely that they could form an intimate pair-bond required for mutually satisfying husband–wife relations.

Male informants tended to perceive males as more honest than females, but the difference was slight (ten perceived males as more honest, eight perceived females as more honest and four perceived the two genders as equally honest). Fourteen females, on the other hand, perceived females to be more honest, while only two marked males as more honest (four marked the genders as equal). Honesty is perceived not as a 'naturalized' ingredient of gender but uniformly seen as something 'situational' or one 'tries' to be. For men, women can be 'two faced'; for women, men 'just tell lies' to manipulate or seduce women. Cumulatively, informants tended to see women as more honest than men (for all informants the female to male ratio on honesty is 22:12).

Gossip is less ambiguous, all twenty-two male informants marked women as more gossipy than men; while women were distributed across male and female options equally ($n=6$), and the majority ($n=10$) considered males and females to be equal gossips. Gossip is the only trait for which all men were unanimous that it was a female trait and the centrality of the image of women as 'gossipers' was also emphasized in their responses: 'I need two days to explain how women gossip'; 'every second conversation they gossip'; 'they enjoy gossiping'; 'they are just like that'. Most women do not accept this characterization of themselves, but acknowledge it as a semiotic filter through which men see women. For this to be a divisive trait that hinders intimacy, one would have to investigate what it is that women are perceived to gossip about. Gossip has also been referred to as a 'weapon of the weak' (James Scott 1985), and perhaps male association of females with 'gossip' relates to their sensitivity to women using this weapon against them. Interestingly, in Western societies where there is presumptively gender equality, women were not seen as being more gossipy than men, whereas gossip was a defining characteristic of Muslim women (this is from survey data taken in the United States and Sri Lanka).

Sixteen Macedonian men indicated that women argued more than men and six indicated they argued equally. On the other hand, twelve

Macedonian women noted that men argue more, four that women do, and six that both argue equally. Thus, the response to 'who argues more' is gender biased with informants rating the other gender as more argumentative than one's own gender. Males who said women are more argumentative noted that women 'think on everything more', 'we cannot relax when women are like this', 'they are like that, soft and sensitive'. Women are depicted by men to by hyper-focused on the things that men do. Arguing is something women do naturally, it is part of their way of scrutinizing relationships and it is something males do less than women, in terms of their own self-appraisal. As one male informant noted, 'God save you from those kind of women' and another 'it is natural [to them]'. Not all women are 'like that' but males seem to think that most are.

Females who also noted that they argued more than men, blamed men for this predicament noting that 'we ask for things and males are just lazy and don't respond, then we become aggressive'. Women explained that they were exasperated by the general ineptitude of men and it was not their nature to argue more than men. A similar discrepancy in perceptions was observed with jealousy where men also viewed women as 'naturally' more jealous than males but women saw jealousy as a consequence of males' more promiscuous behaviour.

When women indicate that males argue more, they are usually referring to either the subject of sex or male images of their 'manhood'. Males argue more than women because women don't 'give them sex' or because women 'show up their manhood'. Both men and women sometimes made references to 'soft-hard' or 'soft-rigorous' dichotomies, where women are emotional and thus get angry but men are rational and don't argue.

Interestingly, men saw themselves as more intelligent ($n=14$) than women (no male respondent indicated that women were more intelligent than men), while women saw themselves as more intelligent ($n=10$) or as equal ($n=10$). Both males and females who indicated that males are more intelligent would rely on either observations (e.g. economic and political leaders are predominantly male) or presume it an inherent quality of males ('what else do you expect', 'they are born that way'). However, 18 of the 44 responses (41 per cent) said males and females were equal. This is a significant number. Also the explanations by males for why males were more intelligent were defensive declarations that struck us as hollow (as the above, 'what else...'). We suggest that the strong patriarchal entitlement of male intellectual superiority is not what these answers reflect, but rather a reluctance to let go of a traditional engendered world view.

A few males and females noted that females were strong in 'social reason' and males in 'logic' or 'rational reasoning'. This distinction in intelligence is expressed in the explanations for other questions (such as argues). We suggest that Macedonians recognize a cognitive distinction between males and females, with females better at emotional and relational reasoning and males at logical rational reasoning.[6]

Responses to who manages money better, more or less parallel the responses to the 'intelligence' question. Males think males manage money better ($n=16$) and females think that females manage money better ($n=12$). There is quite a bit of variability for this answer, as four males noted that female managed money better while six females noted that males did. Males who noted that males are better at managing money better explained their answer through various disparaging qualifiers of females: they are 'foolish', 'waste money', 'buy stupid things' and the like. Females who noted females were better at money management said either that males 'lack control', or that as 'housewives' women must manage money carefully. The gist of their answers were reminiscent of Schubert's argument in 'Too Many Men' – that Macedonian males enjoy a bachelor sort of lifestyle (even when married) and often do not consider family needs when they have money at their disposal.

The question 'What is it better to be born as?' is key to perceptions of how gender and the quality of one's life are affected by patriarchy. Twenty males indicated that it was better to be born a male (two indicated 'equal'), and eight females also indicated male (ten indicated 'equal' and four 'female'). These responses imply that Macedonians recognize that males receive certain social entitlements or privileges not readily available to females. Men who indicated that it is better to be born male noted that males are more 'free', 'have less obligations', 'men can find better work', 'men would not like being pregnant', 'men are leaders and head of the household' and so on. Freedom, greater political and economic clout, and biological benefits influence informants' responses to this question. Women who *favoured* being born female often explained their decision because they 'love children', 'it's nice to be a woman' and 'it's easier to pick somewhere to go if you are a woman'. These answers also segue with Schubert's findings that rural women are more able to migrate to urban areas or even abroad because they have employment and marital opportunities. The reason why women abandoned the villages was that they did not want to stay there and had a greater chance to get married in the cities than did the men. A man also is responsible for the family land and resources, which he traditionally and still by custom inherits and cannot leave without losing claim to them.[7] Tradition requires that males provide a place for women to live and so women who come to urban areas usually go where there is a male member of the family who is obligated to take them in.

This concludes our discussion of the results and analysis. In the next section we synthesize these findings and provide a portrayal of how they influence gendered aspects of life for women, particularly in Skopje.

Conclusion: Discussion on the Significance of the Findings

Males perceive themselves in terms of a bundle of positive traits and perceive females as a bundle of negative traits except for those associated with the conceptually 'natural' roles of 'wife' and 'mother' for women – i.e. attractive, sympathetic and care for children. The remaining traits males identify with women are all negative: jealous, gossip and argues. The constellations of traits males attribute to males and to females indicate that most of our sample of educated males conceptualizes gender through a patriarchal lens.[8] By contrast, Macedonian women have quite a different conception of gender. Their view fits more with a Western 'enlightenment', one that is relatively free of gender biases.[9] Our main reason for concluding that women have a less patriarchal, indeed non-sexist conception of gender is that they rated ten of the nineteen traits as 'equal'. Perhaps this comes as no surprise, but we base our claim on unambiguous empirical data, systematically collected, rather than conjecture or anecdotes for our claim. A much larger sample across different areas of Macedonia would bolster this claim and we hope to do so in the near future.

The non-sexist view of gender by females is hardly surprising and is indicative of the national and indeed global rise in female status, largely spurred on by the global rise in educational opportunities opened to women and their achievements. For instance in 1990, 48.9 per cent of Macedonian university students were female. That trend steadily rose until by 2005, 56.7 per cent of all university students were female, and undoubtedly the rate has continued to increase (Magno and Silova 2008: 7). Such a rise in the educational status of women closes the gap between females and males and thus claims of equality, whether 'real' or idealized, reflect an imagined possible future, seeded both by educational attainments of women and, as Thiessen (2006) has shown, by women entering traditionally male-only domains.

Actions should follow expectations, and in some cases they have. However, in many domains of work one can observe the patriarchal and egalitarian views of gender seamlessly meld. For instance, in the workplace women who hold the same official status as men are still expected to enact nurturing and housewife roles by bringing coffee, listening and remaining passive, usually making their points in dyadic and intimate rather than in public settings. Men fill the public spaces of high-status workplaces as entitled members; women often fill those spaces nervously and timidly. Once the default assumptions of males as legitimate keepers of the flames of power are no longer fuelled, and more women enter those work and public spaces, the flame, like the Olympic flame, will be passed from one to the other and ultimately controlled by neither gender.

Notes

1. Complementarity is frequently associated with a biblical principle of the articulation of the sexes. In this chapter we are using the term to have a similar meaning but stripped of its religious connotations. Thus, complementarity refers to viewing males and females as 'having different roles and

fitting together' in a way that complements each other and makes a larger functioning social unit (i.e. parents usually).
2. Originally the survey was conducted among Sri Lankan Sinhalese (mostly Buddhists) and Muslims (a distinct ethnic group in Sri Lanka), US citizens, and was subsequently extended to include Turkey, Lithuania, Russia, Nigeria and Norway.
3. For more extensive discussions on consensus analysis see de Munck, Cardinale and Dudley (2002); Romney and Wells (1986) and Borgatti (1992). For a critique of the method see Garro (2000).
4. When we conducted a consensus analysis within gender we also obtained eigen value ratios under 2.0.
5. For visual clarity we only mapped half the respondents, adding the other half would not alter the interpretation of the MDS.
6. Given our educated sample it is unclear if this is an extension of traditional understandings of gender or because they have been exposed to expositions about the 'the female brain' (Brizendine 2007) in popular or scholarly writings.
7. The traditional custom was that sons inherit all the land and farm resources; however, since independence, daughters were also legally entitled to the estate. However, it is present-day practice for daughters to forfeit their rights to the family house and estate, giving their share to their brothers. This is usually at the urging of the parents and, of course, brothers. Inheritance practices are undergoing rapid change and many women are also claiming their share of the inheritance. Seldom do these women enter the sex trade according to a 2007 UNICEF sponsored study unless they are from dysfunctional families (see Risteski et al. 2007: 32–48).
8. We note that a minority, but a significant minority, of males had adopted a view of gender in accord with that of females and what I am referring to here as a Western European normative view of gender.
9. We realize this may be construed as an ethnocentric statement, however we take the position that an egalitarian and non-sexist view would perceive all answers except for 'strength' and 'care for child' to be equal. Our female informants fit this non-sexist construction much better than did the men. We hope and presume that this is an 'enlightened' view and held at least 'ideally' in Western Europe.

REFERENCES

Borgatti, Stephen P. 1992. ANTHROPAC. 4.0. Columbia, SC:Analytic Technologies.
Brizendine, Louann 2007. *The Female Brain*. New York: Broadway Books.

Brown, Donald 1991. *Human Universals*. Philadelphia, Temple University Press.
Danforth, Loring M. 1995. *The Macedonian Conflict: Ethnic Nationalism in a Transnational World*. Princeton, NJ: Princeton University Press.
De Munck, Victor C., J. Cardinale and H. Dudley. 2002. 'Cultural models of gender in Sri Lanka and the United States'. *Ethnology*. 41 (3): 225–61.
De Munck, Victor C. and Andrey Korotayev 2007. 'Wife-Husband intimacy and female status in cross-cultural perspective'. *Journal of Cross-Cultural Research*. 4: 307–35.
———. 1999. 'Sexuality and gender relations: a reanalysis of Rosenblatt's study on the function of romantic love'. *Journal of Cross-Cultural Research* Vol. 33(3): 265–77.
Denich, Bette S. 1974. 'Sexual power in the Balkans.' In M.Z. Rosaldo and L. Lamphere (eds). *Women Culture and Society*. Stanford: Stanford University press. pp 243–262.
Dimova, Rozita 2006. 'Consuming the "Other:" The South-Eastern European case'. *EthnoAnthropoZoom* (Journal of the Department of Ethnology at the Faculty of Natural Sciences), University Cyril and Methodius, Skopje, Macedonia.
——— 2003. 'Lost objects: ethnicity, consumption, and gendered spaces in contemporary Macedonia. PhD Thesis'. *Department of Cultural and Social Anthropology*. Stanford University.
Dubisch, Jill (ed.) 1986. *Gender and Power in Rural Greece*. Princeton, New Jersey: Princeton University Press.
Ensminger, Jean and Knight, Jack 1997. 'Changing social norms: common property, bridewealth, and clan exogamy.' *Current Anthropology* Vol.38,1.
Friedl, Ernestine 1967. 'The position of women: appearance and reality.' *Anthropological Quarterly*, Vol 40 (3) July: 97–108.
Friedman, Victor A. 1993. 'Macedonian.' In B. Comrie and G.G Corbett (eds).
Friedman, Victor 2005. 'Macedonia'. *Encyclopedia of the World's Minorities*, Vol. 2 (G-O), ed. by Carl Skutsch (pp. 763–65). New York/London: Routledge.
Frisick, Jasminka and Mariana Duarte 2007. Women's Rights in the Former Yugoslav Republic of Macedonia (a Briefing) Geneva: Human Rights Committee
Garro, Linda. 2000. 'Remembering what one knows and the construction of the past: a comparison of cultural consensus theory and cultural schema theory'. *Ethos* 28: 275–319.
Gilmore, David E. (ed). 1987. 'Honour and shame and the unity of the Mediterranean'. *Special Publication of the American Anthropological Association* No. 22.
Gilmore, David E. 1983. 'Anthropology of the Mediterranean area'. *Annual Review of Anthropology*. 11: 175–2005.
——— 1987. *Aggression and Community: Paradoxes of Andalusian Culture*. New Haven: Yale University Press.
Halpern, Joel M. and Kerewsky-Halpern, Barbara 1972. *A Serbian Village in Historical Perspective*. New York: Holt, Rinehart and Winston.

Halpern, Joel, M. and Kideckel, David, A. 1983. 'Anthropology of Eastern Europe'. *Annual Review of Anthropology*. 12: 377–402.
Hammel, Eugene A. 1968. *Alternative Social Structures and Ritual Relations in the Balkans*. Englewood Cliffs, NJ: Prentice-Hall.
Holy, Ladislav 1996. *Anthropological Perspectives on Kinship*. London: Pluto Press.
———. 1989. *Kinship, Honour and Solidarity: Cousin Marriage in the Middle East*. Manchester: Manchester University Press.
Karakasidou, Anastasia 1997. *Fields of Wheat, Hills of Blood: Passages toNationhood in Greek Macedonia 1870–1990*. Chicago: University of Chicago Press.
Kosev, Sasho 2007. 'Unemployment in the Republic of Maceodnia-specifics and possible solutions'. *Facta Universitetas Series: Economics and Organization* Vol 4(2): 153–60.
Lindholm, Charles 1998. 'Love and structure'. *Theory, Culture & Society*, Vol. 15, No. 3, 243–63.
———. 1995. 'Love as an experience of transcendence'. Jankowiak, William (ed.) *Romantic Love: A Universal Experience?* New York: Columbia University Press.
Loizos, P. and Papataxiarchis, E. (eds.) 1991. *Contested Identities: Gender and Kinship In Modern Greece*. Princeton University Press.
Magno, Cathyrn and Iventa Silova 2008. 'Divergent trends in higher education in the post-socialist transition'. *International Studies in Education* 9: 6–10.
Ramet, S.R. 1996. *Balkan Babel: The Disintegration of Yugoslavia From the Death of Tito to Ethnic War*. Boulder, CO: Westview Press.
Rheubottom, David B. 1996. 'Land, labour and the Zadruga: the economic viability of peasant households in Macedonia.' *Manchester Papers in Social Anthropology* No.3.
Risteski, Ljupcho S. 2007. Mapping and Community Based Research Study On Most At-Risk Adolescents To Hiv/Aids/Sti. http://www.iea.pmf.ukim.edu.mk/ENG/ UNICEF_MARA_ Research.pdf
Romney, A. K., S. C. Weller, and W. H. Batchelder. 1986. "Culture as Consensus: A Theory of Culture and Informant Accuracy." *American Anthropologist* 88: 313–38.
Schubert, Violeta 2005. 'Dynamics of Macedonian kinship: contextualizing ideologies and pragmatics of agnation'. *Journal of Mediterranean Studies* Volume 15, Number 1: 2005.
———. 2011. 'Too many men: the problem of bachelorhood in a contemporary Macedonian village'. Unpublished Manuscript.
Scott, James 1985. *Weapons of the Weak: Everyday forms of Peasant Resistance*. New Haven: Yale University Press.
Simic, Andre 1983. 'Machismo and cryptomatriarchy power, affect, and authority in the contemporary Yugoslav family.' *Ethos* 11: 66–86.
Thiessen, Ilka 2006. *Waiting for Macedonia: Identity in a Changing World*. Toronto: University of Toronto Press.

6

IS IT JUST A SONG THAT REMAINS? REFLECTIONS ON TURKISH MINORITIES IN MACEDONIA

Burcu Akan Ellis

Everybody wants to know about the Albanians. Wouldn't it be better if someone wrote about us instead? If only someone wondered about us...[1]

The Turkish community in Macedonia, a significant element of the rich and diverse multi-ethnic tapestry of Macedonia, resides in the shadows. It often seems invisible and appears both economically poor and politically under-represented. In this context, Turks often find themselves stereotyped as either villains in Macedonian history books or a 'docile' third leg of interethnic relations in contemporary Macedonia. Many question the authenticity of their identity, underestimate the challenges they face, and may expect Turks to 'go back' to Turkey if they are discontent in modern Macedonia.

Meanwhile, Turkish remains a native language for roughly 23,000 people beyond the ethnic Turkish population, with many more who can partly speak the language or understand it (Çayırlı 2008). Among this cadre, Turkey is commonly regarded as a friend of Macedonia;

meanwhile, close to 200,000 Macedonian citizens visit Turkey each year for economic trade, to visit family and spend vacations.[2] Turkish products are readily available in Macedonia, Turkish television programmes and music are considered a staple, Turkish cooking and food valued and Turkish investments in Macedonia are welcome. There are no visa requirements between the two countries, and the two governments have agreed, for instance, that the Turkish government would fund the repair of old Ottoman architectural monuments that have eroded over the years or that were destroyed during the local armed conflict in 2001.

The transformation of an old, historical relationship between these two countries is not surprising, especially after significant changes in regional dynamics following the end of the Cold War. It is ironic, however, that apparently sound relations at the diplomatic level have not noticeably improved the living conditions of Turkish minorities within Macedonia or decreased local pressures for them either to assimilate into larger minority groups or to emigrate to Turkey. Turkey continues to be a significant, emergent market with a shared cultural past with the Balkans and remains an important, and often supportive, player at the political level for key regional states. But nowhere except in Macedonia do we see the juxtaposition of perceived value for the Turkish culture coupled with the relative invisibility of its culturally affiliated people.

In general, relationships with previous rulers and with influential cultures are often complex and involve both significant physical and cultural violence while the contours of newer national identities are constructed. Groups accustomed to privilege may find themselves endangered and potentially at risk in the national (re)construction process once the original sources of that privilege erode or disappear. However, it is not uncommon for each cultural identity to adopt and value certain portions of the former legacy even as – and sometimes especially as – the people who can claim direct access to that legacy are diminished or destroyed. Sanja Bahun discusses Yugoslavia in this vein, for example as an 'impossible chronotope', a place and a time that no longer exists yet continues to be present in literature from the region (Bahun 2010). The same can be claimed for the 'Turkish legacy', which has been detached from a specific minority of people and their experience and operates autonomously as an attractive chronotope to many people in Macedonia (Todorova 1995; Ellis 2002). Such an 'appetite' for 'things Turkish', while good for relations between the two countries, may in practice work against Turkish minorities who would want to claim exclusive access to that lifestyle or cultural choice. Moreover, the inherent ambiguity of such legacies (Todorova 1995), which increases the cultural appetite of others to devour them (Lebow 2008), may fare poorly in establishing exclusive ethnic categories that can be politically mobilized to compete with other ethnic groups.

Given the significant regional, cultural and economic force that modern Turkey has become, and given how linguistically and culturally accessible and appealing it is within the Macedonian context, it is very hard for Turkish minorities to emulate a cultural identity that can compete with the influence of modern Turkey. Today, one could argue that there are Albanians who speak better Turkish at home (Ellis 2003), or Macedonian-speaking Muslims who request Turkish schools more forcefully than the Turkish minority themselves (Dikici 2008). Similarly, the authenticity of local-area Turks is, as are other ethnic identities in the region, sometimes questioned by ethnic competitors.[3] The mass migrations from the region that have decreased the number of Turks enable others to argue there are 'no more Turks' here, hence no need to provide rights, schools or jobs for people who do not exist (Drakulic 2009). Divisions among ethnic Turks and a lack of unification between political parties, compounded by demographic and voting trends that consolidate smaller minorities towards the largest group that can fight for minority rights, are likely to persist (Mandacı 2007).

Several perspectives dominate approaches to the issues Turks face. Melancholic Turkish-Ottomanism embraces Turkey as a lost homeland or passively follows the dominant political actors in Macedonia. On the other hand, there are efforts to create ethnic parties that can compete to secure rights for the Turks in Macedonia. However, beyond all of these there is a fledgling effort on the part of civil society organizations to create consensus on the cross-cutting problems that Turks experience, ranging from domestic violence, and education for girls, to the demolishment of an architectural heritage. Turkish organizations in Macedonia are beginning to collaborate with international institutions and their counterparts in Turkey to address issues that are not necessarily 'ethnic', but rather national problems of relevance to this minority population. Such activities are arguably similar to strategies that Turkish minorities in the European Union have used in recent years to emphasize the cultural and economic contributions of Turkish communities. These movements also seek to create expertise in broader civil society issues to become relevant irrespective of ethnic background. Such issue-based efforts find easier counterparts in both the Turkish government and with private Turkish organizations, as well as with European and international organizations that operate in Macedonia. While a long way from achieving full social acceptance for Turks in Macedonia, these efforts may help position Turks well for a scenario in which future Macedonian politics becomes less ethnically based.

Understanding Invisibility: The Problems with 'Nationality'

Balkan Muslims 'enjoyed the legal and social privileges of belonging to the ruling confessional community of the Ottoman Empire' (Mentzel 2000). While numerous traits separated Balkan Muslims from one another, their shared social and legal status transcended their linguistic differences and geographic distances. However, their fate changed dramatically with the rise of predominantly Christian nation-states that regarded them as foreigners who had to either be expelled or assimilated. Consequently, as Peter Mentzel argues, 'Balkan Muslim minorities have faced very different pressures and choices than the Muslims who have lived in a state with a Muslim majority' (Mentzel 2000). The growth of nationalism placed them in the difficult position of building distinct national identities for themselves even though their primary identifications were not necessarily 'national'. This general situation was even more complicated in places such as Macedonia, where minority Muslims were ethnically intermixed and identified principally in non-national terms (Yosmaoğlu 2008). In these instances, the choices facing Muslim minorities were few and all untenable. Whether they sought integration with the non-Muslim majority, inclusion into the larger Muslim group with the more pronounced national identity, migration to another country or seclusion and enclosure in their own private social worlds, Muslim minorities would remain as communities who had a difficult time building vitality (Ellis 2003).

The establishment of socialist Yugoslavia with modern concepts of nation-building, industrialization and education further complicated identity formation in Macedonia. Socialist Yugoslavia separated its citizens into 'nations' and 'nationalities', thus determining the rights of the minority Muslim populations according to their status in one of these categories (Shoup 1968). Fellow Muslims in Macedonia were faced with institutionalized categories of Turkish and Albanian 'nationalities' whose homelands were defined as outside of Yugoslavia, as well as the category of 'Muslim', which could be declared as one's 'nation' following federal constitutional changes in 1974. Turks and other Muslims could integrate into evolving, modern, socialist Yugoslavia, or they could choose to leave for Turkey with the initiation of 'free migration' in 1953 (Kirişci 1996). Within neighbourhood after neighbourhood, families felt compelled to migrate leaving behind scattered family members, the impoverished and the unfortunate.

Those who did not migrate chose to adapt to the new system of governance. Muslim life in Macedonia transformed into a struggle between a choice of nationally mandated categories, which determined which schoolchildren would attend, what sort of employment opportunities would exist and even which television channels they would watch. Many Muslims would adopt then shift their identifications from one national group to the next. Ambiguity became a survival skill, with the particular choices of individuals predicated to a large extent on the prevailing socio-political environment.

Turks in Macedonia

Turks in Macedonia officially constitute 3.8 per cent of the Macedonian population, or approximately 79,959 people according to the 2002 census (Çayırlı 2008). Historically, Turks settled in Macedonia in the form of nomadic warrior tribes called *Yörük,* who established villages.

The Turkish presence increased and became more permanent with the expansion of the Ottoman Empire and the emergence of its administrative and military presence in the Balkans that transformed settlements into townships and urban centres (Mandacı 2007). The Muslim presence in these towns included people from many ethnic backgrounds, including communities that converted to Islam and populations that had lived in these towns for generations. This created a complex social tapestry undergirded by Turkish as a common spoken language. Many of these communities stayed intact until the Balkan Wars, but declined rapidly with ensuing mass migrations to Turkey.

In Macedonia, the remaining Turkish presence took two forms: in Western Macedonia Turks were a common presence in almost all the urban areas, with town-dwelling artisan or administrative populations; in Eastern Macedonia, the Turks were concentrated in villages that traced their ethnic background to various *Yörük* settlers from Anatolia. The distinction between the two sides of the country was reinforced during World War II, when Eastern Macedonia came under the occupation of Bulgarian forces, which ultimately led to discrimination and mistreatment of Turks in the villages (Poulton and Taji-Farouki 1998). The Western Macedonian Turks, on the other hand, experienced German and Albanian occupations as part of World War II and lived in towns where an 'Albanian Renaissance' reigned supreme for a number of years (Vickers 1995). During this period, Turkish groups who intermarried with Albanians and Muslim groups generally tended to assimilate into a rising Albanian identity. Albanian communists remained active in the area even after the establishment of Yugoslavia, and the Albanian influence continued to be strong as Tito envisioned that Albania would eventually join Yugoslavia (Bozbora 1997).

With the establishment of former Yugoslavia, Turks developed their own nationalist group, called *Yücelciler,* to promote their rights and status as a 'nationality' in Yugoslavia (Mandacı 2007). Such efforts came to a halt with the prosecution of *Yücelciler*, as the group eventually became perceived as a risk to Yugoslav socialism when Turkey and Yugoslavia found themselves on the opposite ends of the Cold War era ideological divide. Consequently, in Western Macedonia Turks found themselves caught in the tidal wave of conflicts between Albania and

Yugoslavia as the disagreements between the two led to a cessation of relations. Turkey's admission to NATO created further distance between it and Yugoslavia. This made populations very sensitive to making the 'right' kind of choices to stay out of trouble and led to further assimilation tendencies. Census results from Macedonia often show an unnatural rise or decline in the numbers of 'Turks' in the area, depending on overall political circumstances (Karahasan 1990). In general, when Yugoslav–Albanian relations were on positive ground, Turks found themselves socially and culturally pressured to support the Albanian groups. However, when many Turkish nationalists were persecuted because of their politics, many in Western Macedonia chose to become a loyal part of brotherhood and unity in Yugoslavia. However, when Albanians fell out of grace, Turks favoured their own or integrated with other groups in order to seek access to government jobs, schools and cultural representation in Macedonia (Çayırlı 2008).

The developmental gap between the Eastern and Western parts of the country remained, and resource distribution to Turks was limited to a diminishing population that lived in townships of Western Macedonia. Turkish villages in Eastern Macedonia suffered from neglect and underdevelopment (Mandacı 2007). By the same token, mass migration emptied towns and villages of their population. On the one hand, nationality status brought Turks the ability to have their own schools with instruction in their own language as well as access to a certain quota in government jobs and resources. They also obtained the ability to publish their own newspaper, *Birlik*, have their own radio and television programmes and theatre, and political representation. The problem was that such representation came with strings attached: it precluded meaningful discussion of the social and other challenges faced by Turks, whether in regards to the underdevelopment of the Eastern Macedonian villages or the consequences of the mass migration that ensued in 1953 (Karahasan 1990). Furthermore, this increased scope and level of rights came at a point when so many Turks had either migrated or were planning to migrate that it was originally even hard to fill the positions available for ethnic Turks.[4] In practice, there were not a sufficient number of intellectuals, teachers, doctors or even clergy left to take advantage of the newly available political opportunities. This led to a pattern in which other ethnic groups or fellow Muslims agreeable to the socialist system self-declared a 'Turkish' background in order to qualify for some of these positions. At the same time, others declared themselves Turkish to qualify for the right to migrate to Turkey (Ağanoğlu 2008).

Turkish intellectuals saw a viable place for themselves as a nationality but were also faced with a relatively oblique set of choices.[5] The Turkish culture and language in Macedonia were parts of a social system that emanated from a multi-ethnic urban legacy. It was relatively detached from the politics of Turkey and local Turkish nationalism. Yet, the Turks were now defined as an extension of a homeland that had undertaken significant reforms. The culture that ethnic Turks embodied had much more in common with the final social milieu of the Ottoman Empire than modern Turkey (Ellis 2003). Furthermore, Muslim minorities sought to downplay the role of Muslim clergy and identity because of the dynamics of the socialist system. In that respect, it may have helped that Turkey itself was concurrently engaged in a similar process with the rise of secularism; but 'devout' carried or conveyed different meanings whether one spoke of it in Istanbul, Skopje or Vrapcishte. Meanwhile, Eastern villagers faced a different set of challenges, as they were perceived by Turks in Turkey as those with the 'pure' traditions and should therefore seek to display 'unspoiled Anatolian identity'. This meant the Turkish villagers would have to remain traditional and undeveloped, while other villages from different ethnic backgrounds pursued better educational prospects and agricultural modernization (Mandacı 2007).

The Impact of Migration

The most important issue that frames the identity of Turks in Macedonia is that of the 'free migration' of 1953 that resulted in the permanent, legal and (by design) irreversible migration of Muslims from Macedonia to Turkey. The concept of 'nationality' in former Yugoslavia supported the idea that nationalities may, in fact, prefer to reside in their ethnic homelands and, as such, may want to migrate rather than stay in the country in which they have resided for centuries. For the Turks in Macedonia, migrating to Turkey was a long-standing option often encouraged by the Yugoslav and Turkish governments (Ağanoğlu 2008; Maynard 2009). Today many Muslim families in Macedonia have relatives in Turkey as a result of such migratory patterns.

In 1953, the Turkish and Yugoslav governments reached a gentlemen's agreement to allow for easy migration of people who declared themselves Turkish to Turkey (Kirişci 1996). Unlike previous migrations, this migration was neither officially forced nor was it treated as formal resettlement. It was advertised, however, as a great 'opportunity' for Turks, and the Yugoslav government even supported it with full promotion and advertisements in the newspapers (Ellis 2003). The process remained simple and not selective as to who could apply. Anyone who declared themselves Turkish and spoke a little bit of the language was allowed to migrate. As a result, the number of declared 'Turks' in Macedonia swelled to 203,938 in 1953 from a mere 95,940 just five years before (Çayırlı 2008). Many Albanians, Muslim Macedonians and Roma populations took advantage of the ability to legally migrate to Turkey with approximately 200,000 leaving between 1953 and 1968 (Kirişci 1996). They left behind their savings, their nationalized property, businesses and homes. While the migration was based on an agreement between states, it was not state-sponsored. As a consequence, Muslims who migrated to Turkey would not qualify for the land rights and privileges extended to other immigrants who had migrated from the Balkans.

> Everyone was in a hurry to leave. A few sacks of clothing, maybe a few household items, hardly anything of value; everything else would be sold, in panic and rapidly, nothing going for its worth, nothing worth anything.[6]

The migration that began in 1953 was so pervasive that not a single Muslim family was untouched in Macedonia (Ellis 2003). In some places, whole villages became ghost towns after their inhabitants deserted them:

> The train station... who has not been to the train station? For months villagers flowed to our home, villagers with children and

old grandmothers, with sacks on their backs, sleeping on the floor in our courtyard to catch the train next day. And the departures at the train station, that siren... that long siren in the early morning hours. It would be the last time we would see our cousins, sisters, brothers. How many of us came of age at that train station?[7]

The rapid departure of prominent families transformed the situation into mass panic among the remaining Muslims. Pressures were largely invisible except for the sudden evacuation of homes and departure of kin, only traceable with a call from the local police to the head of a family. Wherever the migration touched, houses quickly became deserted, their doors left open, household items left behind by people trying to get out of 'these places' as soon as they received their paperwork. Insecurity spread among the Muslim populations, the poorer families becoming even more scared by the speed with which prominent families deserted their homes:

> Do you have any idea what it is like to watch people go? Wave after wave, house after house. Like watching fire engulf home after home, coming closer to you. You watch your neighbors, your friends, your family melt away... 10 houses this week, five more next week. You feel lonely, you feel left behind. You feel lost and abandoned.[8]

Since there was no guaranteed state sponsorship at the other end in Turkey, many families did not migrate as a unit. Fractured families became a common phenomenon, with fathers staying behind for married daughters whose family would not migrate or siblings who were either left behind or chose to remain. Now that 'the road to Turkey' had been opened, there was another frame of reference for life in Turkey. Its appearance as a possible choice transformed the rooted self-identification of the Muslims in Macedonia to a state of liminality between 'here' in Macedonia and 'there' in Turkey. Whether they physically migrated or not, the Turkish population in Macedonia became, in effect, psychologically displaced:

> Nothing touched my father like the departure of my sister. After she migrated, every single night he would retreat to his room

and put on a Zeki Muren song and just sit there, rocking and sobbing to the lyrics of the screeching gramophone.[9]

By 1971 the number of Turks in Macedonia had declined to about 6 per cent, a downward trend that continues to the present day (Çayırlı 2008). Entire towns that were once associated with a sizable Turkish presence such as Bitola (Manastır), are today areas where only a handful of Turkish families can still be found. The people who left Macedonia often never came back, even to visit:

> I left an entire life, I lost everything I owned. I'm sorry, but I have no reason to want to go back and visit. Nostalgia is for people who have not suffered in those lands.[10]

One significant result of the free migration was a noticeable decline in the number of people who would declare themselves Turkish in the Macedonian context. Census results are often contested in Macedonia, and data relating to the Turks is no exception. Turks, on the other hand, describe the significant challenges they face in continuing to declare themselves as Turkish given the linguistic and political pressures towards assimilation into the larger Albanian minority (Hugh Poulton and Suha Taji-Farouki 1998). In the modern context, Albanians often perceive any government support towards Turks as an effort to weaken the Albanian population. A common claim about Turks in this context is that 'there aren't any left'. Turkish communities consequently claim that they have become an endangered community (Mandacı 2007).

Contemporary Macedonia: Ethnic and Political Obstacles

The independence of Macedonia was supported by the local Turkish minority, which generally regarded it as an opportunity to achieve enhanced political representation. While the constitution recognized minority rights, ethnic discrimination and issues with the constituent nation status of communities engulfed the country soon after its independence. Tensions between ethnic Albanian and Macedonian groups escalated into armed conflict in 2001. The resulting Ohrid framework agreement favoured balancing out the tensions between Albanians and Macedonians to the exclusion of the Turks, the Roma and other groups (Çayırlı 2008). In this context, while Turks could potentially have been sought-out as a minority group partner for purposes of coalition-formation or other political options, the Turkish experience in practice suggests the group was more of a political afterthought. The integrative role that Turks have played over the years apparently has alienated them from their Albanian counterparts, who today often pressure Turks to vote for Albanian parties. At the same time, Macedonians see Turks as a 'forgotten' ethnic group inconsequential to their political standing (Mandacı 2007).

By the same token, 'Turkish' remains a nationality that other minority groups continue to adopt in order to protect their identities, as it is an institutionalized and non-violent form of interethnic politics in the country. Some members of the Roma and Torbesh populations, for instance, prefer Turkish as a language for education. Muslim Macedonians have sought Turkish schools for their children (Dikici 2008). For Albanians, who harbour memories of perceived divide-and-rule policies by former Yugoslav politicians, any suggestion of Turkish rights is seen as a political device by which to disempower ethnic Albanians. Hence, they resort to a defensive rhetoric that argues 'Turks' are people who wish to hide their Muslim, Macedonian or Roma background, or at best are confused and scared Albanians who many years ago switched to an inauthentic Turkish identity in order to avoid contemporary social problems (Dikici 2008). Not surprisingly, such claims of inauthenticity are offensive to Turks and to other communities who are trying very hard to maintain vitality in an ethnically charged political environment.

The Ohrid Framework Agreement has sought to provide rights and to balance out ethnic grievances by redistricting municipalities, an effort that appears to have facilitated progress for Albanian, but not other, local minorities. The Turkish community argues that their access to rights and a share of resources has declined in recent years (Çayırlı 2008). The Turkish population, at approximately 4 per cent, is below the 5 per cent necessary for a party to be represented in the parliament. Consequently, ethnic Turkish parties have not fared well, having limited political representation. Furthermore, reorganization of municipal boundaries has lowered the number of districts creating larger entities in which Turks find it even more difficult to gain political stature (Mandacı 2007). As a result, for example, while the new political arrangement would allow for ethnic groups to use the symbols of their motherlands in areas where they constitute a majority of the population, this has proven impossible for Turks except in a few locations (Çayırlı 2008). The same is true for gaining the right to education in one's own native language and use of minority languages in official capacities, all of which is tied to the new borders and population dynamics in the region. Government and teaching jobs, which used to be a primary source of income for populations who are otherwise mostly artisans or farmers, have significantly declined due to ethnic favouritism. The dispersal of the Western Macedonian Turkish population in various small towns dominated by ethnic Macedonian or Albanian populations thus continues to limit their options.

The Influence of Turkey

The relationship of Turks in Turkey to those in Macedonia remains complicated. Macedonia was one of the last territories to break free of the Ottoman Empire before its collapse. The 'Macedonian knot' remains a common historical analogy arising from the complex power involvement, intrigue and violence that characterized Macedonia's relationship with the Ottoman Empire (Bozbora 1997). Memories of Macedonian bandits, attacks on villages and convoys of Muslim immigrants are also part of the imagery associated with area. In many respects, Macedonia represents the last frontier of the Muslim Ottoman retreat from lands that they had lived in for generations (Ağanoğlu 2008).

Not surprisingly, Turkish melancholy abounds in this context. Sanja Bahun discusses the idea that melancholy is different to nostalgia, as the latter term suggests something essentially worth missing. Turks do not remember Macedonia nostalgically, as their last memories of the place are evidently too ridden by sadness, loss and violence. Many Balkan immigrants have focused their efforts on becoming part of the 'new' Turkey, a country in which they could start fresh (Maynard and Geniş 2009). The acute difference in relative development levels of Turkey and post-independence Macedonia, one of several important variables, effectively curtails any ambition on the part of the now-settled immigrants to return. For modern Turks, Macedonia remains, simply put, a 'lover lost'.

Culturally, Macedonia still produces immense melancholy, 'a form of protracted and deliberately imperfect mourning' of abstract loss in Turkey (Bahun, 2010). For example, the popular TV series *Elveda Rumeli* (*Farewell Rumelia*) derives its name from a Turkish term traditionally used to describe the Ottoman Balkans. The TV show was set in a village in Macedonia and followed the stories of Sütçü Ramiz and his five daughters, ordinary people who happened to be in the wrong place at the wrong time during the upheavals of the early 1900s. In a complex story line, the show re-created tremendous 'sadness' about Macedonia as a 'love lost', told through the hopeless love stories of the characters involved. Such melancholy, however, does not empower anyone 'left behind' in contemporary Macedonia, as it tends to bury them further in the past, making them an anachronism or an older version of contemporary identities. In fact, while the series was well-received, the show was quietly criticized by immigrants in Turkey from Macedonias as having 'Turkey-washed' the interactions and the linguistic performance that would have reflected a closer reality to the Macedonia from which they migrated (Trix 2010).

When Turkey rediscovered the Balkans in the 1990s, it was arguably torn between strong, post-Ottoman visions of the Balkans as a new 'backyard of influence' and severe anxiety over the potential spill-over of Balkan conflicts to Macedonia that could potentially embroil Greece and Turkey in conflict (Çalış 2001). Ultimately, Turkey opted for policies that provided both economic assistance and diplomatic recognition to Macedonia. Turkey was among the first country to recognize the independence of the Republic of Macedonia and support its claims to its contested name. At a time when there were economic sanctions and diplomatic pressures from a number of other states, Turkey's support was very important for and, of course, well received by Macedonia. The two countries established airplane and bus links, removed visa restrictions and facilitated commerce; businessmen from Turkey made investments in the nascent Republic. Non-governmental actors opened schools and Turkish TV channels and commodities soon became available. Turkey made clear that it supported the territorial integrity of Macedonia. Of course, relations became more complicated with the onset of the Kosovo crisis and armed conflict in Macedonia. However, Turkey, while supportive of the plight of Albanians in general, towed a careful line between ethnic Albanians and Macedonians in the country (Yosmaoğlu and Yılmaz 2008).

Such a political balancing act, however, has very important consequences for Turks in Macedonia. Turkey has traditionally refrained from intervening in the domestic affairs of Macedonia and has proven supportive of past migration trends, doing little for the minority Turkish population in Macedonia despite evident discrimination. This has amounted to a perceived policy of benign neglect over the years, where Turkish officials would travel to Macedonia to make grand speeches about how Ataturk had gone to school there, how the *Yörüks* were the 'purest Turks' and how Turks had 'roots' in Macedonia (Çayırlı 2008). Turks in Macedonia could visit Turkey or migrate at any time, and the Turkish government would support cultural or educational exchanges. But as minorities in the Republic of Macedonia, ethnic Turks had to do what they needed to survive on their own (Çayırlı 2008). Turkey's recent balanced stance between the country's Albanian and Macedonian populations has similarly placed the Turkish minority in an ambiguous position of having to work closely with local parties in the absence of significant political support from Turkey. Ethnic Turkish political parties in Macedonia are somewhat inexperienced compared to their local counterparts and appear divided on various fronts while Turkey remains unwilling, or unable, to assist them in their growth.

Meanwhile, Turkey's citizenry has become more aware of their ethnic compatriots in Macedonia as a result of the Balkan wars. The persecution of Bosnian Muslims, notable socio-economic challenges faced by their ethnic affiliates in Macedonia, and issues such as the refugee crisis in Kosovo has awakened national interest in the ethnic roots of Turkish citizens (Maynard and Geniş 2009). Muslim Macedonians,

Bulgarians, Turks and Albanians, whose parents migrated from the Balkans, began to form ethnic clubs where they would try to learn their grandparents' language, entertain cultural activities and form new bonds with those 'new' countries that had become accessible to ordinary citizens in a post-communist era. Turks in Macedonia were especially appealing to such groups as 'authentic' Turks: they were variously perceived as 'true' Muslims who had been persecuted, the 'true' Turks who resisted ethnic cleansing, or a living museum of 'pure' Anatolian culture (Çayırlı 2008). For businessmen, Macedonia remains a culturally familiar market in need of development. So the Turkish community in Macedonia found themselves faced with foreign nationals (Turks from Turkey, primarily) who wanted to invest in their stores, open up private schools for their children, fund various projects or sell their *kilims*. The natural consequence of this well-intended assault was that each project came with projected identities that emerged from the particular political and economic context in Turkey, which was unfamiliar to the various Turkish groups in Macedonia. Already divided among themselves, Turks in Macedonia began to compete for funds from Turkey and blamed others for accepting funds from the 'wrong' kind of people.[11] On the other hand, access to Turkish resources provided some breathing room for an impoverished minority.

The Beauty of Ambiguity and the Politics of Distinction

While the Turkish minority in Macedonia is struggling with political recognition and economic viability in a society characterized by an ethnically based distribution of resources, 'Turkishness' tends to be a resource in-and-of itself. There is an ambiguity and, hence, a mimetic quality that allows people to voluntarily adopt Turkish cultural qualities as a familiar source of distinction from other ethnicities. In fact, as a cultural mode, 'things-Turkish' tend to benefit from an association with both a past high culture and a contemporary or modern developing country. As a result, it is not surprising that there is what Lebow (2008) might call an 'appetite' for things Turkish in Macedonia.

For ethnic Macedonians, Turkey represents a beacon of hope in the region – an example of successful development. It also represents a

Muslim society that ethnic Macedonians apparently feel some familiarity with, as well as a sense of perceived coexistence. The local existence of relatively docile Turkish communities is an integral component of Macedonia's multi-ethnic tapestry. In an environment where commonalities are destroyed and a religious divide between Muslims and Christians is notable (Mandacı 2007), this cultural affinity strengthens a sense of shared identity. Turkey represents a developing country, an important ally, a close and affordable market and touristic venue, which further increases the country's appeal for Macedonians.

'Things-Turkish' are arguably most appealing to the Muslim communities in Macedonia. The language itself remains one of the most commonly spoken languages in Macedonia (Friedman 2003). Turkish provides a venue of cultural differentiation to a variety of groups. For example, the Roma or Torbeshi groups are known for their adoption of the Turkish language in order to distinguish themselves from Macedonian or Albanian ethnic counterparts (Dikici 2008). Given that there are even more profound claims from various quarters about their identity and the absence of a minority status that would guarantee the survival of their identity, Turkish is a functionally useful language and identity category with schools that provide Turkish as a language of instruction. It is interesting to note that while Turkish schools, in the past, have shown assimilative tendencies towards especially the Torbeshi (Muslim Macedonian) groups (Dikici 2008), contemporary schools do not have a need to increase the numbers of their members forcefully. Hence, 'Turkishness' remains one of the culturally familiar options for those who voluntarily seek to remain 'distinct' from others.

Knowledge of Turkish also makes migration easier for members of the Muslim population that would wish to relocate and gives access to students to continue their education beyond Macedonian institutions. While scholarship opportunities remain limited in Turkish schools, the trends have been positive recently with as many as 200 scholarships available to students in 2009. There has been a rise in the number of Turkish classes available to students, and a handful of fields in Turkish language and pedagogy have become available in Macedonian universities. Turkish higher education institutions in Turkey have also opened to scholarships and enrolment of students from Macedonia. In fact, some students have been able to utilize well-recognized educational institutions in Turkey to build academic careers in Europe and beyond.[12]

Associated with a friendly state and an emerging market, Turkey's value as a high culture remains pronounced especially for Muslim communities in the country. Again, it is not seen as a useful domestic source of power, but perceived, nevertheless, as a high culture that promotes longevity and cultural dynamism of local communities. Western Macedonia's major towns, Tetovo and Gostivar, sustain significant populations whose home language remains Turkish (Ellis 2003). These urban families participate fully in Albanian ethnic politics, yet retain a cultural distinction from other Albanians, especially villagers or newer immigrants, by virtue of sustaining the Turkish language and traditions that they associate with Ottoman high culture. The urban families in Gostivar, furthermore, sustain their difference from the families in Tetovo by emphasizing the larger number of Turks and Turkish speakers in the area. There are villages, such as Vrapcishte, that form a very distinct local identity as a 'progressive' set of people by virtue of their skills in Turkish and the specific traditions they maintain. In the cultural currencies of the Muslim populations in Macedonia, the language and traditions carry value that creates distinction and perceived superiority for the groups that can claim them (Ellis 2003).

Spoken Turkish in Macedonia differs in its dialect from that spoken in Turkey. Given the availability of Turkish television from Turkey's many private channels and the popularity of Turkish pop and traditional music in Macedonia, most Turkish speakers are arguably fluent in two forms of Turkish: their local language and 'Turkey Turkish' as it is referred to in the area. Turks in Macedonia know that those in Turkey expect others to speak the language with a dialect similar to their own. (Trix 2010) Turkish speakers take great care to show off their 'Turkey Turkish' to visitors from Turkey:

> In Macedonia, there are so few of us ethnic Turks, so we think to ourselves, yes, we are a minority. But then I come to Turkey,

and as soon as I open my mouth, they know that I am not from Turkey. For them I am Macedonian, or worse, someone from rural Turkey because I don't speak with the 'correct' accent. So I can't seem to ever escape being a minority – even when I visit the supposed country of my very own ethnicity![13]

Turkish also remains a gendered language in the sense that there are more Turkish-speaking women than men among the Muslim populations. This is partly because school attendance levels generally remain low for girls in Muslim communities, but Turkish elementary schools have traditionally been regarded a gender-appropriate venue for girls. In this context, conservative families perceive that the language exposes girls to a culturally appropriate knowledge base that enables continuity of traditions that distinguish their small local community from others. This is compounded by the consumerist aspects of day-to-day maintenance of local Muslim identities that often benefit from products imported from Turkey. Due to the open bus routes to Istanbul, Muslim women routinely travel to Turkey to visit extended relatives and engage in shopping expeditions. A lack of visa requirements, coupled with the patrilocal residence patterns in Macedonia, make Turkey something of a woman's heaven on Earth – a place where she can stay with her own migrated extended family, visit without feeling restricted by local traditions or pressures, and quite simply take a break from the daily grind in Macedonia. 'Freedom' is the term that many Muslim women associate with Turkey—valuing books, clothes and cultural artefacts from the country as their own. It is especially interesting that women gain higher social status by virtue of their ability to emulate things Turkish, so it is not uncommon to find women in Macedonia who can cook Turkish food or model their homes after Turkish houses and designs:

> This was an old run down house, but this was the portion of the inheritance that we had to use. I studied houses carefully in Turkey because I wanted to make it better. Every time I was in Turkey, I looked at the houses in Istanbul and came back with scores of decoration and design magazines because I wanted this house to have character; I wanted this house to become mine.[14]

The passion to steep girls and women in things Turkish has increased literacy among women by virtue of them having to read books and magazines in the Turkish language:

> When I was young girl, my favourite book was *Çalıkuşu*, the Turkish novel about that young girl who became a teacher. One of my relatives in Turkey had given the book to me. I remember that I would imagine I was her. And do you see this, I became a seamstress and I, too, have been teaching the girls in this town for the last 30 years. They have all learned that art from me, every single one of them. Just like *Çalıkuşu*.[15]

For those who emulate things-Turkish culturally, there is a determination but lightness to the various interpretations they can create. However, for someone who is an ethnic Turk from Macedonia, what strikes them when they visit Turkey is the difference in culture, attitudes and language. Ethnic Turks are a minority in Macedonia, and when they visit Turkey, they remain a minority – this time from Macedonia. Their local Turkish may be perceived as 'uneducated' or 'villager-like' by Turkish citizens; their dialect is quite different than the Turks, their behaviour and attitude also different. So the 'otherness' they feel in Turkey, irrespective of their ethnic background, eventually suggests to some that they may be better off within the smaller communities in their hometowns. Visiting Turkey often underscores just how different the Turks of Turkey are from their homeland compatriots:

> You attend a wedding here in Tetovo, you look around and say to yourself, it is as if no one has left... Then when you attend a wedding in Istanbul, then you realize no one has stayed behind. Everyone is somehow there.[16]

Bringing the Turks Back In

It is not easy to claim an identity as an exclusive category when that identity and things associated with it are in some ways co-opted by other actors in a society. Such co-option may deny the existence of the population that associates with that identity marker and can override their interpretation and experience of what it means, in this case, to be 'Turkish'. The more popular 'things-Turkish' become as expressions of identity politics, the more erosion exclusive groups such as Turkish minorities may sustain to their identity and prospects. However, depending on how resourceful that group is, they can arguably use the attention given to aspects of their culture and claim rights to it themselves as part of an agenda that has become, for other reasons, appealing to others.

A recent topic that seems to generate agenda-building possibilities in Macedonia has been architecture or, in other words, the Turkish 'legacy in stone' (Hartmuth 2008). Just as elsewhere in the Balkans, a number of mosques, towers and bridges constitute the 'older' portion of the towns in Macedonia. Some of the older architectural and culturally important buildings were nationalized and demolished during the Yugoslav years, including many Islamic institutions and their *vakıf* (endowments). However, because some of the mosques and bridges were in old neighbourhoods outside the areas of socialist reconstruction, they survived – albeit in run-down form. During the armed conflict in 2001, nationalists attacked and destroyed some of these buildings, despite the fact that ethnic Macedonians in general consider this older Ottoman architecture to be part of their common cultural heritage. The Islamic Union, which has an interest in maintaining and rebuilding such entities as well as eventually re-invigorating some of the nationalized Islamic property, has actively argued for their reconstruction. Non-governmental organizations also took an interest in the issue as it resembled some of the ethnic-based destruction seen during the wars in Bosnia and Kosovo, and it was seen to signal a decrease in inter-religious tolerance. Eventually, the Turkish and Macedonian governments signed agreements, allowing Turkey to help rebuild some of the destroyed architecture – part of a common heritage.[17]

The activities of non-governmental organizations that involve Turks also appear to have exceeded the activities of Turkish political parties in Macedonia to date. Acute differences of opinion plague this small, dispersed and economically underprivileged community, and Turkish political parties have had a hard time consolidating votes in Macedonia (Mandacı 2007). Consensus seems to be easier to generate on the nongovernmental front, and Turkish NGOs have been able to build active civil society organizations as a way to create solidarity and establish a more visible presence. From active Turkish women's organizations such as MATUKAT (the Macedonian Turkish Women's Organization) to the network of Young Macedonians, from the literary and cultural Köprü organization to the Macedonian Turkish Businessmen's association, Turkish civil society organizations have proliferated over the last decade. These NGOs became increasingly important after the closure of the government funded Turkish institutions such as the state-owned Turkish media, as well as the decline in the number of government jobs available to Turks in an environment of ethnic favouritism. As large private businesses are rare among the Turks in Macedonia, non-governmental organizations that have been able to tap into international or Turkish funding have begun to make a difference. The Turkish Embassy, which keeps a distant interest in these communities so as not to negatively influence their relations with the Macedonian government, hosted an effort to create a mechanism of coordination between various Turkish NGOs in 2003. The resulting institution, MTUSITEB (Union of Macedonian Turkish Nongovernmental Organizations) has more than 40 institutions involved in the coordination process[18] and has served an important consensus-building role in recent years. Such efforts tend to maintain seasoned individuals who have experience in the NGO domain and attract young people in a way political parties have not (Çayırlı 2008).

The viability of these efforts ultimately depends on their ability to engage international organizations as well as keep their focus on crosscutting problems that affect Turks and other ethnic groups, such as unemployment, corruption, migration and poverty. Women's NGOs from Gostivar, for example, have been influential in their community development projects. As 'being Turkish' is a gendered activity, Turkish women have begun to claim this ground with projects that looked at problems that were important for Turkish minorities but also for other minority groups as well.[19] Issues such as the education of girls, women's inheritance rights, domestic violence, poverty, education, unemployment and lack of nutrition affect Turkish and other communities. In focusing on specific social problems in Eastern and Western Macedonia and tackling different dynamics than the ethnic divisions between Albanians and Macedonians, the Turkish NGOs were able to establish a voice for their counterparts in the Eastern villages. Such issues also attract attention from international institutions and non-governmental organizations that promote country-wide efforts rather than ethnically divided projects. Women's organizations have fared very well as consensus-building mechanisms. Such issue-based efforts have also gained support from NGOs in Turkey. Increased educational scholarships and funding for capacity-building projects from Turkey enhance the Turkish minorities' efforts and improve the performance of the younger generations. On the educational front, the establishment of a Turkish university and other educational projects are being considered as Turkey and Macedonia both aspire to European Union standards in human rights and education. Hence, the Turks in Macedonia may in the long run find themselves well-situated for a future in which democratization and politics in Macedonia cease to revolve around an ethnic axis.

Conclusion

'Things-Turkish' are appealing to many citizens of contemporary Macedonia 'as if in an art play...in which the content-laden forces of reality reverberate only dimly, since their gravity has evaporated into mere attractiveness' (Simmel 1950). For those who are culturally affiliated with it, Turkey represents a dynamic country that can offer opportunities to those who are linguistically and culturally fluent. As an institutionalized form of difference, 'things-Turkish' currently serves the purpose of distinguishing those who do not comfortably fit within an Albanian-Macedonian focused dialogue. The legacy of the Ottoman past is likely to be deconstructed and reinvented to serve a variety of identities and interests within contemporary Macedonia. Investments, cultural and linguistic affinity, and closer relations between the two countries are likely to lead to more economic and cultural collaboration.

For the Turks in Macedonia, migration is still a contemporary problem; long-standing trauma has not yet been fully reconciled between those who 'left' and those were 'left behind'. Turkey has rediscovered itself as an immigrant nation which generates interest in the story of the Turks in Macedonia. However, if those 'who left' continue to guide collective memory in Turkey, the Turks in Macedonia will likely be trapped in a state of Turkish melancholy that 'compulsively turns to the now vanished nation' (Bahun 2010). When those in Macedonia are able to foster their own identity as people of a contemporary Balkan homeland, with its distinct identity and ultimately local and global concerns of their own rather than as people who are bound by the trappings of a homeland with which they have an ambiguous relationship, their efforts are more likely to be noticed. One may argue that this may only be possible outside of the current dynamics of ethnicity in Macedonia and, by definition, in diaspora – this time to Europe and beyond (Simmel 1950). Those who believe in this option celebrate the fact that today there is, indeed, a dynamic Vrapcishte Macedonian Turk organization in Switzerland. Others will argue for an end to displacement – mental, economic and physical – as a starting point, so that the Turks are not trapped in increasing liminality of 'here' and 'there'. Either way, imagining Turks in Macedonia as more than just 'an old song that remains' will require a Macedonia that can actively reconcile its past with its future.

Notes

1. Interview with the head of the Turkish women's association in Gostivar.
2. Numbers are reported from the website of the Turkish consulate in Macedonia. http://Üsküp.be.mfa.gov.tr.
3. Interviews by the author with members of Albanian political parties in Gostivar, Tetovo and Skopje.
4. Interviews by the author with members of the Turkish community in Skopje.
5. Interviews by the author with a Turkish journalist, and a well-known author and representative of the Turkish community, Skopje.
6. Interview with an Albanian nurse in Bitola (Manastır). These interviews were originally included in Ellis (2003).
7. Interview with a Turkish teacher in Bitola (Manastır).

8. Interview with a Turkish lawyer from Veles (Köprülu).
9. Conversations with a Turkish journalist in Skopje.
10. Turkish immigrant from Köprülü (Veles) who lives in Istanbul, Turkey.
11. Interview with members of a women's organization, Gostivar.
12. Interviews and correspondence by the author with graduate students in Turkey.
13. A young female Macedonian-Turkish college student in Istanbul, Turkey.
14. A young Albanian bride in Gostivar.
15. A middle-aged Albanian seamstress in Tetovo.
16. A Turkish-speaking Albanian woman in Tetovo.
17. Information available on the website of the Turkish Consulate in Skopje.
18. More information is available at www.matusiteb.org.mk.
19. Zerrin Abbas, for example, became the first ethnic-Turkish female diplomat to be appointed from Macedonia to Turkey in 2010.

References

Ağanoğlu, Yıldırım 2008. *Üsküp Kitabi*. Istanbul: Filde Yayınları.

Bahun, Sanja 2010. 'There was once a country: an impossible chronotope in the writings of Slavenka Drakulic and Dubravka Ugresic'. *European Journal of English Studies* 14, no. 1: 63–74.

Banac, Ivo 1984. *The National Question in Yugoslavia: Origins, History and Politics*. Ithaca: Cornell University Press.

Bozbora, Nuray 1997. *Osmanli Yonetiminde Arnavutluk ve Arnavut Ulusculugunun Gelisimi*. Istanbul: Boyu Kitaplari.

Çalış, Saban 2001. 'Turkey's Balkan policy in the early 1990s'. *Turkish Studies* 2, no. 1: 135–46.

Çayırlı, Necati 2008. 'Turks in Contemporary Macedonia'. *TURKSAM*: 1–23.

Dikici, Ali 2008. 'The Torbeshes of Macedonia: Religious and National Identity Questions of Macedonian Muslims'. *Journal of Muslim Minority Affairs* 28, no. 1: 27–43.

Drakulic, Slobodan 2009. 'Anti-Turkish obsession and the exodus of Balkan Muslims'. *Patterns of Prejudice* 43, no. 3–4: 235–49.

Ellis, Burcu 2003. *Shadow Genealogies: Memory and Identity Among Urban Muslims in Macedonia*. Boulder: East European Monographs. New York: Columbia University Press.

—— 2002. 'The Turkish Saatli Maarif Calendar: Tradition-making between Urban Muslims in Macedonia and their Diaspora in Turkey,' in Armando Salvatore (ed.) *Muslim Traditions and Modern Techniques of Power*. Hamburg: Lit Verlag: 57–72.

Friedman, Victor 2003. *Turkish in Macedonia and Beyond: Studies in Contact, Typlogy and Other Phenomena in the Balkans and the Caucasus*. Wiesbaden: Harrassowitz.

Hartmuth, Maximillian 2008. 'De/constructing a "Legacy in Stone": Of Interpretive and Historiographical Problems Concerning the Ottoman Cultural Heritage in the Balkans'. *Middle Eastern Studies* 44, no. 5: 695–713.

Karahasan, Mustafa 1990. 'Migration and the Problem of Identity'. *Birlik*, June 7: 6.

Kirişci, Kemal 1996. 'Refugees of Turkish Origin: Coerced Immigrants to Turkey since 1945'. *International Migration* 34, no. 3: 385–412.

Lebow, Richard Ned 2008. *A Cultural Theory of International Relations*. Cambridge: Cambridge University Press.

Malcolm, Noel 1998. *Kosovo: A Short History*. New York: New York University Press.

Mandacı, Nazif 2007. 'Turks of Macedonia: The Travails of the "Smaller" minority'. *Journal of Muslim Minority Affairs* 27, no. 1: 5–23.

Maynard, Kelly and Şerife Geniş 2009. 'Formation of a Diasporic Community: The History of Migration and Resettlement of Muslim Albanians in the Black Sea Region of Turkey'. *Middle Eastern Studies* 45, no. 4 (July): 553–69.

Mentzel, Peter 2000. 'Introduction: Identity, Confessionalism and Nationalism'. *Nationalities Papers* 28, no. 1: 7–11.

Norris, H.T. 1993. *Islam in the Balkans: Religion and Society between Europe and the Arab World*. Columbia: Columbia University Press.

Poulton Hough and Suha Taji-Farouki 1998. *Muslim Identity and the Balkan State*. London: C. Hurst and Co. Publishers Ltd.

Shoup, Paul 1968. *Communism and The Yugoslav National Question*. New York: Columbia University Press.

Simmel, Georg 1950. 'Sociability: An Example of Pure or Formal Sociology'. In *The Sociology of Georg Simmel*, by Kurt H. Wolff. New York: Free Press.

Todorova, Maria 1995. 'The Ottoman Legacy in the Balkans'. *Balkans: A Mirror of the New International Order*, by G.G. Ozdogan and K. Saybasili, 55–74. Istanbul: Eren.

Trix, Frances 2010. 'Contesting Immigrant Voices in Istanbul: Mass Media, Verbal Play, Immigrant Channels'. *Language and Communication* 30, no. 1: 7–18.

Vickers, Miranda 1995. *The Albanians: A Modern History*. New York: I.B. Tauris.

Yosmaoğlu, Ipek and Şuhnaz Yılmaz 2008. 'Fighting the Spectres of the Past: Dilemmas of Ottoman Legacy in the Balkans and the Middle East'. *Middle Eastern Studies* 44, no. 5: 677–93.

7

WHY A GYPSY IN MACEDONIA DOES NOT KNOW 'CORRECT' ISLAM

Galina Oustinova-Stjepanovic

Introduction

My fieldwork took place among the members[1] of a *tekke* (dervish lodge) in a Macedonian town in 2009–10. I have researched the experiences, perceptions and circumstances of failure among Muslims who aspired to excel as 'true' Islamic mystics, but whose efforts were not successful. I have explored many inflections of performative failure:[2] rituals would go wrong; interpersonal relations were a disappointment; people self-critically bemoaned their lack of theological knowledge and laxity in prayer and acts of worship. It is beyond the scope of this chapter to discuss in detail people's experiences of performative failure, their reflexive meta-commentaries and the search for solutions. Instead, I will single out one aspect of people's self-understanding of why they have not become 'true' mystics so far. Without exception, these aspiring mystics were Gypsies.[3] In unison, people claimed that they did not know Islam and could not perform satisfactory rituals because Ottoman Turks had excluded Gypsies[4] from learning their religious tradition, *dervishluk*. Here, I would like to tease out the significance and implications of this historical perception on people's reforms of their lodge. I will also show that despite people's grievances against the Ottoman shaykh, their perceptions were marked by ambiguity.

Dervish Orders in Macedonia

In the thirteenth century dervish orders either entered Rumelia (today's Balkans) as missionaries and military Ottoman scouts, or followed in the footsteps of the later imperial expansion (Baer 2004: 183). Geographically Macedonia was a territory of the Ottoman Empire until the end of World War I and the signing of the Treaty of Versailles, so the Macedonian dervish orders are in some sense a colonial heritage of Ottoman rule. The relationship between diverse dervish orders and the historically changing Ottoman administration was a pendulum swinging between favouritism and repression. For example, in the sixteenth century Bektashi dervishes led Ottoman Janissary warriors to conquest, then in the eighteenth century they were released from this role in favour of a sultan-preferred 'meek' Mevlevi dervish and in 1826 were banned and prosecuted. In addition to politically motivated disapproval of the lodges, dervish orders and their 'unorthodox' rituals were consistently opposed by groups and agents of other branches of Islam of the Empire (Baer 2004: 184; Norris 2006: 20–21), with the end result that the numbers and vitality of dervish lodges progressively waned in the Ottoman Empire from the eighteenth to the twentieth century. Dervish lodges were made illegal shortly after the emergence of Republican Turkey (Silverstein 2007), but this is another story. In the early twentieth century, Turkey and Macedonia parted ways.

Between the two World Wars, Macedonia belonged territorially to Royal Yugoslavia. There is precious little published on the ethnographic history of dervish lodges at that time, but we know the lodges were open for worship, divination and spiritual healings (Elezovich 1925). After World War II, fledgling socialist Yugoslavia underwent something like a secular restructuring, i.e. religiosity was permissible as private faith, but not as an institutional and civic force in public politics. The 1953 Law on the Status of Religious Communities promoted the ousting of religious institutions not only from Yugoslav state politics (ibid: 122) but also out of the quotidian administrative lives of Yugoslav citizens, for example, by placing the life-cycle duties of registering birth, marriages and death into the secular hands of a registrar. This had the effect of restricting the applicability of Shari'a laws among Muslims. Religious freedoms were guaranteed, yet religiosity was interpreted as a personal matter of Yugoslav citizens. Departments of Theology existed but were removed from national universities; mandatory secondary secular education was extended to all children and religious education in secondary state schools gave way to Marxist socialist education. Religious education was allowed to be organized in religious institutions, churches, mosques and seminaries, not all of which were nationalized (Alexander 1979: 230).

The loss of property and land was the major blow to Yugoslav religious organizations that plunged churches and mosques into penury. Already in the nineteenth century sources of dervish income from pious endowments, supplementary funds from the state budget, property rent, salt mines and so on were severely curtailed by the centralizing policies of the Ottoman administration that attempted to consolidate its control of the imperial economy (Barnes 1992: 33–48). Socialist nationalization policies further aggravated the financial hardship of Macedonian dervish orders. Until the early 1960s, many religious institutions including the Vatican-affiliated Catholic Church, Serbian Orthodox Church and the Islamic Organization were receiving only reduced subventions from the Yugoslav government and faced grave financial crises. For example, the Yugoslav Islamic Organization, which had no external transnational sources of income, was made dependent on irregular handouts from the socialist government. The increasing liberalization of the socialist stance in the 1970s opened overseas channels for financial and practical support of Islamic education, which remained organized, however, outside state schools. It became possible to receive a scholarship and a permit to study Islamic theology in Egypt and Iraq, countries linked to Yugoslavia through non-alliance (neither Soviet, nor American) agreements.

In addition to the 'socialist state versus. religion' complications, some harsh policies affecting dervish orders had internal, Islamic origins. For example, in 1952 the Islamic Organization of Yugoslavia banned all dervish orders in Bosnia, another federate state of Yugoslavia, in order to consolidate its monopoly over religious matters (Algar 1971: 196–97; Duijzings 2000: 112–20). After early days of austerity, the socialist regime in the 1960s underwent a considerable thaw, and in the 1970s an independent association of dervish orders was formed in Kosovo to the severe discontent of the Islamic Organization in Sarajevo (Popovic 1994: 17). The struggles of the latter for exclusive control over dervishes and over the affairs of all Muslims of Yugoslavia were cast in the theological language of the 'perversion of the original Sufi' ideas by contemporary dervish practices. The Kosovo lodges retaliated with moral accusations of corruption, sinfulness and ignorance among the members of the mainstream Islamic institutions. Those recalcitrant lodges seemed to be registered as ethnically Albanian and were 'disliked' by Sunni Bosnian Muslims (ibid: 128), while a number of informal orders with Gypsy members that were burgeoning in urban Kosovo and Macedonia since the 1980s did not figure prominently in the debates.

In the past hundred years, Macedonia has gone through dramatic permutations from being part of the Ottoman territory, to the province and federal republic of royal and socialist Yugoslavia to eventually become the independent, but challenged, nation-state. In history books and in daily parlance, the Ottoman past in Macedonia has been regarded as an 'occupation', but Muslims of different ethnicities, such as Albanians, Turks, Vlachs, Torbeshi and the Roma, continue to live in Macedonia and adhere to Islam and practical cultural legacies of Ottomans. These people are surrounded by the homogenizing and essentializing processes of the consolidating nation-state. Today Macedonia, a former multi-faith territory of the Ottoman Empire, is nationally defined as an independent country of the distinct ancient people of the Orthodox Christian faith. Nevertheless, Macedonia is a constitutionally defined secular state.

'Gypsyness' and the Roma Religion

Against this backdrop of national history, Muslim Gypsies I worked with were trying to learn 'correct' Islamic mysticism, Sufism, in order to reform the relations within their lodge and their ethical subjectivities. I will sidestep the discussion of Gypsy ethnic origins and the analysis of their political and economic struggles in urban Macedonia (Kenrick 2001: 405–25). Many scholars have made their contribution to the understanding of Gypsyness as performative practices and moral discourses unfolding through the interplay between an inner dynamic of self-identifications and an outer political, cultural and economic dynamic between Roma and non Roma (Gay y Blasco 1999; Tong 1998; Marushiakova and Popov 2001; Stewart 1997; Gmelch 1986; Williams 2003; Polansky 2008: 297–355; Barany 2001). Sometimes, scholars make historically essentializing references to traditional Romani holidays of Erdelez, their traditional clothing of *shalvari,* or traditional musical instruments of drums and flutes (e.g. Silverman 1995), which are part of the cultural repertoire of other ethnic groups in the Balkans. I agree with Aspasia Theodosiou (2007) that Gypsy practices, relations and experiences are often discussed as a manifestation of some essential Gypsyness rather than a participatory claim to a time and 'place-based tradition' (ibid: 154). My interlocutors had copyright stakes in certain 'cultural' practices, songs or narratives described to me as their 'authentic tradition' even though they did not exercise a monopoly on those rituals (Lucassen and Willems 2003; cf., Ellis 2003). Gypsies I worked with had stakes in the mystical Islam of the Ottoman Turks.

In this ethnography, Gypsyness is a salient aspect of people's self-knowledge and self-analysis of their conjectural history and religious practices (Stewart 2004). Ethnicity was frequently cited as the reason why Gypsies did not know 'correct' Islam and could not perform their rituals with confidence. These Gypsies claimed that Ottoman Turks denied them the right to learn Islam and, as a result, their theological ideas and ritual practices were full of fallacies, superstitions and mistakes. They complained that their dervish credentials were precarious, that they had no 'aptitude' for coping with a variety of theologically defined obligations. Sometimes, their self-deprecation took the tragic hue of self-hatred (cf., Robbins 2004) and aspirants would reiterate the Ottoman scorn of Gypsy levity with Islamic prescriptions (Barany 2001). For the Ottoman authorities, the fact that Gypsy women refused to wear a veil smacked of disloyalty and transgression of the formally required Islamic morality (ibid; Delaney 1991: 130). Kept ignorant of the theologically 'correct' Islam, Gypsies were moralistically put down as 'improper' Muslims. Gypsies were (and still are) frequently associated with superstition and witchcraft (Marushiakova and Popov 2001: 14–16; Abbot 1903: 187). Their eclectic participation in monotheistic religious traditions was negatively highlighted by travellers in the Balkans, even though religious syncretism has always been a habitual Balkan phenomenon (Čelik 2003: 73–75; Duijzings 2000: 66–79; Elezovich 1925: 79–80; Hasluck 1929; Mazower 2005). These historical studies of Ottoman Gypsies lend credence to my interlocutors' perceptions. Indeed, Ottoman Gypsies were categorized in ethnic terms and as such were distinct from Muslims, Christians (Greek Orthodox, Gregorian Armenian, Roman Armenian, Roman Catholic, Protestant), and Jews – the principal classifications in Ottoman legal discourses[5] – regardless of which religiosity, Islam or Christianity, Ottoman Gypsies professed (Čelik 2003: 63). Conversion to Islam did not mean assimilation or equality of all Muslims in the Ottoman Empire (see Poulton 1997b: 85) and Gypsies were a testimony to this.

Because of this negative differential treatment, Gypsy dervishes had a grudge against 'Turks'.[6] However, they were not alone. Historiographical conventions in a number of Balkan nation-states, including Macedonia, describe the Ottoman regime as a 'yoke' or 'exploitation' (e.g. Trajanovski 2005; crit., Todorova 1996: 48). Certainly, the reality of injustice and discrimination in the Ottoman Empire was significantly more complex than the oppression of non-Muslim populations by 'Muslim Turks'.[7] The case of Gypsies in the Ottoman Empire is a fascinating example of these complexities because, despite being Muslims, aspirants were fluent in this 'anti-Ottoman' discourse. Yet, aspirants' understanding of their failure was partially shaped by the perception that 'Turks' excluded Gypsies from learning Islam. According to my interlocutors, under the Ottoman regime, Gypsies had no preachers of their own, and the fact that a few Gypsies have recently completed their formal theological education or acquired impressive religious knowledge through self-education is tantamount to a 'miracle'. Aspirants told me that Gypsies were prohibited from entering a mosque or a dervish lodge, for the Ottoman fear of infestation of the holy places with jinn spirits. A similar exclusion from intellectual and embodied learning of religiosity and caste-specific skills was applied to domestic bondsmen in Islamic Senegal (Dilley 2010: 181, 183).[8] Being a Gypsy mattered to aspirants in their perception of the historical hurdles to learning theology and its performance, which they had to overcome to succeed as 'true' dervishes. Thus, their experiences of postponed accomplishment as 'proper' dervishes could be related to being barred access to, and the efforts to recover, denied secret knowledge under the conditions of post-colonialism.

The Gypsy Lodge and Departed Teachers

In this section, I will show how one dervish lodge suddenly changed hands from Turkish to Gypsy shaykhs. Aspirants picked up a discarded mystical tradition of their former 'masters', Ottoman Turks, and found themselves in the position to carry on with these practices in the previously inconceivable role of theological leaders. Aspirants felt they were serendipitous leaders, and that their lodge and their religious tradition was a historically fortuitous appropriation. They also felt that Gypsy dervishes were less authentic than Ottoman dervishes. My interlocutors suspected that, despite the empowering transition, something remained concealed from them. Aspirants thought there were ritual technologies beyond what their Gypsy ancestors had gleaned from 'Turks' (Ottoman dervishes) who allegedly denied explicit pedagogical instruction in Sufi religiosity to Gypsy Muslims.

The Sa'di tekke was supposedly founded in 1880, but the year was gathered from the inscription on a stone accidentally stumbled upon in the courtyard during the reconstruction of the tekke that had burnt to cinders twice in the past 25 years. The founder, shaykh Vefa Baba, might have travelled to Konya to establish a lodge there, but returned and built the lodge in Gorno Malo.[9] One of the contested miracles of Vefa Baba was rumoured to be a feat of flying over the local rumbling river, now a polluted brown streak. The tekke was always poor, as the current Shaykh Mehmed explained, but the dervishes lived together like a commune. They worked, ate and slept in the tekke, and tried to feed the poor out of the scant earnings they made cultivating their fields and with healing and lifting spells. And so it continued until the end of World War II and the emergence of socialist Yugoslavia, which saw a departure of many self-declared Turks abroad. In the early years of the Yugoslav socialist regime, Muslims were subtly accused of being an ideological fifth column and reluctant participants in the young socialist federation (Hopken 1994: 222–25); they were made unwelcome in socialist Yugoslavia[10] and were nudged (and inclined) to migrate, especially to Turkey. However, the migration of Muslims from the Balkan territories to Anatolia was a long-drawn, coercive (Hirschon 1998) or permissive process[11] (Ellis 2003: 41–59), spinning out over several centuries (Karpat[12] 1990: 131–52). Some were displaced by conflicts and wars; others were beguiled by the ideas of pilgrimage and relocation (*hijra*) to Istanbul or Anatolia, which was attractive in political, economic and religious terms (Karpat 1990: 133). It is important that demographics shifted and Yugoslav dervish lodges and mosques were rapidly depopulated following the departure of many Turks and Albanians, who were often members of those dervish orders.[13]

Around this time, but perhaps for personal reasons, the last Turkish shaykh of the Sa'di tekke set off on a journey to Istanbul, but allegedly died on a ship and was buried at sea. Mehmed's grandfather, Shaban, a respected blacksmith and a shop owner, was picked as an interim trustee until a better candidate was found. No one better came along and a series of divinatory dreams confirmed his elected status as a leader of the tekke. The tekke was an unpredicted godsend, although no divine intention was read into the events and the death of the Turkish shaykh and was rarely seen as anything but a quirky accident. Shaykh Shaban was initiated as a shaykh by another shaykh from Kosovo and, according to the principle of blood descent (*evladiya*), the tekke passed from the grandfather to Mehmed's father. The departure of the Turkish shaykh enabled Shaykh Mehmed's grandfather to inherit the tekke from its previous leader. The current Shaykh Mehmed is the third shaykh in his family, succeeding his father shaykh Ali Refik, and his grandfather shaykh Shaban.

Mehmed's father, a swaggering man known for his sartorial elegance and a succession of wives (which made little Mehmed feel neglected by his stepmothers), was emotionally devoted to the tekke. However, Mehmed's father did not pay much attention to the reigning idolatry and other *haram* (forbidden) practices among his followers. Piercing with skewers, drinking alcohol and the burning of votive candles (an act reminiscent of Orthodox churches), fetishizing the tombs and misattributing the powers of intercession on behalf of the dead or ill to the saints instead of Allah alone were regular occurrences. All changed with the proclamation of Mehmed as a shaykh when his father passed away.

At some point in his life, Shaykh Mehmed recognized the *nekompletni* (incompleteness) of his dervishes and started wondering what was wrong and whose fault it was (*koj e kriv*). Eventually, he concluded that the main reason for the incompleteness of Romani dervishes in Gorno Malo was their neglect of theological education and scorn of books. Shaykh Mehmed's common refrain was:

> Roma nation, (*Romska natsiya*), should start for real...should start reading...not to be a low nation. We are sharp-witted. This tekke burnt down twice...so poor, it aches [to think] about the tekke. Books give you everything...To become a dervish, first learn Arabic.[14] Our mistake is that we do not know religion (*din*), but we have already decided that it is not necessary to learn. Even when we read and we do not understand what is written. That's illiteracy (*nepismenost*).

Adherence to 'correct' Islamic practices and discontinuation of local initiation rituals as a road to the modernity of airplanes and Muslim spirituality was preached unsuccessfully by a Mende pilgrim returning from Mecca (Ferme 1994: 27–45). Shaykh Mehmed saw theological learning as a key to empowerment, education and knowledge. Religious illiteracy was the key factor, according to Shaykh Mehmed, for why Romani Muslims were 'backward' with religiosity. Earlier Turks, he would explain to me time and again, did not share their knowledge with Gypsies. Turkish preachers and shaykhs used to hide books from Gypsies. Now books were easily available, not cheap, but abundant, so Roma dervishes were learning something on their own.

What was the point of hiding knowledge from somebody if one could get a poster with the beautiful names of Allah on every street corner? Everything became public. It happened to be an astute comment on the technologically enhanced 'universal accessibility of religious texts', books, DVDs, records and so on (Hirschkind 2001: 3; van de Port 2006). Today, the ancient secrecy around theological knowledge could not be maintained; the breakdown of secrecy was a result of the democratization of theology that in multiple forms (books, tapes, web pages and TV programmes) was available to all rank and file worshippers. A shaykh who used to be a keeper of secrets might have been reading the same book as an uninitiated student. Today's shaykhs would be hiding secrets in vain. They became the 'dated' guardians of theological knowledge (Meyer 2006: 432). According to Shaykh Mehmed, the reformed authority of a shaykh was rooted not in his secretiveness, but in the quality of his scholarship.

There were inconsistencies in Mehmed's perception of Ottoman shaykhs. For example, Mehmed's teacher, his Gypsy shaykh, was not teaching him any *dova* (prayers), would not give him anything to read or even let him fast because he did not know theology. In contrast, however, Mehmed was encouraged to take religion seriously by another informal teacher. That teacher was a very old Turk, shaykh Zeko, who knew Mehmed's grandfather. Without shaykh Zeko, a knowledgeable Turkish shaykh, Mehmed would have remained *djahil* (ignorant), knowing only how to perform a howling *zikir* ritual and ritual piercing. Shaykh Mehmed could not explain why that particular Turkish shaykh agreed to teach a Gypsy while others refused. It was Mehmed's fortune that shaykh Zeko recognized Mehmed's hunger for knowledge, and gave Mehmed a commentary to the Quran (*tefsir*), and a few other books. He also coached Mehmed in the interpretations of the Quran, its meanings and symbols, going through the Book word by word. Shaykh Zeko taught Mehmed how to read books. The Turk suffered from flatulence, so could not enter a dervish lodge or a mosque. He would just sit on the threshold, crying and listening to the sounds of the rituals inside, unable to practise religiosity because of his old age. Paradoxically, it was a Turkish shaykh who supervised Shaykh Mehmed's first steps into Islamic theology.

Learning, for Shaykh Mehmed, meant reading books for the authoritative interpretations of the Quran and the *hadith*. Mehmed liked reading books and gained the strength of the reformist convictions that his ancestral tradition had rested on superstitions, ignorance and hearsay. He persisted in re-educating himself and his followers in the theologically correct ways of being a dervish, placing unconditional trust in the efficacy of education, which was augmented by his gratitude to Marshal Tito for the increasing years of Romani schooling during the Yugoslav socialist regime. Reading the vernacular translations of the Holy Book and learning its theological commentaries for Mehmed were essentially an activity of interpretation of scriptural meanings and symbols. Theological texts became indispensable for Mehmed. Books were something he 'could not run away from'. The shaykh's attraction to the semantic meanings of theological propositions and his penchant for intellectual talk and book learning were part and parcel of his 'teach-yourself' religious regime (Aishima and Salvatore 2009: S46). He did not want to learn the saintly techniques of flying, becoming invisible, lifting curses and finding lost objects (cf., Horvatich 1994: 813). He wanted to know exactly what the Quran said about 'correct' religious rituals and about mundane tasks of daily life without deviating from ulema prescribed Islamic 'norms' that were grounded in the Quran and the sayings and deeds of the Prophet (*hadith*).

As Shaykh Mehmed advanced in his theological knowledge, he started to remove signs of idolatry in the tekke. The place used to be cluttered with pictures of saints and skewers for ritual piercing, but Shaykh Mehmed disposed of those objects together with the ritual practices of jinn exorcism and trance-inducing rituals. The members of his lodge stopped piercing their flesh with long and thick metal needles and daggers during the *zikir* rituals. Shaykh Mehmed was interested in mystical experiences, but they were not on the list of priorities for him. Above all, he sought precise theological knowledge. Through self-education, Shaykh Mehmed reviewed the precepts and mystical practices of the inherited dervish religiosity and joined the ranks of highly reflexive Muslim proponents of the re-examination and elimination of 'traditional superstitions' of Muslim faith, dubbed the 'Islamic Reformation' by Dale Eickelman (2002: 246–56).

The theological reforms in Gorno Malo went against the grain of anthropological expectations, historical records of dervish orders and, maybe even, my fantasies about nominally ecstatic religiosities. Inspired by what he had read, the shaykh grew determined to cast away theological mistakes and to learn how to practise Islam without extremes of dervish ecstasy. However, these efforts resonate with many 'modernizing' global trends in Islamic reforms, especially Sufi (Howell and van Bruinessen 2007). A few reformist Sufi schools even received an appellation of 'Neo-Sufis' because they were distinguished by their advocacy of shari'at prescriptions, rejection of ecstatic practices, suspicion of innovations and 'rational interpretations of Islam' (Howell and van Bruinessen 2007: 10–11). Shaykh Mehmed launched a shar'at-centred reform of a Sufi tradition, resembling the movement of Tablighi Jama'at in India (Sikand 2007: 129–48). Gypsy dervishes wanted to reform their associational life and their ethical subjectivities. My interlocutors aspired to embrace theologically 'correct' ways of being a Sufi in order to enrich their religious life rather than to renounce mystical Islam. Nevertheless, aspirants pursued reform that de-emphasized and banished many dervish devotions and habits such as meditative seclusion or dependence on a Sufi teacher. Shaykh Mehmed and his supporters struggled to ground their practices in the values of science, education, rationality of Quranic interpretations and modernity (Hefner 2001: 494). They were apprehensive of the theologically dubious innovations in dervish orders (Bowen 1993).

Paradoxically, the books that Shaykh Mehmed was reading had been written by Turkish theologians. Thus, the shaykh had eventually gained access to the knowledge of the 'Ottoman masters' in a different, textually mediated form. The authority of those texts was unquestionable. Despite grievances about restricted access to Islamic knowledge, the shaykh had a profound respect for Turkish theological scholarship. He wanted to instil that respect for theological books in others. Shaykh Mehmed was strongly influenced by Turkish theological traditions that had formulated several foundational principles of Islamic modernity, including rationalism, enlightenment and anti-superstition, modernization, privatization of worship, trust in the inerrancy of scriptures and a particular valorization of a work ethic[15] (Tapper and Tapper 1991: 56–83). Mehmed's reform had a paramount *ratsionalno* objective (rational). Above all, his dervishes had to be prepared for *dervishluk* intellectually. They 'should' break away from ancestral tradition of ecstatic rituals and relearn 'correct' theology. Shaykh Mehmed argued in favour of 'modern' and 'scientific' interpretations of the Quran. In his search for 'true Sufism', Shaykh Mehmed was not blind to the controversies and the pluralism of Islamic viewpoints. He explained that some Muslim theologians might be mistaken or too innovative; others might have a sound scriptural argument in support of their opinion and still disagree with each other. The most reliable way to learn Islamic theory was to read from many different sources to piece things together (*spoyuvash argumenti*). The best *teolog* (theologian) would look at Islam rationally, in the light of the present world. Such a theologian should have a 'Professor Doctor' title in front of his name, and his books should be reviewed by a group of other Professor Doctors. Professional, theological credentials of the authors would guarantee the accuracy of the scriptural interpretation. The shaykh did not aspire to his autonomy of interpretations because he said that without books one might get lost in knowledge. He did not want to stray away from the scholars' opinions. Instead of being adventurous with their own interpretations, dervishes had to read books and have confidence in their authors; 'if professors do not understand, who are we [to understand Islam]?' Thus, Shaykh Mehmed read Turkish theological texts and watched Turkish satellite programmes, in the hope to finally learn Islam from digitally mediated Turkish shaykhs.

Yet, the shaykh was disappointed with the pace of his reform. According to Shaykh Mehmed, Gypsy Muslims did not have a long-established tradition of serious reading and learning from books, instead they were *igrame igrachke* (playing games), with *dervishluk*. They all were 'making a travesty' of *igrame majtab* (religiosity). Mehmed was sceptical if aspirants could ever accomplish mystical religiosity. 'They were so far from the ancient ideals,' he would say, adding an emphatic gesture of dismissal. The shaykh was irately or humorously disparaging of people's aspirations to become Sufis, their lack of endurance in worship and pragmatic participation in financial or administrative affairs of the lodge. He used to stress people's 'insincere' longing to achieve spiritual betterment and ecstasy in rituals without any effort. He joined in the popular banter about people's *habit of missing* their prayers and rituals and scolded, even humiliated, his dervishes for their apathy, flirtatiousness with religious obligations and non-participation in ritual performances. Five daily prayers in Islam are perceived as a mandatory practice in the shaping of an unfailing moral and spiritual self (cf., Simon 2009). However, a Muslim might find himself 'prayer-free' without any particular reason, spending months without praying (ibid: 261, 267–69). Theological appeals to strict submission did not eradicate ambivalence, reluctance or failure of people to manage their Muslim religiosities (Schielke 2009). Some Muslims find themselves surrounded by conflicting moral, religious, familial or political registers, which are so complex that a pious observance achieved by some during the month of Ramazan is a limited and temporal commitment. However, Shaykh Mehmed and his dervishes felt they were exceptional in their laxity. They had every wish to pray but failed to work on their desire. This was a perturbing experience. This absence of commitment to praying was interpreted as a sign of people's personal failing to realize a mystical ideal. Instead of becoming enraptured in God by performing additional rituals (prayer, fasting, seclusion), people were unwilling to set their alarm clocks for early morning prayers, to adhere to a fast, to rehearse their rituals with physical tenacity. Dervishes though they fell short of a dervish ideal. Learning theology from books and television screens proved interesting to my interlocutors. They enjoyed theological debates and jousts, derived pleasure from dropping names of famous Sufis such as Al Ghazali in their conversations, flaunted the acquired Sufi terminology and esoteric language of Sufi metaphors. However, rituals caused nothing but frustration.

Failed Ritual

Shaykh Mehmed had two sons. One moved to Germany with no intention of returning. The younger son, Ali Refik, would be the shaykh's heir but the affectionate father worried that his son might not be able to maintain the tekke after his death. The younger son was unemployed and was financially dependent on his father. Intellectually,

Ali Refik followed in his father's reformist footstep. Ali Refik was an advocate for learning, although he preferred slightly more 'traditional' interpretations of the Quran. He had the knowledge of Sufi terminology and the meaningful interpretations of the Quran at his fingertips. He knew multiple stories from the lives of Sufi saints and tricksters. He had a gift of the theological gab, his father's genealogy and imposing attire. Yet, when he ventured into ritual, it did not have the same valence and popular appeal as his theological talk. Rituals floundered.

One event showed promise. A preacher from the southern town of Strumica had arrived unannounced and asked Ali Refik if he could sleep one night at his house. The preacher had an ill wife and they came to Gorno Malo to see a doctor but were delayed in the hospital and missed the last bus home. Ali Refik immediately saw an opportunity to gather people for a *zikir* in the tekke. A *zikir*, that conventionally long ritual of remembering and recitation of Allah's names and singing, was a scheduled ritual. A *zikir* would take place once or twice per week in the tekkes or smaller semanas, scattered in the suburbs. The unexpected arrival of the preacher from another town occasioned Ali Refik's desire to open an ad hoc *zikir* that night. He started sending out sms messages inviting people to come to the tekke at 8 p.m. for the ritual. The word about the impromptu *zikir* was spreading and people began to arrive; some friends and acquaintances, members of the lodge, were smoking in the living room, others were waiting for Ali Refik in the tekke a few hundred metres away from Ali Refik's house.

Before the ritual commenced, people were talking about mystical Islam with the authority of self-educated theologians. A *zikir*, Ali Refik was explaining, 'has its energy, which circulates among dervishes like water in pipes. But this energy could be felt only if people who participate in a *zikir* are sincere Muslims.' Another dervish said that a *zikir* also had its *vedjd* (state of being), like a state of ecstasy, which was 'like a wind that flares up the embers already glowing. It is inspiration, breathed into some people but not all.' Another person added that a *zikir* cannot be mechanical; one had to have a feeling. All men agreed. Someone preferred a heartfelt *zikir* (*kalbi*), inner, quiet, secretive, outside a particular time and space when Allah would inspire a dervish: 'Inspiration (*ilham*) could be felt if one knew Allah and tried to remember Allah in a *zikir*.' A *zikir* was the *duhovnost* (spirituality) sent from Allah, when the body would start thinking Allah, when a dervish would contemplate the intricacy of his own movements linked together so well as to create a spider web of organs and veins. 'Blood flows through our veins like energy flows in a *zikir*.' These metaphors and definitions were common descriptions of mystical experience in theological and Islamic hagiographical literature that people would usually read.

It was time to go to the lodge for the *zikir* itself. Shaykh Mehmed was not in the lodge and was not invited to join the *zikir*. The father and son were at loggerheads and cross with each other at that moment. The feeling of the importance of the upcoming event was enhanced by an unusual turnout of worshippers, at least 30 men. Ali Refik's rituals usually gathered five to ten participants. Those who arrived at the lodge looked nervous, or solemn, or slightly short of breath. They were shaking hands and hugging each other cordially. The men gathered in the room on the second floor of the lodge where the lessons of Arabic had been held. Ali Refik was giving instructions left, right and centre: 'Robert, close the gate. All of you switch your mobile phones off. You, start the electric heater.'

Ali Refik was telling the arriving men where to sit, choosing who should be next to him. Once they were seated on their knees in two circles, the men fell silent; some of them just waiting for the beginning of the ritual, others trying to attune themselves to the approaching moments of the *zikir*. One man was slouching over a string of *tespiyi* (prayer beads), which he was flicking slowly with the fingers of his right hand. The main lights were switched off; the room was illuminated by the dim red shimmer of an electric heater. Outside, cars were revving up their engines at the traffic lights. The men started swaying their kneeled bodies from one side to another, then back and forth, singing Allah with repetitive *bismillah i rahman i rahim, la illahi illalah allah* or lowering their voices to hoarse abrasive *allahallahallah*. The rhythm was set by the monotonous thumping on a drum pierced by the high-pitched notes of the visiting preacher's voice singing in imitated unintelligible Arabic. One dervish was asked to read a few passages about the Day of Judgement from the Quran, translated into Macedonian. To be able to hear him, the men grew still and silent but one of them, a teenager, carried on bellowing the words *la illah la illah,* eventually beginning to resemble a barking dog. We were all waiting for him to stop and when he finally did Ali Refik sounded irritated. 'Allah is not deaf', he snapped.

The ritual resumed only to be interrupted again by an uncontrollable sobbing and wheezy sighing of one of the dervishes somewhere in the dark room. The man was somewhat notorious for his violent temper because, people said, he had been aggressively possessed by a jinn spirit as a child. A few jumbled minutes later a *fatiha* prayer was slurred, the *zikir* was wrapped up, and about 15 of us returned to Ali Refik's house for a late meal. One of the participants whispered in my ear that the *zikir* was not good because it lacked exaltation and *ruhaniyet* (spirituality). There were doubts about the sincerity of the crying dervish. Despite high expectations, the ritual had not reached a satisfying resolution; the *zikir* had left everybody dissatisfied. The morning after I asked Ali Refik what he thought of the *zikir*. He and other participants were *razocharani* (disappointed).

This ethnographic episode is only one in a series of many that I have observed and participated in during my fieldwork. My question is how to account for failed rituals when these Gypsy dervishes had finally gained access to textually mediated theological knowledge. I would like to argue that the intellectual engagement with theological books did not compensate for the exclusion from the Ottoman relations of transmission of Islamic knowledge and ritual savvy. The simple reason for this is that texts have limits to transmission of performative knowledge.

When Shaykh Mehmed initiated his reform, he wanted to teach himself and other dervishes the 'correct' propositions of Islamic mysticism. He argued that earlier Gypsies could not learn 'correct' religion, and Ottoman shaykhs were accused of secretiveness and prejudice against Gypsies. This generation of religious autodidacts gained direct access to the Quran in translation and the exegetical commentaries. Their dependence on teachers diminished, although it is more accurate to say that the mode of transmission of religious knowledge had shifted from a living embodied teacher to objects, i.e. books. A peculiar consequence of this theological reform was people's entanglement in theological discourses; they were reluctant to perform physical acts of worship prescribed to them in the Quran. When these dervishes ventured into ritual participation, many performances failed. Despite advanced theological knowledge, Gypsy dervishes found it difficult to master the ritual forms.

Theological language as *talking about God as a proposition* was experienced intellectually rather than performatively in the form of embodied utterances, or speech acts, creating effects or presences (Csordas 1990: 26). The difference between theological language as discourse and 'liturgical utterances' is that 'theological discourse does not necessarily induce religious dispositions...Discourse involved in practice is not the same as that involved in speaking about practice' (Asad 1983: 243). My interlocutors were adept at learning, citing and debating theology. Theologies, however, like cosmologies and cosmogonies, have performative entailments. Theologies are thoughts and language to be translated into practise (cf., Tambiah 1985: 4, 13, 133), and in the process, perhaps, losing some of their explanatory meanings and doctrinal propositions (ibid: 138). However, people said they did not have the *method* that could enable them to convert theological propositions into performances.

The method could be restored from books or learned from a teacher through instruction or imitation. For the theologically inclined aspirants, the textual transmission of the method seemed more reliable, but they also recognized the difficulties of learning religiosity from theological texts that obscured performance techniques and methods of self-work. There are limits to the textual transmission of performances and to the restoration of an original performance from its record in a script (cf., Barber 2007: 29). Aspirants encountered theological propositions written down as texts. From these propositions, aspirants were trying to restore performances, ritual in their embodied form and ethical in the form of dispositions (Bloch 1991: 186). The books of ancient Sufis or Turkish theologians at hand seemed contradictory, convoluted and dated because they contained no hints of the mystical methodology that would work in the context of contemporary Macedonia. At the same time, books contained abstract instructions and normative prescriptions (what a Muslim should or should not do) in abundance, but the 'dervish method' and the practical technologies of self-work could not be easily retrieved either from the available secondary theological books or from the Quran itself.

Aspirants saw no alternatives to scouring theological books in search for the lost method because there were no authoritative teachers in their midst. A theological mistake could creep into the method transmitted by the old Gypsy shaykhs and dervishes, who were disparaged as morally perfidious and theologically ignorant of the 'correct' meanings and proper performative techniques. Many aspirants had misgivings about the intellectual and spiritual qualifications of Gypsy shaykhs in their vicinity, because of the ease with which a shaykh diploma could be purchased rather than earned through stages of training and initiation. I already have stressed that the grim serendipity of the departure of the Turkish shaykh suddenly dropped the tekke into the hands of the family of Shaykh Mehmed. Rapidly, the tekke became a religious space of exclusively Gypsy Muslims, and Shaykh Mehmed became its first theological reformer, who discontinued the mystical tradition of his father that might or might not have borne some semblance to the ritual precedents of the Ottoman Turkish founders of the tekke. The death of the last Turkish shaykh in the Sa'di lodge marked a moment of rupture in the lineage of Ottoman shaykhs. The family of Shaykh Mehmed was well respected but its members had no spiritual cachet[16] provided by the recognized claims to the *silsila* (prophetic or saintly lineage). The death of the Turkish shaykh disrupted the chain of transmission of theological knowledge and ritual methods.

People's turn to theologically bookish intellectualism at the expense of and in the absence of experiential learning from advanced mystics was seen as a promise of the mastery of 'real' and 'purified' Sufism, but aspirants soon understood that the method, the how-to (Geertz 1968), was not known. One aspirant mentioned that the method was the *batin* (esoteric 'mystical' knowledge) that a dervish covets. He compared knowing that 'there is a tasty cake' to 'trying to learn what it is made of and how to bake it'. The recipe that could be recovered from theological texts, i.e. becoming an excellent dervish, was beyond aspirants' reach because of the quality of textual transmission of performative savvy. My interlocutors speculated that Ottoman shaykhs might have known the method. Had they been around, those ancient shaykhs could have transmitted the method to Gypsy aspirants.

Theologically, learning from a teacher was an appropriate mode of accomplishing *dervishluk* because religious knowledge and ritual prowess could be mastered experientially through mimesis of and instruction by a competent teacher. Instead of memorizing the lists of rules and recondite Sufi terminology published in books, aspiring dervishes could have been learning religious actions in the embodied proximity to a teacher (Humphrey and Laidlaw 1994: 120). In sum, learning from a competent teacher would have been an acceptable mystical methodology of becoming a dervish. One Sufi method is *sohbet* (companionship in conversation) (Silverstein 2008). Turkish Naqshbandi shaykhs say the method works through contagion of ethical dispositions in the presence of good people. Learning under the supervision of a shaykh would result in the subtle attunement of a student to the ethical virtues and habits of thought of his teacher (e.g. of Bektashi in Albania; Trix 1993). A teacher and a student forge a personal relationship and knowledge is a result of the gradual coordination, or in Gadamer's terms 'fusion of horizons', between a teacher and student (ibid: 18–19, 22). Aspirants did not object to following a powerful shaykh, provided he could discipline them and warrant against the transgression of 'correct' divine norms (cf., Trimmingham 1971: 149). Perhaps real religious lessons can be learned only through those who embody those norms (Metcalf 1993). Together with doctrine, such a teacher could teach 'performance texts' (cf., Schechner 1985: 234), articulated performance techniques and masses of non-reflexive details (cf., Mauss 1992 [1934]: 464) that aspirants could infer.

Aspirants' grandparents might have learned something from the old Turkish shaykhs, but the impression that Gypsies were excluded from the ritual knowledge of their masters was resilient. Aspirants suspected that the Ottoman shaykhs had withheld mystical performative savvy from Gypsies. On the other hand, aspirants had niggling doubts that the old Ottoman shaykhs themselves did not know the method. Aspirants wanted to become more like Ottoman dervishes, specifically through learning of theology and self-reform, but they also wondered if Ottoman dervishes themselves fell short of the ideals of early Muslims of Arabia. What if the former Ottoman shaykhs, who lived in Macedonia and Turkey, were as dissipated and inadequate as local Gypsy shaykhs? Aspirants did not trust Ottoman shaykhs, but they had no confidence in their own abilities to advance as 'real' dervishes either.

Since his grandfather had become a shaykh by chance, Mehmed was distressed that the tekke might not have been rightfully his, that he might have been a 'hanger-on' rather than an 'original shaykh' (Lidner 2001: 81–91). He had the air of a person who was in fortuitous possession of something which wasn't securely or rightfully his, and he wasn't confident as to how long he would be able to continue acting in his role as a shaykh (cf., how Giriama in Kenya wished for their own Quran and poached Swahili Islam; McIntosh 2009). For the shaykh, becoming well-versed in theological knowledge, which in the popular view had been denied to Gypsies or not cherished by them during the Ottoman times (Barany 2001), was a strategy to fortify his legitimacy as a shaykh. This position he found questionable and insecure in the absence of secure genealogical lineage from earlier shaykhs, or the Prophet's family. Shaykh Mehmed spoke highly of education, theological or secular, as an avenue to prosperity: material and spiritual. In addition, he saw theological literacy as a safeguard against malicious strangers, Turks, Albanians, state officials and Wahhabis, who might feel like reclaiming his tekke. In part, knowing theology assuaged the shaykh's fear that in the imagined future the children of the last Turkish shaykh would take the tekke away. Shaykh Mehmed consoled himself by saying that he could challenge them to a theological duel and defend his position as a competent shaykh and thus be allowed to keep the tekke. However, he could not be sure about the outcomes of his strategy, and this anxiety about the loss of the tekke was harrowing and historically substantiated if not with reference to the 'rightful' Ottoman heirs then to the lodge. Once, in the early 1970, the urban planning authorities wanted to bulldoze the tekke to extend a road straight to the local Ottoman fortress and museum, but the dervishes organized a sit-in protest and won. The road was shifted a few metres and now it skirts the lodge like an urban noose.

Conclusion

Like colonial subjects who have learned the traditions of their masters through mimicry (Bhabha 1994: 121–31), Gypsy dervishes wished to be similar to, but not quite like, Ottoman dervishes. Their recurrent language of play-acting and pretending to be dervishes, as well as their concerns with becoming 'real', indicate aspirants' evaluation of their own efforts as mimicry. Mimicry is ambivalent; it is a confirmation of the desire of colonial subjects to bring themselves closer to the 'original' and is a menace to the normalcy of the division between masters and subjects (ibid: 126). This chapter has described how Gypsy 'colonial subjects' exercised their historical imagination to conceptualize the relations between them and their 'masters' and teachers, Ottoman shaykhs. The Gypsyness of my interlocutors illuminates the specificity of their self-knowledge, their efforts to reform, their inherited Gypsy tradition, to learn and perform Islamic theology and to cope with faltering ritual and theological confidences. In their view, their reformist efforts were hampered by their not knowing their own religious tradition. The blame was placed at the feet of the Ottoman dervishes and shaykhs who had allegedly denied theological knowledge to Gypsy Muslims. This chapter has explored the conditions and experiences of post-colonialism and the challenges to learning the ways of former 'masters' and their secret knowledge by colonial subjects or slaves (cf., Dilley 2010). The study is not exhaustive and it slants towards the perspectives of my interlocutors, Gypsy dervishes. More research is needed in the future.

Concluding, I would like to stress that I have borrowed many ethnographic and theoretical insights from ethnographies outside the Balkan region. It is with regard to my choice of ethnographic theory and literature that I would like to make a small methodological comment. Perhaps it is time to revise the regionalism of the Balkan anthropological scholarship and to attempt the comparative analysis of Balkan experiences to the realities and their ethnographic interpretations in other parts of the world (c.f., Strathern and Lambek 1998). Of course, one needs to proceed with caution, but in trying to figure out what it means for people to learn a particular religious tradition and why failure is a possibility, I have found it productive to expand beyond the geographical region and to consider the themes of 'performative failure', 'learning' and 'post-colonialism', which are much more commonly discussed in African contexts. This audacious comparative work can help us generate new questions and fresh perspectives into local traditions, especially global ones, like Islam.

Notes

1. I will refer to them as *aspirants, Gypsy dervishes* or *my interlocutors*.
2. *Performative failure* is a postponement of achievement. It captures the difficulties that aspirants experienced as they tried to actualize their ambitions to become 'true' dervishes. *Performative failure* is my analytical gloss but *failure* is not a label I am trying to pin on my interlocutors or their practices. Failure is a person's negative self-appraisal of their temporal inability to move from learning theological propositions to being 'proper' dervishes experientially, thus completing their ritual and ethical reform of their tradition and their subjectivities. I cannot elaborate these issues further in this chapter.
3. Gypsy and Rom has been used interchangeably by many of my interlocutors. Gypsy is not an intrinsically offensive term of address, although it could be infused with negative connotations by my self-critical Gypsy interlocutors and some non-Gypsy persons I have met. Many Roma activists and their political and scholarly elites would prefer the term Rom.
4. This does not apply to all Gypsies in Macedonia because, like Catholic, Orthodox and Muslim Albanians, Romas professed different faiths, crassly Islam (Arlija Roma) and Christianity, with further splintering within these religious traditions.
5. The *millet* system that divided the population on religious ground was subject to a failed *Tanzimat* reform in the 1860s. The reform attempted to create a more unified Ottoman citizenry and locally governed units of administration, *vilayets* (Stavrianos 1956: 387). I simplify, so bear in mind that the *millet* system took distinct local and historical forms and arrangements (Poulton 1997a: 16).
6. The switch from Ottoman dervishes to today's Turks indicates the historical shift from imperial to national regimes. Inalcik reminds us that until

the early twentieth century, 'the Ottoman Empire was not the "Turkish" empire' in today's national sense (1996: 19). Being a Turk today has different connotations from being an Ottoman Muslim. *Turci* (Turks) meant 'adherents of Islam'. *Turkuşı* or *Osmanli* was an ethnic category (Rusinow 1996: 93). A Turk, by contrast to Osmanli, could have negative connotations of uneducated peasantry (Poulton 1997a: 18). Today, people who self-identify as Turks in Macedonia speak Turkish, Macedonian and often Albanian. Their religious affiliation is Islam, mainly Sunni Islam. A few families I knew arrived in Macedonia from Bulgaria or Bosnia. Most had extended family in Turkey. Turkish-speaking Gypsies sometimes declare themselves as Turks in the official census but self-identify as Rom or Gypsy in informal conversations.

Some Gypsy dervishes disliked Muslim Albanians. There is a small number of Catholic Albanians in Macedonia as well, but aspirants only mentioned their aversion to the 'ethnic' Albanian Islam. For aspirants, mosque Islam was Albanian and was unfairly put down as militant and corrupt, being a fence to gun running and human trafficking. The impression was sometimes a nod at the memories of the past dangers of having been caught in the crossfire of the armed conflict between Albanian rebels and Macedonian military in 2001. A few aspirants were conscripted into the Macedonian army during the conflict and had endorsed the Macedonian nationalist discourses that describe Albanian populations as a threat to national security. Aspirants disparaged and stereotyped Albanian Islam as aggressive, greedy and dull.

7. Muslim peasants suffered from Ottoman regulations while Jews and Christians complained about the misgovernment of their own civic and ecclesiastic leaders (Stravrianos 1959: 383).
8. By comparison, women in Saudi Arabia in the early twentieth century were not allowed to pray in mosques and had to find their own ways to draw God's attention to their requests (Doumato 2000).
9. I have used a fake name for their town where my research was carried out in order to protect my interlocutors.
10. The category of 'Muslim' has a complex genealogy in Yugoslavia. There are Muslim Turks, Muslim Albanians (but also Orthodox and Catholic Albanians), Macedonian-speaking Muslims, Bosnian-speaking Muslims and more. These issues are beyond the scope of this chapter. Early socialist policies in Yugoslavia were influenced by the perception that Yugoslav Muslims seemed reluctant to participate in the communists' partisan activities during World War II. Some Yugoslav Muslims joined the SS divisions during World War II. The Handzar SS Division No.13 in Bosnia and Skandebeg

Albanian division were responsible for many war crimes in the Balkans and were investigated during the Nurenberg trials (Shay 2007). Some violent activities against the supporters of the new socialist regime continued in Macedonia as late as 1949 (Pettifer 2009: 202). In addition, Turks were suspect Yugoslav subjects for their presumed loyalty to the 'West'-oriented Turkey (Poulton 1997b: 96).

11. After 1953, Turks in Yugoslavia were not forced to leave but had to apply for a state-issued permit to be able to do so.
12. Kemal Karpat, a Turkish-speaking Muslim born in Romania, felt that his migration to Turkey in the 1940s was a politicized aspiration to be a Turk in the nation-state of Turkey rather than a member of a Muslim minority in his country of birth (Karpat 1990: 149).
13. See Chapter Two, this volume.
14. None of my interlocutors knew Arabic.
15. Islamic reforms have been repeatedly compared to Puritanism of Western Christianity (see Gellner 1981: 149–73). To ward off misunderstandings, the analogy between the particular Islamic and Protestant Reformation is undeniable but has to be placed in their historical context. Evolutionary or diffusionist theories of 'monolithic Islam' becoming like 'Protestantism', teleologically or through unilateral culture contact, strike me as a specious explanation, blind to the possibility that 'protestant-like' ideas and practices could have been immanent to any religious tradition at any time and place. Many reformation efforts within the cognate religiosities of Islam and Christianity have continuously demonstrated theological resemblances and historical interaction (see Goffman 2002).
16. Aspirants did not talk about spiritual energies or blessing emanating from a teacher (*baraka*).

References

Abbot, G. 1903. *The Tale of a Tour in Macedonia*. London: Edward Arnold.

Aishima, H. and A. Salvatore 2009. 'Doubt, faith, and knowledge: the reconfiguration of the intellectual field in post-Nasserist Cairo'. *Journal of the Royal Anthropological Institute* (N.S.), 41–56.

Alexander, St. 1979. *Church and State in Yugoslavia since 1945*. Cambridge: Cambridge University Press.

Algar, H. 1971. 'Some notes on Naqshbandi tariqat in Bosnia'. *Die Welt des Islam*, New Series 13:3 / 4, 168–203.

Asad, T. 1983. 'Anthropological conceptions of religion: reflections on Geertz'. *Man, New Series* 18:2, 237–59.

Baer, M. 2004. 'The conversion of Christian and Jewish souls and space during the 'anti-dervish movement of 1656–76'. *Archaelogy, Anthropology ad Heritage in the Balkans and Anatolia: The Life and Times of F.W.Hasluck, 1878–1920.* Vol.2 (ed.) D. Shankland, 183–200. Istanbul: The Isis Press.

Barany, Z. 2001. 'The East European Gypsies in the Imperial Age'. *Ethnic and Racial Studies* 24:1, 50–63.

Barber, K. 2007. 'Improvisation and the art of making things stick'. *Creativity and Cultural Improvisation* (eds) E. Hallam and T. Ingold, 25–45. Oxford and New York: Berg.

Barnes, J. 1992. 'The dervish orders of the Ottoman Empire'. *The Dervish Lodge. Architecture, Art, and Sufism in Ottoman Turkey* (ed.) R. Lifchez, 33–48. Berkeley, Los Angeles and Oxford: University of California Press.

Bhabha, H. 1994. 'Of mimicry and man'. *Location of Culture,* H. Bhabha, 121–31. London and New York: Routledge.

Bloch, M. 1991. 'Language, anthropology and cognitive science'. *Man. New Series* 26:2, 183–98.

Bowen, J. 1993. *Muslims Through Discourse.* Princeton: Princeton University Press.

Čelik, F. 2003. *Gypsies (Roma) in the orbit of Islam: The Ottoman Experience (1450–1600).* A Master of Arts Thesis submitted to the Faculty of Graduate Studies, Institute of Islamic Studies, McGill University, Montreal.

Csordas, T. 1990. 'Embodiment as a paradigm for anthropology'. *Ethnos* 18:1, 5–47.

Delaney, C. 1991. *The Seed and the Soil. Gender and Cosmology in Turkish Village Society.* Berkeley, Los Angeles and Oxford: University of California Press.

Dilley, R. 2010. 'Reflections on knowledge practices and the problem of ignorance'. *Journal of the Royal Anthropological Institute* 16, S176–S192.

Doumato, E. 2000. *Getting God's Ear. Women, Islam, and Healing in Saudi Arabia and the Gulf.* New York: Columbia University Press.

Duijzings, G. 2000. *Religion and the Politics of Identity in Kosovo.* London: Hurst and Company.

Eickelman, D. 2002. 'Inside the Islamic Reformation'. *Everyday Life in the Muslim Middle East* (eds) D. Lee Bowen and E. A. Early, 246–56. Bloomington and Indianapolis: Indiana University Press.

Elezovich, G. 1925. *Dervishki redovi Muslimanski. Tekije u Skoplju* (Muslim dervish orders. Tekkes in Skopje). Stara Srbija.

Ellis, B. 2003. *Shadow Genealogies. Memory and Identity Among Urban Muslims in Macedonia.* Boulder: East European Monographs.

Ferme, M. 1994. 'What 'Alhaji Airplane' saw in Mecca, and what happened when he came home: ritual transformation in a Mende community (Sierra Leone)'. *Syncretism/ Anti-Syncretism. The Politics of Religious Synthesis.* (eds) Ch. Stewart and R. Shaw, 25–43. London: Routledge.

Gay y Blasco, P. 1999. *Gypsies in Madrid: Sex, Gender and the Performance of Identity.* Oxford: Berg.

Geertz 1968. *Islam Observed. Religious Development in Morocco and Indonesia.* Chicago: Chicago University Press.
Gellner, E. 1981. *Muslim Society.* Cambridge: Cambridge University Press.
Gmelch, S. 1986. 'Groups that don't want in: Gypsies and other artisan, trader and entertainer minorities'. *Annual Review of Anthropology* 15, 307–30.
Goffman, D. 2002. *The Ottoman Empire and Early Modern Europe.* Cambridge: Cambridge University Press.
Hasluck, F.W. 1929. *Christianity and Islam Under the Sultans.* Oxford: Clarendon Press.
Hefner, R. 2001. 'Public Islam and the problem of democratization'. *Sociology of Religion* 62:4, 491–514.
Hirschon, R. 1998. *Heirs of the Greek Catastrophe: the Social Life of Asia Minor Refugees in Piraeus.* New York: Berghahn Books.
Hirschkind, C. 2001. 'The ethics of listening: cassette-sermon audition in contemporary Egypt'. *American Ethnologist* 28:3, 623–49.
Hopken, W. 1994. 'Yugoslavia's communists and the Bosnian Muslims'. *Muslim Communities Reemerge. Historical Perspectives on Nationality, Politics, and Opposition in the Former Soviet Union and Yugoslavia.* (ed.) E. Allworth, 214–41. Durham and London: Duke University Press.
Horvatich, P. 1994. 'Ways of knowing Islam'. *American Ethnologist* 21:4, 811–26.
Howell, J. and van Bruinessen, M. 2007. 'Sufism and the "modern" in Islam'. *Sufism and the 'Modern' in Islam* (eds) J. Howel and M. van Bruinessen, 3–18. London and New York: I.B. Tauris.
Humphrey, C. and Laidlaw, J. 1994. *The Archetypal Actions of Ritual. A Theory of Ritual Illustrated by the Jain Rite of Worship.* Oxford: Clarendon Press.
Inalcik, H. 1996. 'The meaning of legacy: the Ottoman case'. *Imperial Legacy. The Ottoman Imprint on the Balkans and the Middle East* (ed.) C. Brown, 17–30. New York and Chichester, West Sussex: Columbia University Press.
Karpat, K. 1990. 'The hijra from Russia and the Balkans: the process of self-definition in the late Ottoman state'. *Muslim Travelers. Pilgrimage, Migration, and the Religious Imagination.* (eds) D. Eickelman and J. Piscatori, 131–52. Berkeley and Los Angeles: University of California Press.
Kenrick, D. 2001. 'Former Yugoslavia: A patchwork of destinies'. *Between Past and Future. The Roma of Central and Eastern Europe* (ed.) W. Guy, 405–25. Hertfordshire: University of Hertfordshire Press.
Lidner, R. 2001. 'The constructing of authenticity: the case of subcultures'. *Locating Cultural Creativity* (ed.) J. Liep, 81–91. London: Pluto Press.
Lucassen, L. and W. Willems 2003. 'The weakness of well-ordered societies. Gypsies in Western Europe, the Ottoman Empire, and India 1400–1941'. *Review* 26 (3), 283–313.
Marushiakova, E. and V. Popov 2001. *Gypsies in the Ottoman Empire.* Centre de recherches Tsiganes: University of Hertfordshire Press.
Mauss, M. 1992 [1934]. 'Techniques of the body'. *Incorporations* (eds) J. Crary and S. Kwinter, 454–77. New York: Zone.

Mazower, M. 2005. *Salonica, City of Ghosts: Christians, Muslims, and Jews, 1430–1950.* New York: Knopf.
Metcalf, B. 1993. 'Living hadith in the Tablighi Jama'at'. *The Journal of Asian Studies* 52 (3), 584–608.
Meyer, B. 2006. 'Religious revelation, secrecy and the limits of visual representations'. *Anthropological Theory* 6, 431–53.
McIntosh, J. 2009. *The Edge of Islam. Power, Personhood, and Ethnoreligious Boundaries on the Kenya Coast.* Durham and London: Duke University Press.
Norris, H.T. 2006. *Popular Sufism in Eastern Europe. Sufi Brotherhoods and the Dialogue with Christianity and 'Heterodoxy'.* New York: Routledge.
Pettifer, J. 2009. 'The Gligorov regime in former Yugoslav Macedonia and the development of religion'. *Quo vadis Eastern Europe? Religion, State and Society after Communism* (ed.) I. Murzaku, 197–207. Ravenna: Longo Editore.
Polansky, P. 2008. *One Blood, One Flame. The Oral Histories of the Yugoslav Gypsies Before, During and After WWII.* Vol. III. KRRF.
Popovic, A. 1994. *Les derviches balkaniques hier et aujourd'hui* (Dervish orders, yesterday and today). Istanbul: Les Editions Isis.
Poulton, H. 1997a. 'Islam, ethnicity and state in contemporary Balkans'. *Muslim Identity and the Balkan State.* (eds) H. Poulton and S. Taji-Farouki, 13–32. Washington Square, New York: New York University Press.
Poulton, H. 1997b. 'Changing notions of national identity among Muslims in Thrace and Macedonia: Turks, Pomaks and Roma'. *Muslim Identity and the Balkan State.* (eds) H. Poulton and S. Taji-Farouki, 82–102. Washington Square, New York: New York University Press.
Robbins, J. 2004. *Becoming Sinners. Christianity + Moral Torment in a Papua New Guinea Society.* Berkeley and Los Angeles: University of California Press.
Rusinow, D. 1996. 'The Ottoman legacy in Yugoslavia's disintegration and civil war'. *Imperial Legacy. The Ottoman Imprint on the Balkans and the Middle East* (ed.) C. Brown, 78–99. New York and Chichester, West Sussex: Columbia University Press.
Schechner, D. 1985. *Between Theatre and Anthropology.* Philadelphia: University of Pennsylvania Press.
Schielke, S. 2009. 'Being good in Ramadan: ambivalence, fragmentation and the moral self in the lives of young Egyptians'. *Journal of the Royal Anthropological Institute.* 15 (Special Issue), 24–40.
Shay, S. 2007. *Islamic Terror and the Balkans.* New Brunswick and London: Transaction Publishers.
Sikand, Y. 2007. 'The reformist Sufism of the Tablighi Jama'at: the case of the Meos of Mewat, India'. *Sufism and the 'Modern' in Islam* (eds) J. Howell and M. van Bruinessen, 129–48. London and New York: I.B.Tauris.
Silverman, C. 1995. 'Roma in Shuto Orizari, Macedonia: class, politics, and community'. *East European Communities. The Struggle for Balance in Turbulent Times* (ed.) D. Kideckel, 197–215. Boulder, San Francisco, Oxford: Westview Press.

Silverstein, B. 2008. 'Disciplines of presence in modern Turkey: discourse, companionship, and the mass media of Islamic practice'. *Cultural Anthropology* 23:1, 115–53.

Silverstein, B. 2007. 'Sufism and modernity in Turkey: from the authenticity of experience to the practice of discipline'. *Sufism and the 'modern' in Islam* (eds) J. Howell and M. van Bruinessen, 39–61. London and New York: I.B.Tauris.

Simon, G. 2009. 'The soul freed of cares? Islamic prayer, subjectivity, and the contradictions of moral selfhood in Minangkabau, Indonesia'. *American Ethnologist* 36:2, 258–75.

Stavrianos, L. 1959. *The Balkans Since 1453*. New York: Rinehart & Company, Inc.

Stewart, M. 2004. 'Remembering without commemoration: the mnemonics and politics of Holocaust memories among European Roma'. *The Journal of the Royal Anthropological Institute* 10:3, 561–82.

Stewart, M. 1997. *The Time of the Gypsies*. Boulder, Colorado and Oxford: Westview Press.

Strathern, A. and Lambek, M. 1998. 'Introduction. Embodying sociality: Africanist-Melanesianist comparisons'. *Bodies and Persons. Comparative Perspectives from Africa and Melanesia*. (eds) M. Lambek and A. Strathern, 1–25. Cambridge: Cambridge University Press.

Tambiah, S. 1985. *Culture, Thought and Social Action. An Anthropological Perspective*. Cambridge, Massachusetts and London: Harvard University Press.

Tapper, R. and Tapper, N. 1991. 'Religion, education and continuity in a provincial town'. *Islam in Modern Turkey. Religion,Politics and Literature in a Secular State*. (ed.) R. Tapper, 56–83. London and New York: I.B.Tauris.

Theodosiou, A. 2007. 'Disorienting rhythms: Gypsyness, "Authenticity" and place on the Greek-Albanian border'. *History and Anthropology* 18: 2, 153–75.

Todorova, M. 1996. 'The Ottoman legacy in the Balkans'. *Imperial Legacy. The Ottoman Imprint on the Balkans and the Middle East* (ed.) C. Brown, 45–77. New York and Chichester, West Sussex: Columbia University Press.

Tong, D (ed.) 1998. *Gypsies. An Interdisciplinary Reader*. New York and London: Garland Publishing.

Trajanovski, A. 2005. *Istorija na Makedonija: kratok pregled na istorijata na Makedonija i na makedonskiot narod ot antika do denes* (History of Macedonia: a Short History of Macedonia and Macedonian People from Antiquity to Modern Day). Skopje: Menora.

Trimmingham, S. 1971. *The Sufi Orders of Islam*. New York and Oxford: Oxford University Press.

Trix, F. 1993. *Spiritual Discourse Learning and an Islamic Master*. Philadelphia: University of Pennsylvania Press.

Van de Port, M. 2006. 'Visualizing the sacred: video technology, "televisual" style, and the religious imagination in Bahian Candomble'. *American Ethnologist*. 33 (3): 444–61.

Williams, P. 2003. *Gypsy World: the Silence of the Living and the Voices of the Dead*. Chicago and London: University of Chicago Press.

8

ABSENT ROMA, IMPORTED INTEREST: 'ROMA' AS SUBJECT AND AGENT IN THE REPUBLIC OF MACEDONIA[1]

Shayna Plaut

'I am proud of being representative of the country in which the Roma have perhaps the highest level of rights compared to all the other European countries.' – *Mr Branko Crvenovski, former President of Macedonia in Budapest discussing the Decade of Roma Inclusion*

Introduction: Macedonia as a Test Case for Donors and Western Governments

For nearly a decade the disintegration of former Yugoslavia (and particularly the unrest in Kosovo) has generated much *international* and, albeit limited, domestic interest regarding all ethnic groups, including the Romani population, in Macedonia. The war and subsequent bombing in 1999 in Kosovo between ethnic Albanian insurgents and the predominantly ethnically Serbian Yugoslav army created a dramatic demographic reshuffling in the region (Bideleux and Jefferies 2007). Although small, Macedonia was in some ways seen as the last bastion of stability in former Yugoslavia. After 1999, many members of the international community who had previously focused on Bosnia and Kosovo turned their eyes and dollars to Macedonia (Macedonian Institute for the Media 2003). The Organization for Security and Cooperation in Europe (OSCE) and other international organizations set up 'spill over missions' from Kosovo to assure that Macedonia would remain both intact and multi-ethnic. Much of the journalistic and formal research published since 2000, with the support of international funding, presents Macedonia as the model state for minority (including Romani) rights. In fact, according to an in-depth 2006 analysis by *Radio Free Europe/Radio Liberty* (RFE/RL), Macedonia's 'treatment' of its ethnic minorities is often directly promoted as a positive example to other governments in the region (http://www.rferl.org/content/article/1065965.html). It's desirability as a model is often further emphasized in a juxtaposition against Kosovo. By presenting itself as a multi-ethnic and peaceful country in a sea of bloody transitions, Macedonia serves as an example of the benefits of intervention by various actors within the international community. This results in real and tangible material benefits such as funding, programming and loaned expertise. However, I argue that such a limited cost-benefit analysis can, in fact, be short-sighted and limit the creativity and power that leads to ideas and practices of domestic socio-cultural and political change.

In order to justify such funding and programming, Macedonia hosts and participates in countless research projects, forums and programmes, which, on the surface, appear as if there is an *internal* interest in understanding the complexities and nuances of the different ethnicities that compose Macedonia. Upon closer analysis, one must question where this 'interest' is coming from and whose 'interests' are in fact being satisfied and subsidized. My research demonstrates that the interests driving many of the projects focused on the Roma in particular are primarily crafted to benefit external interests – primarily those of Western Europe and, to some extent, the United States. This is not to argue for Cold War conspiracy theories, but rather to explain the need for the West to justify a proportionally large and long-term presence in a rather small country. This is done primarily in the name of what international relations scholars term as republican liberal 'democracy building' projects as well as preventive security in a region of the world that has been historically volatile (Moravcsik 2000). But these projects also justify an internationally focused development regime where Western notions of capitalism and governance remain the unquestioned ideals painted with a heavily protected veneer of neutrality and expertise (Barnett and Finnemore 2004).[2] Lastly, the fall of socialism and subsequent, rapid fall of living standards for the Roma have brought a large number of immigrants into Western Europe, a region that has faced its own domestic pressures often fuelled by fear and racism.

In the Balkans, one can see this process emerging with full force in the wake of the Yugoslav wars and intensifying with the Decade of Roma Inclusion – an initiative funded primarily by the World Bank and the Soros Foundation. I argue that this has created a dependence on such actors and funds, thus inhibiting a domestic sphere of scholarship and activism. For sustainable change to take place, the responsibility for improvement must be recognized as the responsibility of the state. The much needed role of the international community is not to *do* for the state, for this is where dependency and complacency get nurtured, but rather to play a 'watch-dog role' and to support the state, if needed, in caring for its own citizens.

Brief Background and Demographics

Macedonia is an economically impoverished country with an average unemployment rate of 40 per cent (ECMI 2004 citing Nanevska 2002) but with a comparatively high primary education and literacy rate of 84 and 92 per cent, respectively (ECMI 2004 citing Statistical office of Macedonia 1997).[3] With a population of 2.2 million people, the Republic of Macedonia is a multi-ethnic country that is 'home' to six officially recognized 'nationalities' living together in varying degrees of harmony.[4] Macedonia is the only country that recognizes its Romani citizens in the original constitution; however, as noted by the Project on Ethnic Relations (PER), the United Nations Development Program (UNDP), the World Bank and the Macedonian government itself, official recognition does not always translate into a positive reality (PER 2001). The majority of Roma consistently survive below recognized standards for health, economic viability and education. In fact the Roma, with an official population of 52,000 and an unofficial population estimated between 60,000 and 260,000, are consistently regarded as the most marginalized population within Macedonia (Barany 2002; CEDAW Shadow Report 2005; UNDP 2005).[5]

As Mark Twain (1924) so aptly put it, 'there are lies, damned lies and statistics' and demographics and identity in Macedonia are no exception. In Macedonia everything from money, political positions, state jobs, municipal power and even university admissions are allotted on the basis of ethnic demographic saturation – thus how one claims ethnicity becomes crucially important. Does one identify as 'Roma' in an area where there may not be many Roma or does one identify with another, larger ethnic group? It is important to note that, according to the 2002 census, 91 per cent of the Roma population in Macedonia consider themselves Muslim – as do the vast majority of ethnic Albanians. In the western part of Macedonia it is not unusual for someone who is Romani to declare themselves ethnically Albanian, thus not only reducing the severity of ethnic stigma but also possibly increasing their employment and educational opportunities. In the eastern part of Macedonia many Roma will declare themselves Turkish and may even speak Turkish as a first language at home (Friedman 1996: 81–105 & 119–26). In a country heavily dependent on census data for economic and political allotments, such identity switching can be seen as potentially beneficial for ethnic Albanians and Turks and potentially threatening to the ethnic Macedonian majority.[6]

That said, the hatred and fear that has resulted in organized violence such as pogroms and forced sterilizations of Romani, which can be found in some Eastern European countries such as Hungary, Romania and Slovakia, is rare or non-existent in Macedonia (Friedman 1999; Friedman 2002; Plaut 2010). The Roma face 'mere' marginalization in Macedonia as compared to physical violence that is endemic and growing, in many other parts of Central and Eastern Europe. As Eben Friedman explains in his 2002 dissertation, Macedonia is often mentioned as the 'best case' for the Roma in the former socialist countries.

According to the 2001 Ohrid Agreement, if a municipality has a population of over 20 per cent of any of the officially recognized ethnicities, then the language of that ethnicity becomes one of the official languages of the municipality. Municipal services as well as all classroom instruction must be offered in that language. Based on the demographic makeup of the country, Albanian and Macedonian are the two official languages of the Republic of Macedonia. There is one municipality in Macedonia, Shuto Oriziri, where Romani is an official language; however, there are no schools where Romani is the dominant language of instruction. The language and cultural instruction that is offered is nearly all funded by NGOs rather than the state institutions, which not only violates Macedonian law, but is also symptomatic of the larger cycle of seeing the Roma as an international point of concern ('interest') rather than an important domestic constituency.

Macedonia, the Roma and the Lack of Academe

There is an increasing amount of work published by Macedonian academics and highly regarded members of civil society on Romani issues; however, this research is rarely initiated by the Macedonian academics/policymakers themselves, but rather commissioned by and for international organizations to craft and evaluate internationally initiated policy. In fact, the bulk of the research falls into two categories: justifying various internationally funded programmes or speaking to the stability of the region as a whole.[7] Marija Tasseva, Professor of Sociology at University of Skopje, explains the academic presence of Roma as a 'topic' within the academe as such:

> Roma have a different culture but they have been present in our society for so long that we feel that we know them. We know the differences but we have agreed that they have a right to live their own lives; to be different. They have very good symbiotic relations with other groups so there is no interest in studying them because it (the relationships/dynamics) is not problematic...12 or 13 years ago a foreign researcher presented his research on Roma. He was so excited about his research and we tried not to

laugh. We were all thinking 'we know this already, why he is so excited about it?' (pc. 16 May 2004)

According to Tasseva, she and some of her colleagues in the Sociology and Social Work faculties have often participated in internationally initiated (and funded) studies on the Roma. However, as of 2004 there has never been a single Masters thesis or PhD dissertation in the Department of Sociology at the University of Skopje written about the Roma (personal communication, 16 May 2004).[8] Although there are periodic special courses offered at South East European University, as of 2004 there was no class on Romani issues in any of the public universities. This phenomenon of 'the international community...pushing Romani issues' but a 'complete absence within the Macedonian academic discourse' was reiterated by Professor Ilo Trajkovski, also from the Department of Sociology, who was recently recruited to work on projects addressing the sociology of poverty in rural eastern and southwestern Macedonia for the World Bank. As Trajkovski stated, '...if you want to read current research on Roma in Macedonia you read things published by the international community, not the Macedonian journals' (personal communication, 19 May 2004).[9]

Although there are six officially recognized nationalities in Macedonia, the majority of the *domestic* attention and political capital addressing multi-ethnic issues is focused on the large ethnic Albanian population which, according to the 2002 census, comprises 26 per cent of the population. This was true even before the 2001 conflict, but it has only intensified since then. Prior to 2004 there was little, if any, official attention paid to the Roma by either the government or academe. When the state did create policy directives that affected the Roma, it was most often within the wider fields of social welfare and citizenship regulations, thus affecting them based more on their socio-economic position than as a distinct population (ECMI 2004). There were programmes designed for the Romani population but they were *exclusively* designed and funded with mostly international money.

The Macedonian government is very conscious of its international reputation and works hard to cultivate a tolerant, multi-ethnic presentation. That said, how things are portrayed and how people actually live can vary widely. Domestically the attitude of politicians, academics and 'public figures' towards Roma in Macedonia can most easily be labelled as a lack of interest or, more accurately, institutionalized marginalization. I consciously employ the term 'marginalization' rather than 'discrimination' because marginalization means 'being pushed to the side' and not recognized as a worthy object of discrimination. It suggests a passive neglect; in other words, to be marginalized is to be simply ignored.

Ensuring a 'Multi-kulti' (...and Romani Friendly) Macedonia: Internationally Approved and Funded

Macedonia is a 'country in transition'. The economy, media and social services are all transitioning from state-centred socialism to a fledging capitalist democracy. NGOs and international funders have been crucial in this transitional process, often providing financial support to initiatives as diverse as raising awareness on domestic violence to establishing the trilingual South East European University (www.osi.org and www.osce.org, respectively). That said, the state is still recognized as the main source of centralized power and validity in everything from education to media consumption (pc. Plaut 2010). Such a belief in the power of the state and in the need for the state to take a stand and implement change was seen most clearly in the Albanian insurgents' demand during the 2001 conflict. Their demands for more *formal recognition* of Albanian socio-political rights was not a demand for more NGO funding, or a stronger civil society, rather it was a demand for amendments in the constitution that would then change state policy.

According to the republican liberal view of international relations, people may attempt to affect the behaviour of their own government. The state should, therefore respond if it is in the state's interest to do so. So what happens when certain issues aren't acted on or, to borrow a term from Keck and Sikkink, when these actors are 'blocked' from being able to affect their government and thus fail to gain 'traction' (1998: 12)? When this occurs, according to republican liberal views, the issue should die, or perhaps lay dormant for a more opportune time when the leaders will be more responsive. But something else is happening: non-state actors, often NGOs, in one state are affecting the behaviour of other states and, according to many international relations scholars, they are doing so in consistent patterns.

Keck and Sikkink attempt to create a blueprint for this system of influence by identifying what they term the 'boomerang pattern' (1998: 12–13). The boomerang pattern is activated by activists in one state (A) who, after failing to affect their government, reach out to activists in another state (B) with information and a plea for solidarity asking those actors to exert pressure on their behalf. Activists in state B will then lobby their government to take a stand on the issue concerning the people in state A. This may occur by state B holding direct discussions with state A or another forum such as an International Organization (IO), of which they are both members. Power dynamics are often rife within these arrangements – not only in terms of the states but also between the activists themselves.

According to this dynamic, articulated in *Activists Beyond Borders*, the lobbying still takes place primarily on a state-to-state or NGO to NGO level rather than non-state actors directly lobbying states (ibid: 12–14).[10] Keck and Sikkink recognize that the primary form of 'currency' in this process is that of information, which they term 'information politics'. NGOs in state A provide information about what is occurring on the ground to the NGOs and other activists in state B. This information is then turned into a campaign whose audience is often twofold: activists in the global North who are fighting 'on behalf' of those in country A as well as a campaign to shame the government of state A. What occurs then is the deployment of four different types of politics: information politics, symbolic politics, leverage politics and accountability politics (Keck and Sikkink 1998: 18–24).

Although Central and Eastern Europe would not traditionally be considered the global South, in this situation they are often cast in that position as the partner with less agency and power. Much can be learned from Keck and Sikkink's analysis of the dynamics of international NGOs, international organizations (including funders) and Western European states in their attempt to direct Central and Eastern European government attention to the Roma. By wishing to access the political and economic advantages of the European Union, many Central and Eastern European states have been persuaded, if not forced, to address their most marginalized citizens. But where is this pressure coming from? Is it a form of domestic activism from the Roma or from those non-Romani citizens advocating for equal treatment or dignity of all citizens, or is it rather a form of not-so-covert international coercion? The questions become *who* is directing the attention of *which* states for *what* reasons?

The Decade of Roma Inclusion as a Continuation of International Influence and/or Socially Progressive Neo-colonialism?

A large portion of this chapter is devoted to exploring the Decade of Roma Inclusion (the Decade), a multinational initiative funded by the Soros Foundation and the World Bank. Launched in February 2005, it serves as an example of the 'imported' interest in the Roma. There are only two full-time staff at the Decade, and its impetus is supposed to be to assist state governments in implementing their own Roma-focused strategies. There are currently 12 governments that have 'signed on to' the Decade including Albania, Bosnia-Herzegovina, Montenegro, Spain, Czech Republic, Slovakia, Hungary, Serbia, Bulgaria, Croatia, Romania and Macedonia.

The goal of the Decade is stated as follows:

> The Decade of Roma Inclusion 2005–2015 is an unprecedented political commitment by European governments to improve the socio-economic status and social inclusion of Roma. The Decade is an international initiative that brings together governments, intergovernmental and nongovernmental organizations, as well as Romani civil society, to accelerate progress toward improving the welfare of Roma and to review such progress in a transparent and quantifiable way. The Decade focuses on the priority areas of education, employment, health, and housing, and commits governments to take into account the other core issues of poverty, discrimination, and gender mainstreaming. (http://www.romadecade.org/about)

The financial compensation offered under the Decade is minimal, although substantial funds are offered with its twin project, The Roma Education Fund, which focuses exclusively on projects to aid Roma in primary school through university.[11] There is evidence, however, to support the notion that compliance with the goals established by the Decade of Roma Inclusion (the Decade) may be tied to larger goals of European and international integration.[12]

The Decade was promoted as an opportunity for the states with large Roma populations to do better by its citizens. As Azbija Memedova, a sociologist, Romani activist and member of the National Working Group for the Decade of Roma Inclusion explained in 2004, 'The Decade is what started the dialogue between Roma and non-Roma... the purpose of the decade is to incorporate positive models from the informal (NGO) sector into the state system... we'll work, we'll wait and we'll see what happens.' The emphasis on the need for state affirmation is crucial on three levels. First, as noted above, the state is the only legal means of ensuring that proposed change is implemented. Changes in educational or health systems – two of the goals outlined in the Decade–are solely controlled by the state; the other two, employment and housing, are heavily influenced by state regulation and monitoring. Second, it should come as no surprise that although international donor funding is extremely helpful, it is also fickle and cannot be relied on as the sole source of income (Smillie 2001). Lastly, by the Macedonian state responding to Romani needs, it is taking a proactive and public stance in recognizing that the Romani population is a valuable member of the larger Macedonian citizenry. The 'problems that Roma face' will no longer simply be a 'Romani problem' but rather reflective of the failings of the Macedonian state to ensure that all its citizens enjoy the rights they are entitled to.[13] When Memedova was asked nearly two years later 'what happened?' now that the Decade was under way, she pointed to the budget outlined in the 'Action Plan' and shook her head – all the funding was coming from international funding sources: 'There is no state accountability' (personal communication, 20 January 2006).

There are many debates regarding the motives behind the launching of the Decade and, as time progresses but the policies do not, it appears that the cynics may be right – the purpose of the Decade is to help Western Europe keep the Roma out. In 2004 Natasha Gaber, Senior Researcher and Analyst at the Institute for Sociological, Political and Juridical Research and author of the Macedonian National Strategy on Roma Inclusion, offered the following direct assessment of Western interest in Romani issues, 'Roma are interesting to the international community because they are the worst off economically [and] Western Europe does not want the Roma to leave here and go there' (personal communication, 23 May 2004). There is much truth in this statement, particularly in light of the Sarkozy government's forced expulsion of ethnically Romani Bulgarian and Romani citizens in August 2010.

Unlike statements made by the political leaders of other countries involved in the Decade, the public statements by non-Romani politicians in Macedonia, though few, have generally been supportive of the Roma as both a people and 'an issue'. In 2004, the current President Branko Crvenkovski (at the time the Prime Minister) spoke before other Eastern European heads of state, the World Bank and the Open Society Institute proclaiming his country's commitment and support to the Romani population (Memedova and Plaut 2005: 21).[14] Crvenkovski was specifically addressing Macedonia's involvement in the Decade and proclaimed that his government would support civil society (Romani and non-Romani) in addressing four key points: education, health, employment and housing in addition to two 'cross-cutting' issues. He also added gender and discrimination.

I emphasize the term 'support' because at no point was the Macedonian government obligating itself to offer the financial or political backing needed to ensure change in policy and proper implementation. Instead, changes in the socio-economic status of the Romani population continue to remain the responsibility of those outside of the formal state structure. This is an important abdication of responsibility that comes up repeatedly and that, I argue, allows the Macedonian state to treat the Roma as less than full citizens. The funding, attention and intellectual commitment that have characterized the Decade have nearly all focused on analysis with no clear goals beyond specific project benchmarks specified. Just as importantly, there are no consequences to the state if such goals are not met. In fact, the official 'watchdog' of the Decade of Roma Inclusion, 'Decade Watch' is funded by the Soros Foundation and the World Bank, the same funders of the Decade itself.[15]

In 2006 I assisted in designing a research mission for Amnesty International focusing on the double discrimination faced by Romani women and girls. This research took place in November 2006, nearly 24 months after the official 'launch' of the Decade. The results are startling. In the country that is often lauded as the 'best case' for the Roma in Europe, the violations of human rights in terms of education, work, health and domestic violence are stark:

- Nearly 40 per cent of Romani women had either an incomplete or complete lack of primary education as compared to 22 per cent of Romani men and 8 per cent of the non-Romani population.
- 83 per cent of Romani women and 65 per cent of Romani men had never been employed in the formal economy as compared to 50 per cent of non-Roma.
- 31 per cent of Romani women suffered from chronic illness as compared to 23 per cent of non-Roma.
- As many as 70 per cent of Romani women report they have experienced some form of domestic violence by either their partner or in-laws.

As evidenced by the report and recommendations that I helped draft, there was no accountability to the Roma by either the state or the funders. More shocking, however, was the lack of interest or attention by the Macedonian state authorities in investigating or responding to this information. We were unable to get a single meeting with the Ministry of Internal Affairs, Ministry of Health or Ministry of Labor and Social Welfare. Although there were many NGOs present at the launch of our report in December 2007, the only government officials who met with us, or who showed interested in the release of the report were those officially mandated to focus on Romani issues and the Minister of Gender Equality. After six months of concerted letter-writing, the then Minster of Health and the Ministry of Labor and Social Welfare agreed to investigate our concerns, specifically addressing the lack of issuing health cards to those who had not completed primary school, which disproportionally affected Romani women.[16] That said, nearly five years later, there has been little to no improvement of the concrete violations of human rights first documented in our original research in 2006. Why?

Put simply, the reason why things have not changed is that the people and institutions that hold sway in the country, the state officials and ministries, do not have a vested interest in changing the conditions themselves but rather see Roma as an 'issue of concern' for internationals rather than fellow citizens who are living a life of dignity. This feeling of 'outsourcing the problem' is exacerbated by the international focus of the Decade. This is clearly evident in a simple conversation with a former maths teacher who was working as the decentralization coordinator for the municipality of Gorce Petrov. When discussing why some Roma students don't go to school, the issue of transportation costs came up. She stated that the Roma Education Fund was not funding transportation for Romani students. When I asked why the municipalities' responsibilities under the Decade of Roma Inclusion are seen as a separate issue rather than as part of the decentralization process, she paused:

> Because of Budgeting? I am not sure. The municipalities are not getting funded by Soros…as a local municipality we cannot apply for Soros funding. We only get our money from our own budget and from the state (personal communication, 28 November 2006).

This statement is powerful; it shows that the education of Romani students is not recognized as part of the larger educational plans of Macedonia and, I would argue, is representative of how the Macedonian population is responding to Romani people in general. They are seen as separate, as a separate issue, as a separately funded issue, not as their fellow citizens.

If not properly monitored, the Decade may continue to provide a politically correct form of racist, socially progressive, neo-colonialism where external economic interests are creating a market for easily digestible 'problems and solutions' to Romani issues – packaged and delivered by 'Romani experts' to the international market without the time, money or political/intellectual investment needed to ensure proper implementation.[17]

Conclusion: So Why 'The State' is Important Anyway; Shouldn't Change Come from the Bottom Up?

The international community funding these initiatives is not providing the proper pressure so that *the Macedonian state* follows through on its basic commitments afforded to all its citizens under international and domestic law. One can argue that failure to do so is a breach of the core principles of sovereignty, where one has control over the territory because one takes care of 'one's own' people. This pressure cannot be applied 'after the fact' but rather needs to be encouraged in the actual drafting of the plans and the implementation of various programmes and in assessing funding allocation. This was one of the stated goals of the 'Action Plan' drafted by the Macedonian Ministry of Education to address Romani needs in education as required by the Decade of Roma Inclusion.[18] However, after the 'Action Plan' was drafted, the projects were to be implemented by a governmental agency without a reappropriation of funding. By not allocating funding for overheads and staff, the projects are simply words on paper; in fact, according to the 2005 report submitted to the CEDAW commission, none of the programmes have been put into practise. According to the grant report offered by the Foundation for Open Society in Macedonia, FOSIM's Education programme detailing the projects specifically targeted at Romani students, all the funding allocated originates from international donors (personnal communication, Spomenka 15 February 2006).

For sustainable change in the socio-political and economic position of the Roma to take place within Macedonian society, it is crucial that the Macedonian state be held accountable by the international community and for those who create the norms to be held accountable by its own population – Romani and non-Romani. Citizens must be taught to expect, and thus demand, that their government respond to their needs. One of the clearest ways to do this is to hold the government accountable economically. There are positive models for this within Macedonia's history, namely the heavily monitored implementation of the Ohrid Agreement. There are also international examples of this – including the federally mandated desegregation and anti-discrimination policies of the United States in the 1950s and 1960s and South Africa's post-apartheid transition. One should not disregard the international community's ability to assist in this process; one should look to harness the strength of its economic clout.

A partnership between the Macedonian state and funding for the Decade is crucial. This can be manifested in many ways including the creation of something as mundane as a 'matching fund programme' to assist families throughout a child's education or a state/donor programme that can support a student through university, guaranteeing secured, if temporary, employment upon graduation. These are models that have proved successful in multiple countries, cultures and economies and can only help to cultivate a stronger and more experienced Romani population that can be integrated into the state structures and civil society. What will prove unsustainable is the international communities' continued influx of attention and funding for research and policy proposals 'studying' Roma in Macedonia as a subject without ensuring that the various actors – the state, the domestic civil society and the 'Romani elite' – are active agents in implementing change.

Notes

1. I thank the US Fulbright Program for the financial means to conduct research on this chapter. Versions of this chapter have been presented at the 2006 International Studies Association and the University of British Columbia's Transitional Justice Workshop in 2010. I also thank Enisa Eminova and Denis Durmis for both assisting with Macedonian to English translation and helping locate the appropriate people for the appropriate information. Lastly, my thanks to the people who agreed to be interviewed for this chapter and to Eben Friedman, Victor Friedman, Andy Graan, Spomenka Lazerevska and Amanda Loos who agreed to review my (multiple) drafts and offer suggestions.
2. *Radio Free Europe/Radio Liberty* provides excellent news on a region often ignored by mainstream English language media but it should not be forgotten that they are funded by the US State Department.
3. The poverty and illiteracy rate for the Roma, especially Romani women, is much higher than the national average. According to the 2005 CEDAW

Shadow report submitted by the Roma Centre of Skopje, European Roma Rights Centre and the Roma Women's Initiative (OSI-Network Women's Programme) although it is the state's responsibility to ensure equal and complete education through primary school, over 50 per cent of Romani women leave school prior to completing 8th grade. According to the same shadow report, however: 'Despite alarming data about the educational status of the Romani community – and especially Romani girls – in Macedonia, during 13 years of independence, state institutions have not proposed or implemented any specific programs for [Roma], especially at the pre-school, primary and secondary school levels.' (7.2.10: 19)

4. 'Nationality' is a literal translation of the official Macedonian term 'drzhavnost'. However, in English 'nationality' also means 'citizenship'; therefore, in my own work, I will use the term 'ethnicity'.
5. The 2002 census states that there are 52,000 Roma in Macedonia; however, this is consistently recognized as an inaccurate number.
6. The Macedonian government is aware of this 'identity-switching' and some international researchers, including Victor Friedman and Eben Friedman, cite this 'fear' that the Roma are 'potential Albanians' (thus a possible demographic 'threat') as one of the motives for the Macedonian government's relatively 'benign' treatment of them compared to other European countries. (E. Friedman 2002)
7. During May and June 2004 I went to the National Library in Skopje (affiliated with the University) and examined the electronic and manual card catalogues (from 1946–present) for all references to 'Roma' and 'Cigani' from 1946 (under Yugoslavia) in Macedonia or by Macedonian authors.
8. There are four state universities in Macedonia, the largest being the University of Skopje. In 2001 South East European University, a private university funded mostly by Western European and American governments and the OSCE, was opened in Tetevo (a predominantly ethnic-Albanian city in the western part of the country), offering trilingual instruction in Albanian, Macedonian and English.
9. This is not to say there is no literature written by people from Macedonia regarding the Roma – there is, it just is not commonly known nor sought after. Throughout the 1970s and 1980s the majority of literature written in Romani consisted of poetry from throughout the Yugoslav republics and in 1981 'Romani literature' appeared as a separate topic in the Macedonian National Library's card catalogue and was gone by 1982. There was then a dearth of Romani topics (most often 'Roma' or 'Cigani' would be referenced only in Pushkin's work) until 1983 when Dr. Trajko Petrovski, at that time a student in the ethnography department at the University of Skopje, published a mimeograph regarding the Roma in Macedonia.
10. This is one part of their work that I believe could benefit from further revision; for although states often do lobby other states regarding their

behaviour (particularly if there is an uneven power relation between the two), there are also many cases where NGOs and activists themselves participate in lobbying and other action-based campaigns without state mediation (de Jong et al. 2005; Orenstein and Schmitz 2005; Fraser 2009). Various forms of more direct communication – through email, cell phone videos and YouTube – also increase the capability for direct communication (Howely 2010, especially parts V, VII and Chapter 27).

11. For more information regarding funding distribution please see http://www.romadecade.org/decade_trust_fund. It is interesting to note that although George Soros has allocated $30 million, the eight governments which have 'pledged their commitment' have collectively pledged only $13 million.
12. This linkage between international monitoring bodies and the Decade was most recently seen in the response issued by the UN Committee monitoring Macedonia's compliance to the Convention for the Elimination of Discrimination against Women (CEDAW) on 3 February, which instructed Macedonia to follow directives laid out in the Decade. That said, the CEDAW report is not requiring follow-up monitoring until 2011.
13. Both Romani and non-Romani NGOs are currently given a role in influencing the multiple 'working groups' that are connected to the recent (symbolic) interest in the Roma on a state level partially because they are the ones that have been working on the issues. Two of the members of the National Working group, Ljatif Demir and Zaklina Durmish, run education-based NGOs for Romani children. The largest, and arguably most effective, Romani NGOs in Macedonia are focused primarily on preschool, supplementary and remedial education. Based on the NGOs' experience, and accumulated data, they have been active and vocal in expressing their opinions regarding the needs of Romani students. What has been largely absent, however, is how to reach out and affect non-Roma teachers and students regarding their level of knowledge or ignorance concerning the Roma. As Memedova stated, 'All of our projects are dealing with Roma and for Roma, I wonder if we realize what we are doing... we are putting ourselves in our own box.' (pc. Memedova 2006).
14. The full text was formally submitted in 2003 to the World Bank and can be found here http://info.worldbank.org/etools/library/view_p.asp?lprogram=1&objectid=19815
15. http://www.romadecade.org/decade_watch
16. For the full report please see http://www.amnesty.org/en/library/info/EUR65/004/2007/en. For information on the campaigns to affect change please see http://takeaction.amnestyusa.org/siteapps/advocacy/index.aspx?c=jhKPIXPCIoE&b=2590179&template=x.ascx&action=15687
17. Although I conducted the majority of my research in the spring and summer of 2004 at the dawn of the Decade of Roma Inclusion, I have been in contact

with various non-Romani and Romani actors via email for the past two years. For up-to-date information regarding the Decade of Roma Inclusion please see www.soros.org/iniatives/roma.

18. When asked why the Department for Development and Promotion of Education in Languages of Minorities is rendered impotent he answered frankly, 'In the Ohrid agreement it states that there needs to be equal representation of the "other" ethnic groups in Macedonia. In reality this means "Albanian" only.' Nedeljkovic believes that the ethnic politics of both ethnic Macedonians and Albanians has created a situation where the 'other', including the Roma, are non-existent because they are not politically valuable (personal communication, 17 March 2004).

References

Amnesty International 2007. *'Little by Little We Women Have Learned Our Rights': The Macedonian Government's Failure to Uphold the Rights of Romani Women and Girls.* London, England: Amnesty International.

Barany, Zoltan 2002. *The East European Gypsies – Regime Change, Marginality and Ethnopolitics.* New York: Cambridge University Press.

Barnett, Michael and Martha Finnemore (2004). *Rules for the World: International Organizations and Global Politics.* Ithaca, NY: Cornell University Press.

Bideleux, Robert and Ian Jefferies 2007. *The Balkans: A Post-Communist History.* New York: Routledge.

Brunnbauer, Ulf 2002. 'The Implementation of the Ohrid Agreement: ethnic Macedonian resentments'. Retrieved April 12, 2004: http://www.ecmi.de/jemie/download/Focus1-2002Brunnbauer.pdf.

Constitution of the Republic of Macedonia (English Edition).

De Jong, Wilma; Shaw, Martin Neil Stammers 2005. *Global Activism, Global Media.* London: Pluto Press.

Demir, Ljatif Mefaileskoro 2002. *'Roma* People in the Macedonian Literature, Music and Film'. RCEC 'Darhija', Skopje, Macedonia.

ECMI and MRG 2004. 'Shadow Report on Minority Issues'. Skopje, Macedonia.

Elezovski, Ashmet 2003. *Pomegju fikcijata I realnosta/Between the Fiction and Reality/Maskar I fikcija thaj o realitoteto,* 'DROM'; Kumanovo, Macedonia.

Engstrom, Janny 2002. 'The power of perception: the impact of the Macedonian Question on inter-ethnic relations in the Republic of Macedonia'. *The Global Review Of Ethnopolitics* Vol. 1, no. 3: 3–17.

European Roma Rights Center 1999. 'Competing romani identities'. *Roma Rights,* Vol. 3. http://www.errc.org/cikk.php?cikk=965.

Foundation Open Society Institute Macedonia 2002. *Do We Know Each Other Well? – The OTHER in the Higher Education Curricula in the Republic of Macedonia.* Jelena Luzina (ed.), Skopje, Macedonia.

Fraser, Nancy 2009. 'Abnormal justice'. *Scales of Justice: Reimagining Political Space in a Globalizing World.* New York: Columbia University Press, 48–75.

Friedman, Eben 2002. *'Explaining the Political Integration of Minorities: Roms as a Hard Case',* PhD dissertation.

Friedman, Eben 2002. 'Political integration of the Roma minority in post-communistic Macedonia'. *Southeast European Politics*, Vol.III, No 2–3: 107–26.
Friedman, Victor 1999. 'The Romani language in the Republic of Macedonia: status, usage and sociolinguistic perspectives'. *Acta Lingusitica Hungarica*, Vol. 46, No. 3–4.
Friedman, Victor A. 1985. 'Problems in the codification of a standard Romani literary language'. *Papers from the Fourth and Fifth Annual Meetings: Gypsy Lore Society, North American Chapter.* New York: Gypsy Lore Society.
Friedman, Victor 1999. 'Observing the observers: language, ethnicity, and power in the 1994 Macedonian census and beyond'. *Toward Comprehensive Peace in Southeastern Europe: Conflict Prevention in the South Balkans*, Barnett Rubin (ed.). New York: Council on Foreign Relations/Twentieth Century Fund, 81–105, 119–26.
Keck, Margaret and Kathryn Sikkink 1998. *Activists Beyond Borders*. Ithaca, NY: Cornell University Press.
Koinova, Maria 2000. *Roma of Macedonia*. Center for Documentation and Information on Minorities in Europe – Southeast Europe (CEDIME-SE), Greek Helsinki Committee.
Macedonian Institute for the Media 2003. *Macedonia: The Conflict and the Media*. Skopje, Macedonia.
Memedova 2005. Roma's Identities in Southeast Europe: Macedonia. Rome: Ethnobarometer
____ 2006. Shifting from Terminology to Substance. *Roma Rights Quarterly* 4: 15–18.
Moravcsik, Andrew 2000. 'The origins of human rights regimes'. *International Organization, 54(2)*. doi:10.1162/002081800551163.
Ohrid Framework Agreement http://faq.macedonia.org/politics/framework_agreement.pdf
Plaut, Shayna 2010. 'Mapping communication patterns between Romani Media and Romani NGOs in the Republic of Macedonia'. *Understanding Community Media*, Kevin Howley (ed.). Thousand Oaks, CA: Sage, 116–26.
Project on Ethnic Relations 2001. *State Policies toward the Roma in Macedonia*. Princeton, NJ: Project on Ethnic Relations. http://www.per-usa.org/Reports/MacedoniaRoma.pdf
Risse, Thomas and Kathryn Sikkink (eds) 1999. 'The socialization of international human rights norms into domestic practices: introduction'. *The Power of Human Rights: International Norms and Domestic Change*. New York, NY: Cambridge University Press, 1–38.
Romani and the Census in the Republic of Macedonia. *Journal of the Gypsy Lore Society* 6(2) 89-101.
Smillie, I 2001. *The Alms Bazaar*. London: IT Publications.
www.president.gov.mk/eng/info/dogovor.htm
www.romadecade.org
www.worldbank.org

9

TOPOGRAPHY OF SPATIAL AND TEMPORAL RUPTURES: (IM)MATERIALITIES OF (POST)SOCIALISM IN A NORTHERN TOWN IN MACEDONIA

Rozita Dimova

Introduction: The '"Wild" District' Exposed

Divo Naselje (Wild Settlement) is the first eye-catching district in Kumanovo when one drives north on the main freeway that connects Skopje and Kumanovo. Only the backs of houses can be seen. Often children play in the large patch of green surface between the two lanes of the freeway, a frightening sight given the speed of the passing automobiles. The name *Divo Naselje* is the widely accepted toponym for this neighbourhood. First used mainly by Macedonians, it now circulates among and is used by Albanians and other ethnicities too. The meaning of *divo* is ambiguous; it is referred to as *divo* (wild) because most of the houses were built without permits. Those districts without official urban permits in Macedonia were designated as *divi* and the state officials considered them 'illegal'. But the meaning of 'wild' in this Kumanovo district also derives from the widespread view that I heard from many Macedonians that law is absent and that people in this district – mainly Albanians – 'are wild without respect for law outside of their own "wild horde".'

Many of the houses in *Divo Naselje,* built or remodelled in the last two decades, are impressive in size and style. My first walk through this neighbourhood in the autumn of 1999 convinced me that the transformation of style and size of the houses reveals an important shift in wealth and power in Kumanovo in particular, and in Macedonia in general. Stylish columns fence the large balconies tiled with porcelain or marble tiles. The sporadic presence of swans or lions guarding the entrances creates uneasiness. The overall impression is that a lot of money, attention and the professional advice of exterior (and interior) designers and architects were behind the construction. This is evident even among the old remodelled and refurnished houses. Although not newly built from scratch, they have a minimum of one-storey extensions (often up to three), decorative façade stones covering the front side of the house facing the street, terrace flowers and several exterior armchairs and a coffee table. Unlike some of the other neighborhoods in Kumanovo where Muslim households still have a high fence around the house (rarely a wall and more often a metal fence), the houses in *Divo Naselje*, against the traditional Islamic tradition, stand fully exposed. They often reveal interiors, especially if curtains are pulled back and balcony wings or sliding doors are left open. The houses in *Divo Naselje* are fully exposed and ostentatious, directly contradicting the tendency to wall up and 'hide behind walls'. In contrast to the sumptuous houses, the most neglected part of the district is its infrastructure. The roads are full of potholes. The pavements are used to park cars on, often expensive BMWs and SUVs, leaving pedestrians to walk on the street to squeeze behind one another when a car passes or lean against the parked cars when two cars would pass. On the day of my walk, the drainage was full after the heavy rain from the previous night, and an unpleasant smell rose from the gutter.

During socialism, *Divo Naselje* did not exist with the same connotation and 'civilizational' attributes as it holds today. Most often it was referred to as the 'Tode Mendol' part of town, the name of the main street going through the district. Prior to 1991 this district was also not viewed as exclusively Albanian. Nowadays most Macedonians refer to *Divo Naselje* as a place that needs to be avoided, a place where Macedonians are not safe. Yet, my question posed to many as to 'what kind of danger is out there?' was never directly answered. During the military insurgency in 2001, the police frequently visited *Divo Naselje* to check for illegal weapon possessions, drug laboratories or other allegedly illegal activities. Newspapers and TV news reported several incidents where weapons were confiscated from their owners. But, despite my persistent inquires during the research periods 1999–2005, no one told me of any personal experiences with these types of incidents in *Divo Naselje*. Why then is this district – which has, in fact, become more urbanized, modernized and 'civilized' – called *Divo Naselje*? Why has this district become *divo* (wild) with the disappearance of the traditional Islamic housing elements, and at a time when the newly built or remodelled houses are more 'Westernized' than the ones that had previously existed?

The views and fears that Macedonians have developed of *Divo Naselje* require an explanation that goes beyond the framework of actual experience and justifiable reasons. Elsewhere I have developed the concept of loss as central in explaining nationalism in contemporary Macedonia (Dimova 2010). Here I insist on the role of space as critical in shaping the view that people have of each other. The basis on which this view is formed is the official narrative of spatial and temporal origins, a paramount link in the chain that produces the collective fantasy and fear of the Albanian 'Other'.

The Ottoman past has always been officially acknowledged as an inseparable part of Kumanovo's spatial and temporal origins. The contemporary view of Islam, especially the equation between Islam and Albanians in Macedonia, informs the official narration of the history of Kumanovo and how the town's origin is retold and disseminated. A semiotic reading of Kumanovo's architecture similarly reveals both temporal continuities and ruptures that relate to five centuries of Turkish rule up to present-day political tensions. Ethnographic and historical analyses produced during the Yugoslav Kingdom (Serbian) period (1919–45), the socialist Yugoslav period (1945–91) and independent Macedonia (1991–present) suggest that Kumanovo was indeed founded as a Turkish town with the majority of the population being Turkish. In the pages below I will show how these 'scientific accounts' are shaped by the sense of current ethnic claims of 'ownership' of the town.

Walter Benjamin in his *Theses of History* and support for historical materialism, insists on an appreciation of time that acknowledges how the present informs the past, and vice versa (Benjamin 1999). Writing against linear and teleological versions of historicism, which are inevitably written from the position of the victor to celebrate 'the tales of cultural treasure', he reminds us that what remains unsaid is the barbarism, conflict and violence underlying the celebratory tone of these tales. A tool of his analysis of historical materialism is space and materiality; they are constitutive of and constituted by conflicts between different ideological systems and shifts rendering the violence and tensions visible.

Space in Kumanovo has, indeed, been a literal and symbolic battlefield where Islamic, Christian, socialist and new, late capitalist elements have been in constant struggle shaping, affecting and reflecting popular ethnic, religious and gender distinctions. Although the presence of Islam has been closely linked to larger historical events, generally speaking, since 1919 and the formation of the Yugoslav Kingdom, the official narrative of the town has been told from the perspective of its Christian 'majority'. During this period Kumanovo and central Macedonia were called Juzna Serbia. The Yugoslav socialist rule and the post-1991 independent period have also been anti-Muslim. The present-day nationalistic tension in Kumanovo and independent Macedonia is situated within a similar matrix of a Macedonian (Orthodox) majority and the Albanian (Muslim) minority. It is within this framework that I interpret the multilayered meanings of the *Wild District* and Kumanovo's narratives of the past.

Narratives of the Past: Spatial and Temporal Origins of a Small Town

The first comprehensive ethnographic study of Kumanovo was written by the Serbian ethnographer Atanasije Urosevic (1949). He based his analysis on Hadzi-Vasiljevic's work who, as the first Serbian ethnographer to work on Macedonia and Kumanovo at the beginning of the twentieth century, described the town of Kumanovo as a 'pleasant' place that grew out of a small village and turned into a typical Turkish *kasaba* (settlement) (Hadzi-Vasiljevic 1909).[1]

The town of Kumanovo was initially mentioned by Evlija Celebija, a Turkish traveller in 1660, as a marginal place that did not deserve detailed description – in contrast to Skopje, Veles, Stip, Kratovo or Kriva Palnka (Urosevic 1949). At the time when Celebija passed through the area, Kumanovo was newly built, almost a village and part of the Skopje *vilayet*. According to the tomb in the mosque's yard, the Eski Jami (the Old Mosque) was built in 1659 (Hadzi-Vasiljevic 1909). Kumanovo's meteoric rise begins at the start of the seventeenth century when, during the Austro-Turkish war in 1689, the leader of the uprising in the northern part of Macedonia declared himself to be a *Kralot od Kumanovo* (king of Kumanovo) (Hadzi-Vasiljevic 1909; Urosevic 1949).

Kumanovo earned its good reputation due to its strategic position as an intersection of important trading routes that had its own small *charsija* (commercial centre). At the beginning of the nineteenth century Kumanovo was called *varosica* (small town), and with the revival of the Skopje trading route across the Vardar Valley, Kumanovo began its rapid rise. Although overshadowed by Skopje 20 miles south, both Hadzi-Vasiljevic and Urosevic agree that in the second half of the nineteenth century Kumanovo's progress was remarkable. It grew from a small village with only 600 houses in the seventeenth century, very few of which were made of brick, to develop into a trade centre for the entire *vilayet* (district), especially during the rule of Hivzi-Pasha in the nineteenth century.

Historians, ethnologists and geographers have agreed that the Muslim population was predominant until 1887 and the outbreak of the Turkish-Serb war, when many Muslims left the Balkans and went to Asia Minor (Hadzi-Vasiljevic 1909; Trifunoski 1974; Urosevic 1949). While the early predominance of the Muslim population has been acknowledged in most historical writings on Kumanovo, historians and popular narratives differentiate between the Turks who founded the town and the Albanian population that inhabited it after its foundation (Trifunoski 1988). Many Albanians converted to Islam between the sixteenth and eighteenth centuries and, as Muslims, were part of the ruling stratum and always identified as Turks (or generally as Muslims) (ibid: 22).

Urosevic (1949) provides a more detailed description of the ethnic distinction of the town, indicating that the founders of the town were the Turkish settlers from Asia Minor (Urosevic 1949). Between 1689 and 1737 during the Austro-Turkish wars, most of the Turks left Kumanovo and the town almost disappeared. It was in this period that the 'incursion' of Albanians took place. Although Urosevic mentions that probably many of the Turkish (Muslim) population were from Albania and had an Albanian origin, he nonetheless stresses that the Albanian population arrived in the area from Albania at the end of the seventeenth and beginning of the eighteenth centuries. He makes the distinction between different Muslim ethnicities: Turks, Albanians, Tatars and Cherkez who arrived in this area after the Russians expelled them from Russia in 1864 (Urosevic 1949: 56).

The Macedonian (what Hadzi-Vasiljevic calls Serbian) population started settling down in Kumanovo only at the beginning of the nineteenth century when the town started to develop.[2] Until the second half of the eighteenth century there was not even an Orthodox priest, because of the small number of Christian houses. The bulk of the Christian population settled in Kumanovo between 1878 and 1912. The Greeks moved into the town during the 1847 construction of the St. Nicholas Church. Most of them moved out between the two world wars, and the last household left in 1942. The Vlachs (*Cincari*) moved into Kumanovo from Krusevo, a town in south Macedonia, mainly as innkeepers and traders. The Roma people in 1949 were present with 200 houses only, equally divided between the Muslim and Christian religions. According to the census conducted in 1921 in which the mother tongue was taken as a main criterion, out of a total population of 14,300 only 2,917 (or 21.8 per cent) spoke Turkish while 641 (or 4.8 per cent) spoke Albanian. The proportion between Turks and Albanians soon shifted with Albanians gradually coming to outnumber Turks (Urosevic 1949: 67).

Massive migrations of the Muslim population occurred after the Balkan wars in 1913 when many Turks and Albanians moved out to Turkey. Regardless of migratory movements, Kumanovo continued to develop in the second half of the nineteenth century. Despite its 'youth', Hadzi-Vasiljevic writes that the town did not differ from older towns in Macedonia that possessed 'a proper' distinction between the Turkish and the Serbian (Christian) parts (Hadzi-Vasiljevic 1909).[3] The Turkish houses were pressed one next to the other and circled by high walls with *kapii* (large gates). There were rarely gardens or empty spaces around the houses, except for those few of very rich Turks, such as Ali-Efendi, Zaim and Mula-Jusen. There were twelve *maala* (neighborhoods) in the town. Christians were concentrated around the church of St. Nicholas built in 1847, which is in the southeastern part of the town. Muslims lived in the northern part of town. The western part was the only mixed area with both a Muslim and Christian population (Hadzi-Vasiljevic 1909).[4]

The oldest building in the town is Eski Jami (Eski Mosque), which is also known as the 'old mosque'. The mosque itself was built in 1751 with three *kubes* (domes) and one *minaret*. Hadzi-Vasiljevic believes that the mosque was built on top of a pre-existing church. The belief is that the church was turned into a mosque, and that the Christians from the town could still see a cross on one of the *kube* 'because otherwise the mosque would collapse without the cross to symbolically support it' (Hadzi-Vasiljevic 1909: 49).

Next to Eski Jami was the clock tower, built at the same time as the mosque in the mid-eighteenth century, and a Turkish religious primary and middle school, *Medreza*. Across the street there was the old *amam* (Turkish bath). The second mosque, called *Jeni* (new) *Jami* (mosque), was built in 1803 and was much smaller than *Eski Jami*. The clock tower, the *medresa*, the *amam*, and the *Jeni Jami* do not exist today. The *Jeni Jami* was destroyed during the Balkan wars of 1911–13 while the remaining three buildings were destroyed after World War II.

In contrast to the visible presence of Islam, the Christian legacy was represented only by one church. Hadzi-Vasiljevic (1909) writes about the reluctance of the Turkish officials to allow restoration of the church in the early 1800s. Even the Sultan Mahmud himself sent a prohibition from Tsarigrad (Istanbul). In general, the Turks from Kumanovo were against the erection of the church until 1842 when there was a Christian uprising against the Turkish and Albanian oppression. Immediately afterward a new church was built in 1851 primarily through donations and voluntary work of the town's men. During Orthodox holidays, women and younger children would also participate often by carrying bricks, buckets of sand or other material (Hadzi-Vasiljevic 1909: 42). In 1887 another church was erected by the Serbian patriarchists devoted to the Holy Trinity (Sveta Tojca).[5] Unlike St. Nicholas, which was made in a Cathedral form with three naval divisions, the new church was smaller, more elegant and built in a Byzantine style.

Arguably the most important factor for the development of Kumanovo was the building of state roads and railroad in the 1870s. Kumanovo's territory expanded simultaneously. Territory that previously belonged to Vranje, after 1877, began to gravitate towards Kumanovo attracting merchants not only from Vranje and Kratovo, but also from larger towns such as Skopje and Veles (Urosevic 1949).[6] With the rapid growth of different manufacturers in Kumanovo came great diversity. Probably the most unusual were the intestine retailers that lasted until 1925. In the 1930s there were cheese manufacturers, weavers, and four brick factories. In 1922 two banks were founded (Urosevic 1949).

In 1947, according to the report of the Producers Union, there were 56 different manufacturers with 698 factories in Kumanovo. Kumanovo's role as a major manufacturing centre was solidified by the erection of the *Zanatski Dom* (the Manufacturers' Building) built in 1927. Until World War II, this was the largest and most beautiful building in town occupying a central location. In total, including manufacturers and service providers, Kumanovo had 1,330 stores. After World War II, along with the socialist collectivization, most of these manufacturing resources remained private property. The Yugoslav system also formed a *zadruzen sistem* (communal union) where the manufacturers could join together as a collective body. With the introduction of socialism, state-owned factories overtook the production of particular goods (Urosevic 1949).

Liberation from the Ottomans came after the second Balkan War in 1913, but was fully realized only after World War I in 1918 and the official 'death of the Ottoman Empire'. After the Paris Peace Conference, central Macedonia was placed under the rule of Serbia. Serbian rule in Kumanovo between 1919 and 1941 introduced several important changes in the topography of the town. A concerted effort was made to counterbalance, even camouflage, the Turkish quarters and to minimize the architectural presence of Islam that had previously dominated the town. This was done by constructing new buildings in a modernist or neo-historical style close to the dominant Central European styles. An architect from Russia was commissioned to build the most important buildings, such as the manufacturer's mall the *Sokolana* (the sport hall), and the central *Krug*, an aligned mansion surrounding the central street where the local government and the town Mayor were housed. This row of buildings emerged as the most dominant architectural style, hiding the visibility of *Orta Bunar*, the oldest Muslim quarter of the town, and encircling the edges of the street by forming an L-shaped inner space called the *Kasapski Krug* (Butchers' Circle), which housed around eight butchers' stores.

The 1930s were marked by a significant embellishment of the town with innovations introduced by the Russian architect who followed Western architectural trends. Most traditional Turkish inns and *bezistens* in Macedonian towns built with arcades and oval, atrium-shaped buildings were a common style in Ottoman architecture. Commercial buildings from the 1930s in Kumanovo built by this architect do not contain many oval elements or atrium-style buildings – a distinct effort to minimize Islamic influence within the urban landscape.[7]

Ruptures of the Present: Socialism, Islam and Ensuing (In)visibilities

Socialist ideology in Yugoslavia, which was deeply rooted in the processes of urbanization, and industrialization, considered the 'ideal-type' socialist city to be a combination of economic efficacy, social justice, access to urban goods and services and a high quality of life for the urban population (Smith 1998). This model, however, was better achieved in new towns than in those which had an inherited urban legacy. Kumanovo with its Ottoman and Central European architectural legacy underwent massive changes in order to accommodate the new socialist ideology. The only way to place the newly built and mandatory socialist mansions in the centre of towns was to destroy several central buildings such as the old *bezisten,* on which the new *Kulturen Dom* was built in the 1960s. The old market was also destroyed and the largest retail store, the *NAMA* (*Naroden Magazin* or the People's Magazine) was erected in its place.[8] The new socialist power, with its urban-based ideology, aimed to control the cities and to govern the country from urban centres. Urban and regional planning – like other state socialist policies – relied on negotiations between politicians, bureaucrats and experts and from which the general public was excluded (Enyedi 1996).

The socialist project in Yugoslavia was ultimately one of modernization where religion would play a minimal role. This officially accounts for the destruction of the *saat-kula* (clock tower), the *amam* and the *medresa*. According to several officials working on Kumanovo's urban planning team, the destruction had nothing to do with Islam per se but with a repudiation of religion in general. The public rumours spread in the town claim these monuments were destroyed during the street battles in 1944. However, pictures and official documents suggest that the 'end of the war' and the 'liberation parades' had been performed alongside both the *saat-kula* and the Turkish *amam*. Some of the people I interviewed involved in local governance during the 1960s and 1970s believe that the destruction of these buildings was primarily an anti-religious act. They insist that the Yugoslav socialist government destroyed many churches too. This destruction was conducted in the name of a socialist ideology stripped of any religious elements. In Kumanovo, however, the main orthodox churches remained intact, while the *saat-kula* and the *amam* were demolished and replaced with apartment blocks and the current music school.

Most of my Albanian interlocutors believe that the destruction was a planned anti-Albanian and anti-Muslim act. An Albanian high-school history teacher pointed out that the presence of Albanians was troubling to socialist-controlled Yugoslavia and has continued to be an even larger problem since the 1991 independence of Macedonia. We had the interview in a *cajdzilnica* (tea-house) in Orta Bunar, a place visited only by men. I felt awkward with the gaze of a dozen men staring at us, following every word we exchanged. The size of the teahouse did not allow for a private conversation, and the people sitting nearby could clearly hear everything we said. Fekim bitterly expressed his views, stressing that Albanians and Islam in Kumanovo had suffered tremendously. During socialism there was a constant threat and the destruction of the older buildings associated with the Turkish rule needed to be accounted for.[9]

The interviews I conducted with the town's officials did not identify the specific reasons for the destruction. One of the members, who chaired several committees that created urban plans during the 1950s and evaluated which buildings should be destroyed, mentioned the poor condition of these buildings as the main reason for their demolition. Their restoration would have been too costly, therefore urban planners were forced to tear them down.

In contrast, a Macedonian architect openly disclosed her view that the main Market Street in the town was lined with too many Islamic markers that needed to be erased:

> With all these Turkish buildings, you'd have a feeling that you are in a Turkish town: the Mosque, the *amam*, the *medreza*, the clock-tower... The Ottoman architecture was not very decorative... Not as the Western renaissance style is. It is more backward, less civilized. I don't think it is a big architectural loss if you destroy a simple Islamic building and try to replace it with something more modern.

This street, where the post office and the court justice were erected in the 1960s, had become the central artery for socialist architectural representation. The rows of socialist residential buildings along the central street and state official buildings such as the *Opstina* (town hall) and the post office also cover up the two oldest Turkish districts, Orta Bunar and Jeni Maalo. Indeed, during socialism Kumanovo rapidly became well developed following World War II. It emerged as an important industrial and urban centre. One of the first socialist residential buildings (built for the military personnel of the town) was erected along the main market street on the west side, across from the building of the *opstina* (town hall), where the old *amam* stood before 1948. These buildings have seven storeys and tower over the old Muslim houses in the Orta Bunar district. Only the Jami district around Jeni Jami remains uncovered by socialist residential blocks. The central boulevard, typical for most cities in Macedonia during socialism, passes near the Farmer's Market. It is one of the few places where the Albanian residential quarters are not hidden behind socialist residential blocks. The central districts in Kumanovo where many Albanians live remain 'invisible'.

An interview with an official from the socialist planning committee in Kumanovo pointed out that the local government complied with the requirements of the Macedonian government regarding the spatial division of the town. The town was to have the main socialist buildings resembling those in every other Macedonian large town: a court of justice, post office, the socialist party central committee building, the NAMA (the Central People's Magazine), the people's bank, and the Yugoslav Army *Dom*. Buildings of cultural importance such as the library, the museum and the cinema were neglected. However, the *Kulturen Dom*, as the centre of cultural happenings especially during celebrations of Yugoslav socialist holidays, was left alone.

Socialism (1945–91) elevated Kumanovo into an important and well-developed centre of northern Macedonia. As a result, its infrastructure improved significantly. A modern water pipeline was introduced in 1958–59, and complex road networks including the central freeway *Bratstvo-Edinstvo* (Brotherhood and Unity) that runs throughout Yugoslavia facilitated Kumanovo's economic growth. The collapse of Yugoslavia in 1991, however, caused a collapse of the town's industry. The embargo with Greece, Serbia, and blocked communication with other Yugoslav republics as well as civil wars (Croatia and Bosnia and Herzegovina) caused severe economic crisis. As a consequence Kumanovo faced serious economic decline. Although perhaps not an abrupt and radical cut (see for instance Berdahl 2005), the shift from socialist to the post-1991 system induced massive changes in the town's spatial outlook. The organization of space has altered the urban landscape of socialism, changing its squares and monumental places to commercialism, both of the more organized Western variety and also in forms that are more reminiscent of the 'bazaar economies of Third World' (Andrusz, Harloe and Szelâenyi 1996: 12).

The period since 1991 has been marked by fast readaptation of the pre-existing socialist official buildings into commercialized space. The Central Committee building of the Local Communist Party Branch in Kumanovo, for instance, houses a private TV station owned by a supporter of the nationalist right-wing party. It also hosts three coffee houses that are constantly crowded by people and bursting with loud music. Similarly the *Kulturen Dom* in the centre of the town, built in the place of a former market from the 1930s, is sublet to two of the most famous cafes in the town. The space is usually rented for a long period of time, allowing the renters to restore and change the buildings' interiors (often the exteriors too), adding to it or demolishing it in ways that serve their purposes. Moreover, the central park area that surrounds the *Kulturen Dom* has also been appropriated by one of the renters of the coffee shop – first it was a summer garden for his coffee shop, and during my research it was turned into an Auto Salon for European Cars, with a gleaming Peugeot squeezed inside the glass aquarium-like display space. The frontal view of the *Kulturen Dom* that stood in the central area of the town was dominated by Marlboro and Peugeot billboards.

Cafes and restaurants are the most popular and visible forms of private businesses. Since 1991 Kumanovo has been flooded with night bars that have luxurious interiors. The traditional tea-houses scattered around the Farmers Market and in Orta Bunar and frequented by Albanian men are still popular (although considered old-fashioned). But the young people I talked to find them 'boring because they are still reserved for male-only visitors'. The new cafes, in contrast, are frequently visited by young Albanian women, usually in groups or accompanied by male relatives.

A story I often heard from Macedonians is that the *kafani* – modestly decorated places where people used to meet over drinks and food – have disappeared. In most of the public places for socialization nowadays it becomes an imperative to have luxurious interiors. Several people pointed out that the new fashion had destroyed the spirit of friendship and communication among people. This was especially pointed out to me in relation to the famous place called '7'. Many of my Albanian and Macedonian neighbours and interlocutors shared their memories of '7' in the 1980s. They socialized with each other regardless of their ethnic difference. '7' was opened in 1983 by a half-Albanian and half-Turkish man, and soon became the most popular place for intellectuals and artists. Macedonians, Albanians, Serbs and Turks visited it for drinking, talking and mainly for socializing with 'kindred souls'.

Luan and Tanja, an Albanian man and Macedonian woman of a similar generation who were close friends and important for my fieldwork, stressed that '7' was especially important in the 1980s when Macedonians, Serbs, Albanians and Roma visited it. The 'mixed' relationships, usually between Macedonian women and Albanian mens took place in '7'; it acquired a reputation as being a safe space where members of different ethnicities could meet and develop intimate relationships. Luan befriended most of his Macedonian friends at '7'. In the period between 1983 when the bar/cafe opened until 1991, '7' was a centre of social life that attracted intellectuals and bohemians even from Skopje. In the 1980s, others of Luan and Tanja's generation who were in college and were also involved in the rich alternative movement that had spread across Yugoslavia 'appropriated' '7' as their main gathering place.

However, since 1991 the spirit of '7' has changed drastically. Its interior followed the new polished trend: expensive furniture, art reproductions in gold-plated frames imported usually from Turkey and unbearably loud music. Tanja often remarked that the need for verbal communication seemed to be failing not only between Macedonians and Albanians, but also between members of the same ethnicity.[10] In my field notes, I recorded that in many places communication and conversation were reduced to a minimum or entirely replaced with loud music. It was Tanja's impression too that the fashion of the people in the bars, the expensive interiors, and the latest Western music had replaced the previous conversation and relationships among people.

Neither Luan nor Tanja went to '7' frequently. The pressure of competition imposed itself on the owners to follow the decoration trend of fancy lighting, visual effects and an expensive audio-sound system. Dragan, a cafe owner, revealed that since 1991 the most decisive factor for success was an expensive interior. An Albanian owner similarly mentioned the new taste of Albanians. The modest tea-shops were not 'cool' anymore. The flashier the interior, the more attractive the place becomes. Designed by professional interior designers, most of these places are furnished with tiles and furniture usually imported from Greece or Italy.

If you try to improvise and start a place without the flashy interiors you have no chance to survive. Today if the interior does not 'smell' of money, it does not attract young people. The taste of crowds has changed. To start a cafe you need enormous wealth because an expensive interior is the key to success.

Reshaping Space and Architecture: Material Visibility of the 'Other'

Here I would return to Walter Benjamin. In his attempt to destroy the 'mythic immediacy' of the present and go beyond the affirmation of the present as a culmination on the cultural continuum, Benjamin claimed to be a historical detective. Further, he claimed he could unveil historical knowledge, which is the only antidote that could oppose the dream-like state of consciousness at this time – a time of industrial modernity and conspicuous consumption (Benjamin 1999; Buck-Morss 1989). The relationship between space and material objects, in the post-1991 ideology of a consumption and market economy, allows ongoing desires and fantasies to be constantly produced and reproduced. These, along with the predominant ideology of nationalism in the Balkans, have dwelt within and between ownership claims of social and national spaces. Moreover, nationalism as a dominant ideology affects, even regulates, space in Kumanovo into a rigid category that seemingly isolates people of different ethnicities into fixed compartments. Yet, these compartments are imaginary – stable only in the historical memory of the inhabitants of the town. Space was reshaped during socialism when Macedonians occupied the best central districts, had more money, and dominated the apartment blocks.

After 1991 Albanian 'invisibility' began to change. The market economy and the financial help of relatives from abroad allowed many Albanians to earn good livings, become rich and display their wealth through material objects. The emergence of *Divo Naselje* corroborates how Albanians have reclaimed the urban space in the town. This, in turn, fuels Macedonian experiences of loss and generates fantasies that Albanians are 'wild'. The saying that if it is a big house, it must be '*Shiptarska*' (derogatory for Albanian) reveals the view and often the despair that Macedonians feel in the face of rich Albanians.

Ironically, the managers of the socialist firms – mainly Macedonians – who have become rich by appropriating previously state-owned property have also built conspicuous houses in a district called *Zelen Rid* (Green Hill). An Albanian friend mentioned in one of our conversations that it would be much more appropriate for *Zelen Rid* to be called *Divo Naselje* because this district is 'wild, built out of wealth stolen from the people who had worked during Yugoslavia times. The new and rich houses in Divo Naselje or Orta Bunar were erected primarily with the help of the Albanian diaspora and relatives who work hard, leave their bones abroad and don't see daylight throughout their lives'.

The dualism between 'wild' and 'civilized' has been reinforced through the symbolic meaning of Islam and Orthodox Christianity. Islam as it is linked with the Orient is a foreign influence that connotes 'backwardness and lack of civilization'; Orthodox Christianity, on the contrary, has come to signify 'civilization' and an ethical stance. It is also considered the 'domestic' (autochthonous) religion (see Shubert, Chapter 3). Since the 1920s following the Ottoman Empire, Islam has continuously signified backwardness. However, the contemporary symbolic space reveals something else: the houses built by Albanians are modern, richly decorated and often made with style. In addition to this, another crucial factor that disturbs the balance of power along spatial lines in the town is that many ethnic Albanians now live in apartment blocks – something that was extremely rare during socialism. Their presence thus becomes more visible, while young emancipated women break from the traditional belief that Albanians are backward (Dimova 2006).

I was repeatedly told that Macedonians lived on one side of the main street, Albanians on the other and the Roma people lived in the ghetto near the small river. Yet, I was struck by the fact that the town's population markedly deviated from the prescribed schema along many lines, most notably, along ethnic ones. It became clear that those narratives were imaginary. And yet, this imaginary spatial delineation of the town's topology has dominated the rhetoric of most of the Albanians and Macedonians I have talked to. The vision of Kumanovo continues to be firmly rooted in a nationalistic framework. The fact that the population persists in becoming more mixed and similar is regularly negated and denied. That Albanians have an organized plan for conquering the town with its most prestigious locales remains a dominant phantasmal narrative. A Macedonian architect told me that the centre of town would soon be entirely Albanian:

> They have a very precise way of pursuing their intentions to assimilate us, to draw us out of our town. One would pay an enormous amount of money to get to a certain district. Several others would follow. This community of few houses is so aggressive and holds so tight that the other non-Albanian population moves away. It is impossible to withstand their tricks and strategies to drive everyone out from their demarcated zone that needs to be conquered... What started with a very high price of the real estate for the first who moved ends up with almost giving in, without getting even the minimum of what the house is worth. But they set the rules now... And this is a repeating schema. Once they spread their hands, it is difficult to stop them, to fight them in any way.

We could theorize that the narrative above and the ways that nationalism works as a dominant form of ideology in post-1991 Macedonia serves as a binding cement that ties together space and material signifiers such as specific buildings. Both the peculiar position of Kumanovo near the Macedonian, Serbian and Kosovo border and its demographics with 60 per cent Macedonians, 30 per cent Albanians, and 10 per cent Romani, Serbs and Turks reinforces this among its majority. The link between nationalism and its spatial and visual layout is multilayered perpetuating ethnic tension, spatial, linguistic and cultural divisions in this town.

Skopje has developed striking architectural 'discontinuity' due to the devastating earthquake in 1963 that killed 1,076 and destroyed an estimated 80 per cent of downtown Skopje. The earthquake and the necessity to rebuild the city, being the capital of Macedonia, turned out to be an 'excellent' opportunity to test an entirely new ideological project.[11] Kumanovo, on the other hand, not having undergone natural destruction, has experienced another form of ideological destruction of its architecture. Hence, it has become an ugly and strange mixture of both architectural denial and confirmation in a negation and affirmation of previous times.[12] I noticed from the very outset of my fieldwork that the town had been undergoing a lot of construction and reconstruction. The massive construction work, however, had left people from Kumanovo with a very negative feeling about the overall urban outlook and infrastructure of the town. One of the predominant narratives of ethnic Macedonians was that the town had exceeded any criteria of urban planning: that the infrastructure is awful, mainly destroyed by the 'invasion' of the *wild* people – Albanians from Kosovo and the surrounding villages. This narrative – that the newly arrived Albanians from the nearby villages are guilty for the ugliness of the town – predominates in the narratives not only of Macedonians but also of urban settlers from any ethnicity, thus making class rather than ethnicity a regulatory parameter of the weak urban planning of the town. Coupled with an ongoing criticism of and disbelief in the state, the politicians and their ability to 'regulate and institute a legal framework' remains an ongoing narrative among people from different class, ethnic and gender backgrounds.

Conclusion

This analysis has outlined how space and the architectural representations of different ideologies in Kumanovo affect people's views of each other. I have shown that space in the town is created and conceptualized along several divisive axes such as religion, class and ethnicity.

To grasp the complexities of everyday reality in Kumanovo one needs to perform the role of a 'historical detective', stripping history of its legitimizing, ideological function. But indeed 'if history is abandoned as a conceptual structure that deceptively transfigures the present, its cultural contents are redeemed as the source of critical knowledge that alone can place the present into question' (Buck-Morss 1989: x). Benjamin's goal to take historical materialism so seriously that historical phenomena themselves were brought to speech, in my view, remains the most helpful method to examine materiality of space and architectural representations, which then reveals ruptures, shifts and changes otherwise masked by historicism and contemporary political realities.

It can be successfully argued that any ideological project always aspires towards the conquest of space. Holston (1989) and Davis (1992) have shown this tendency in Brasilia or Los Angeles. A similar analysis could be written about Skopje. The earthquake in 1963 that destroyed the old architecture allowed Tito and the Yugoslav government to make Skopje a playground for the Yugoslav experiment – a unique architectural design that would validate Yugoslavia as having neither a Western nor Eastern orientation, the so-called socialism with a human face.

Bourdieu (1984) argues that social space shapes how different groups interact with one another. Access to capital is the most important feature that shapes which group dictates the rules of the game. The interplay between symbolic and economic capital creates the contours whereby different classes and ethnic groups conceptualize each other's presence. The Marxist philosopher of space, Henri Lefebvre, analysed urban space as a social system that is produced through the primacy of economic relations (Lefebvre 1991). For Lefebvre, the inhabitants of a city have a right to contest this tendency, a 'right to the city' itself. Similarly, Michel de Certeau (1984) emphasized the 'user' of space, describing everyday practices including cultural productions that appropriate spaces to ends other than those for which they were intended (Certeau 1984 [1974]). Kumanovo's space, with its particular historical narrative of origins, has been radically contested since 1991 by the Albanian minority that has more access than previously to both economic and symbolic capital. Historically, the class mobility of Albanians has been fostered through diasporic transnational connections. This has been an effect of the structural isolation and marginalization of Albanians during socialism. It is a mobility which has allowed many Albanians to open private businesses and participate in the market economy of independent post-1991 Macedonia, and display their newly acquired wealth by building large houses and indulging in conspicuous consumption. The contrast of wealthy Albanians and many Macedonians who have experienced economic decline and loss of privileges has revealed social ruptures and generated narratives about 'wild' and 'dangerous' Albanians.

Paradoxically, the more ethnically divided Macedonians and Albanians have become, the more closely intertwined in the domain of social space they are. This is precisely the contradiction of the contemporary nation-state regime. This is especially valid for the new, post-1991 'democracies'. The more integrated in the transnational space the state is, the more it is required to 'embody' and display a distinct national 'essence'.

Notes

1. The Serbian ethnographer Jovan Hadzi-Vasiljevic published a study in 1909 based primarily on his own observations of contemporary practices, oral history, and narratives that were describing past times. His primary intention was to capture the disappearing world. The book entitled *South Old Serbia* (*Juzna Stara Srbija*) provides an ethnographic description of Kumanovo's rural surroundings in which the villages and their clusters, so-called *maala*, were without exact order or planning. While most often named according to the dominant kin living in the *mahaalo*, often a name might be given from the geographic position, such as Upper *Maalo*, Lower *Maalo*, White-Water *Maalo* (Hadzi-Vasiljevic 1909). The section of the analysis on popular consciousness begins by stressing the five-century-old Turkish oppression that had strongly affected the rural population around Kumanovo, precluding a 'highly developed' consciousness. People, he argues, were 'uneducated', on a very low 'civilizational level'. He stresses, however, that Albanians were also the same as the other people – there was no clear distinction on the ethnic differences among people, except the close connection between the Slavic people that made them feel 'inseparably connected to the Serbian people,

as being one of them' (ibid.: 280). Hadzi-Vasiljevic further points out that the Serbian population was aware that the only other ethnic population was the Muslim (Albanians, Turks and Romani people were clustered together). Vlachs, Greeks and Cherkez population were not considered to be 'one of them', because of their different languages. Because the Christian people in the Kumanovo rural surroundings spoke the same language, they were considered to be 'one and the same' (Hadzi-Vasiljevic: 292).

2. Urosevic's account on Kumanovo, which was written in 1947, after the formation of Yugoslavia, uses the term Macedonians, given that they were already recognized as a separate nation with their own republic during the 1943 Constitution of the federation in Jajce.
3. Kumanovo was then part of Serbia, therefore Hadzi-Vasiljevic does not use the term Macedonian, but Serbian to point the differences between Muslim and Orthodox population.
4. The origin story of the town is that Bislim-beg moved in this area and that the first Turkish descents were from this *beg* (a Turkish aristocratic title). There are different versions regarding the name: that it derives from the Turkish word *koma ova*, which means enemies, because of the long battles between the Turks and Serbs in this area. Another version is that the name comes from the village of Kumanichevo, where the population deserted it and settled in the region of contemporary Kumanovo.
5. In 1890 the Bulgarian exarchy was established in Constantinople. Ever since then, all over Macedonia there were struggles between the Exarchists and the Patriarchists who were supporters of the Serbian Church Patriarchy. The church St. Nicolas was won by the Exarchists on 18 April 1897.
6. Kumanovo's market was most famous for its livestock, mainly sheep grown and fed in the surrounding mountainous regions and locally produced wheat. As a consequence of the popularity of the cattle and wheat market, the lodging services became well developed: owners of inns and *meani* (eating places) were Greeks from Janina. Wine and brandy were imported from Skopje because of the bad soil surrounding Kumanovo. Merchants who were transferring wine and brandy were people from Basino Selo, a place near Veles. They would come on Wednesday one day before the market day, then purchase beans, wool and skins, and go back to Veles. They would transport the goods with donkeys. But the real progress of the town began when *zanaeti* (manufacturers) started to develop. Until 1877–78 there were only a few, such as one bakery owned by a Greek family, coal-producers, *terzijski* (production of measuring scales), dying, and saddle-manufacturing (Urosevic 1949: 57–65).
7. Whereas in the West the arcades have become the hallmark of modernity, in the areas under Ottoman rule arcades had been associated with Islamic

architecture. Hence modernity in the Balkans was represented by architectural representations that marked a radical departure from elements prevalent during or associated with Ottoman rule.
8. Every town in Macedonia had a similar style *Kulturen Dom* and NAMA that occupied the central sites of the towns.
9. Many people remember the buildings destroyed after World War II. Hatidza, for instance, a 76-year-old woman, attended the *Medreza* since she received her primary education and learned to speak Turkish in this school. Ramo, a 72-year-old man from Kumanovo, also remembers the *amam* vividly; it was there where he and his siblings would come to bathe. When he was growing up, his family did not have a bathroom and this was the place where people would have their weekly baths.
10. When I visited the place for the first time in autumn 1999, a month after the NATO bombardment of Serbia, I was also struck by the atmosphere: a dim light, people from different generations, foreigners (mainly KFOR soldiers), and unbearably loud music that precluded any conversation. I could not notice a trace of the descriptions and the mood that had been reported to exist among those who attended the cafe in the 1980s and the early 1990s.
11. Skopje was rebuilt with the financial aid of both Western capitalist countries (Sweden, Italy, Spain and the United States) and Eastern socialist ones (Hungary, the Soviet Union and Poland). The old neo-historic style has been replaced with a new real socialist style that intended to keep the capitalist past apart from the Yugoslav present. The old theatre and the army court, which dominated the embankment of the river Vardar in the centre of the city, were replaced with new, administrative socialist buildings (e.g. the central post office).
12. When a friend of mine from Hungary came to visit me in Kumanovo in the first month of my fieldwork, he was flabbergasted when I told him that Kumanovo might as well be considered a town of architects with more than 30 active urban planning firms. 'It is so ugly; one could never imagine that the town has architects at all'. I, myself, had a similar impression in the very first week of my fieldwork. I was meeting mainly architects and I was surprised by their number: in Kumanovo there are more than a dozen architectural studios/offices (*proektanski biroa*).

References

Andrusz, Gregory; Michael Harloe and Ivâan Szelâenyi 1996. *Cities after Socialism: Urban and Regional Change and Conflict in Post-Socialist Societies.* Oxford; Cambridge, MA: Blackwell, xii, 340.

Benjamin, Walter 1999. *The Arcades Project*. Cambridge, MA: Belknap Press.
Berdahl, Daphne 2005. 'Introduction'. *Altering States. Ethnographies of Transition in Eastern Europe and the Former Soviet Union*. M. B. a. M. L. Daphne Berdahl (ed.) Ann Arbor: University of Michigan Press.
Bourdieu, Pierre 1984. *Distinction: The Social Construction of Taste*. London: Routledge/Kegan Press.
Buck-Morss, Susan 1989. *The Dialectics of Seeing : Walter Benjamin and the Arcades project*. Cambridge, MA: Harvard University Press.
Certeau, Michel De 1984 [1974]. *The Practice of Everyday Life*. Berkeley: University of California Press.
Davis, Mike 1992. *City of Quartz : Excavating the Future in Los Angeles*. New York: Vintage Books.
Dimova, Rozita 2006. '"Modern" masculinities: ethnicity, education, and gender in Macedonia', *Nationalities Papers* 34: 305–20.
―— 2010. 'Consuming ethnicity: Loss, commodities and space in Macedonia'. *Slavic Review* 64: 859–81.
Enyedi, Zolt 1996 Hungarian Case Studies: The Alliance of Free Democrats and the Alliance of Young Democrats. In: Paul Lewis (ed.) *Party Structure and Organization in East-Central Europe*, Cheltenham: Edward Elgar, pp. 43–65.
Hadzi-Vasiljevic, Jovan. 1909. *Kumanovoska Oblast (Kniga Prva)*. Beograd: Kolarac.
Holston, James 1989. *The Modernist City : an Anthropological Critique of Brasâilia*. Chicago: University of Chicago Press.
Lefebvre, Henri 1991. *The Production of Space*. Cambridge, MA: Blackwell.
Smith, D. N 1998. The ambivalent worker: Marx, Weber and the Antinomies of Authority. *Social Thought and Research* 21:1-2, 35–83.
Trifunoski, Jovan F. 1974. *Kumanovska oblast; seoska naselja i stanovniéstvo*. Skopje: Privatno piésécevo izdanje.
―— 1988. *Albansko stanovniéstvo u Socijalistiéckoj Republici Makedoniji : antropogeografska i etnografska istraézivanja*. Beograd: NIRO 'Knjiézevne novine'.
Urosevic, Atanasie 1949. 'Kumanovo'. Godisen Zbornik na Filozofskiot Fakultet vo Skopje, Skopje.

10

AFRICA : EUROPE : ALBANIA : MACEDONIA – A ZERO-SUM GAME, ECOLOGICAL FALLACY THEORY OF ETHNIC DIVISIVENESS

Victor C. de Munck and Joseph Moldow

I had been talking with an Albanian taxi driver in the *Bit Pazar* (open market) when he poetically pointed in the direction of the *kamen most* (stone bridge) and said: 'on that side of the river is Europe, on this side is Africa' (Photo 1). 'This side' meant the *Charsiya* and *Ali Baba* districts of Skopje (Photo 3 and 6) where the majority of Albanians (and Roma) live. The 'other side' meant the west side of the Vardar River – the site of the big 'Macedonian Plaza' (formerly called the 'Marshall Tito Plaza') and modern, downtown Skopje, as well as the main hospital and the rich boroughs of the city. Further to the west on top of Vodno Hill is the 66-metre 'Millennium Cross' (see Photo 2), visible from any place in Skopje and neighbourhoods on the 'African side'. The Cross is a none too subtle branding of Macedonia as a Christian nation.[1]

The stark contrast between the two sides of the city is further exemplified by their major markets; on the 'European' side, adjacent to the modern plaza, is the extensive Gradski Trgovski Centre, which is not unlike major shopping malls in the United States, as well as the deluxe Ram supermarket. On the 'African' side is the old Turkish district with its cobblestone streets and quaint one-room stores selling jewellry, wedding and formal clothes (predominantly catering to Albanian tastes), kebab restaurants, mosques, and the large, chaotic *Bit Pazar* (Photo 4).

The *kamen most* (built during Ottoman times) geographically connects these two 'sides' of Skopje, but it cannot span the vast cultural divide demarcated by the Vardar River. This is not a mere intellectualization or exaggeration. Macedonians, Albanians and foreigners can readily perceive the difference between these two sides: one opens up to a modern fashionable plaza, the other to a messy, unkempt area where weeds grow through the concrete and the stores appear from 'Tito' or 'Ottoman times', with old-fashioned and cheap clothes and goods. Even the embankments along the two sides of the river are noticeably different: those on the 'European side' are well kept, with a promenade and benches, the east side is overgrown with weeds and run down – no one walks along that side of the river. Albanians, particularly Shiptarite Albanians (that is 'traditional' and not 'New' Albanians [Neofotistos 2010]), enter 'European' Skopje as tourists, invaders, out for a lark or an illicit date seeking a taste of modernity. In any event, Albanians are cognizant of the fact that they are entering a different world when they cross the *kamen most*. Macedonians feel similarly disconnected when they cross eastward over the bridge into 'Africa'. For the Macedonians, it is as if they've entered the Orient, with the skyline speckled by minarets.

Much ink has been spilled and even more thought, effort and programmes have been devoted to bringing these two communities – Albanians and Macedonians – together, if not to ease interethnic tensions, then at least to arrive at a pragmatic accord between the two. Neofotistos (2004) has written that in daily interactions the two communities find means to put aside their differences and the associated (usually derogatory) stereotypes and work together. However, such interactions are most often merely situationally functional, as when a Macedonian buys produce at the primarily run Albanian-Turkish *Bit Pazar*. While these routine, amicable exchanges offer some rays of hope for a lessening of interethnic tensions, they are perhaps too evanescent and dyadic to serve as a bridge to a multiculturally harmonious Macedonia.

The main 'ray of hope' that has been credited for improving interethnic relations, is the Ohrid Framework Agreement (OFA) of August 2001. The goal of the OFA was to give ethnic Albanians in Macedonia a stake in the nation through proportional representation in all state institutions, including the Macedonian parliament (*Sobranie*). Proportional admission into universities was also instituted, and has served as an affirmative action programme for Albanians. Most importantly a goal of OFA was to have ethnically proportional employment in government agencies.

Indeed, the Ohrid Framework has been an unqualified success as it has given Albanians (as well as other minorities) a stake in the success of the country across a broad spectrum of social, political and economic dimensions. A measure of that success is that there has been no further organized or chronic interethnic conflict in the country since the signing of the Ohrid Agreement. Moreover, one sees Albanian students intermingle collegially with Macedonian students at the University of S. Cyril and Methodius (UKIM, for short).[2] Some recent publications have also suggested that Albanian and Macedonian relations have improved (Neofotistos 2010; Balalovska 2006). Balalovska mentions that in a 2005 survey 'for the first time in seven years, a majority of both ethnic Albanians and ethnic Macedonians held favourable opinions of the other ethnic' (2006: 58). More Albanian youths have entered the Macedonian university system with the expectation of finding jobs in the government, NGOs or other areas of the public sector, and Albanian political parties typically hold around 25 of the 120 deputy seats in the unicameral Macedonian parliament (*Sobranie*). All these improvements in Albanian-Macedonian relationships suggest that the previous interethnic feuding and reflexive hostility are fading and the new generation of Albanians and Macedonians are finding ways to develop cooperative, even friendly ties with each other.

On the other hand, there remains deep-rooted interethnic distrust between the two groups. Our theoretical argument is that interethnic tensions are a result of three conditions: (1) hydraulic, zero-sum game group perceptions both groups have of each other; (2) relative deprivation – that is, higher but unmet expectations (as a result of OFA); (3) the inherent application of the 'ecological fallacy' for attributing personal characteristics onto individuals on the basis of perceived or presumed group differences.[3]

With regard to the first explanation – a chronically high unemployment rate hovering around 35 per cent for the last two decades – would lead Macedonians to perceive any economic successes by the Albanian community to come at their expense. An illustration of the effects of a zero-sum game worldview is as follows: assume that there are 10,000 cows in Macedonia – 3,000 are owned by Albanians and 7,000 by Macedonians – should the Albanian number of cows increase to 4,000 with the number of cows remaining constant (as the unemployment rate does)? Macedonians assume that their aggregate herd has been reduced to 4,000 cows. The success of one group is perceived to come at the expense of the other group. Therefore, any actual or perceived success by one group is met with resistance and hostility by the other group. Similarly, if the unemployment rate for Macedonians remains constant but is increasing for Albanians (or assumed to be increasing in the absence of statistics), then it is rational, but not necessarily correct, for Macedonians to believe that any success in employment for Albanians comes at their expense. In this regard, rumour, news stories, phony statistics and personal knowledge of one Albanian obtaining a government job is generalized to promote or support a perception of collective, undeserved success by Albanians.

With regard to unmet expectations and the ecological fallacy, the Ohrid Framework heightened economic and educational expectations among Albanians (and other minorities) and though many benefitted as a result of the Framework, most did not. Having not experienced any benefits, these latter were likely to conclude that the Ohrid Framework was only minimally implemented and that, in fact, the government was even more corrupt and ethnically biased than it was before they expected to directly benefit from OFA, which became a government policy. We propose that – given the context of a chronic high rate of unemployment, popular conceptions of rampant political corruption, and religious, cultural and historical differences that in (the main) separate along ethnic differences – perceived relative deprivation combined with the ecological fallacy becomes a primary psychological mechanism triggering and maintaining ethnic tensions even in the face of strong government and NGO programmes to reduce the reasons for ethnic tensions.

Let us restate our theoretical position here in a sequentially direct way: (1) Albanians and Macedonians are distinct ethnic groups; (2) the sense of 'difference' is heightened by their respective religious, linguistic, historical and cultural differences; (3) since independence (in 1991) Macedonia has had a fairly constant official unemployment rate ranging between 30 and 40 per cent (unofficially it is higher); (4) people tend to project group characteristics on individuals who are perceived to be members of other groups; (5) if groups are seen as the 'other' – that is as having different cultural, religious and other salient group characteristics – then individuals of that group will be seen as possessing the characteristics attributed to the group; (6) when these groups inhabit the same national ecological niche with relatively constant 'settings', then the groups will be seen as 'in competition' and hence in symbolic opposition to each other for the finite resources that are available to them in that ecological setting;[4] (7) given economic stagnation and finite resources (e.g. good jobs), ethnic groups will perceive their relations as based on a hydraulic model or zero-sum game; (8) in conjunction with the ecological fallacy, the dominant group will interpret any growth or perceived gains by the minority group as aggressive behaviour that threatens their own standing; the minority group will perceive the majority group as seeking to keep them marginalized, poor and relatively powerless within the political economic system; (9) the subordinate group will also perceive the dominant position of the majority group as an entitlement not deserved but obtained and maintained through government collusion.

As a result, the above theoretical position predicts that any action taken by the government and NGOs to resolve tensions through affirmative action or various equity programmes will be ineffective. This is because the basic underlying conditions that have promoted mutual distrust and hostile perceptions of the 'other' – high unemployment, limited national resources, ethnic groups related in central-marginal/in-out group structure – and that have led to the respective ecological fallacies held by members of each group have not changed. The only way to defuse and resolve this situation is through increasing resources and economic opportunities for everyone rather than 'rearranging the chairs on the decks of the Titanic'.

Many would point out that for the last decade at least Macedonians, and particularly Albanians, have found work abroad and send remittances home to lessen the economic problems of families. However, this is a personal solution and one that at least indirectly points to and potentially exacerbates the situation in Macedonia since, at least symbolically, emigration or looking for work outside the nation reflects the failure of the nation to provide jobs for its citizens. Interethnic tensions are exacerbated by Macedonia's semi-closed borders in that it is not a member of the EU, it is not easy to travel to EU countries, it is surrounded by other former Yugoslavian republic nations that are in similar straits as well as countries that it has unfriendly relations with (e.g. Greece and to a lesser extent Bulgaria).

One step towards addressing some of the issues related to Albanian-Macedonian relations is to describe and analyse the effects of what we refer to here as the ecological fallacy – that is to discover the kinds of characteristics each group attributes both to itself and, more importantly, to the 'other'. By describing these group characteristics, it is possible to find areas of tolerance and cooperation as well as dimensions of prejudice and opposition. Given our theoretical position, we expect that the dimensions of prejudice and symbolic opposition will dominate and be associated with the 'zero-sum game' perception of the allotment of national resources (i.e. jobs, education, positions of power and prestige). In the latter part of our analysis we will use this theoretical model to propose 'solutions' or at least means to ameliorate interethnic tensions, not through interactive sorts of activities or affirmative action policies, but through eradicating zero-sum perceptions and delegitimizing ecological fallacy constructions of the other.

The remainder of the chapter is organized as follows: (1) discovering the group characteristics that Albanians and Macedonians attribute to themselves and each other (i.e. the ecological fallacy); (2) analysing the above data in order to discover if the attributes reflect the dimensions of tolerance, opposition and prejudice that we have hypothesized or whether they reflect other sorts of dimensions; (3) discussing the results of these findings; (4) suggestions for how these data can be applied to ameliorating or potentially resolving interethnic tensions; (5) concluding remarks.

The Ecological Fallacy of Group Characteristics: Albanians and Macedonians are...

Primary data was gathered by Victor de Munck; both authors worked collaboratively to gather secondary data and develop the analysis presented in this chapter. It is common in cognitive anthropology and cross-cultural psychological studies to use a simple elicitation frame such as '_____ are...' to obtain lists of characteristics attributed to a group or individual. Albanians and Macedonians were asked to respond to the two prompts: 'Albanians are...' and 'Macedonians are...' Respondents were recruited on the streets and other public areas of Skopje on both sides of the divide. The interviews were conducted with the first author's field assistant, Azam Kastruoti, a multilingual Albanian university student. Informants were asked to list or recite (some verbally responded to the question) as many reasonable responses as they could. It was explained that all the data was collected anonymously and it would be impossible to trace answers to an informant. Informants were fairly relaxed yet took the exercise seriously; most seemed to enjoy doing it and asked questions about the study afterwards. All questions were put to the informants in their native language and then translated into English and back-translated into the native language to see if the translation was accurate.

The four aggregate sets of responses are presented and discussed below. They are referred to as 'freelists' and responses are arranged in terms of frequency (how many of the informants provided the response), and respondent percentage (the per cent of respondents that cited the term). Our description of group characteristics presented in freelist format is sequenced as follows: (1) what Albanians say about Albanians; (2) what Albanians say about Macedonians; (3) what Macedonians say about Macedonians; (4) what Macedonians say about Albanians.

1.1 What do Albanians say about Albanians? There were 40 Albanians recruited for the 'Albanians on Albanian freelist'; they were evenly divided between males and females (20/20) and their ages ranged from 19 to 56. There were a total of 117 responses, for an average of 2.9 responses per person. Most of the older respondents (i.e. over 50) only wrote one term while the younger ones (between 19 and 30 years of age) averaged around five responses; thus the results exhibit a bias towards the views of younger respondents. All the respondents were strangers to the field researcher. For all four freelists, terms that were deemed synonymous by the authors were combined under one of the terms. For instance, 'better than others' was combined with 'proud'; 'uneducated' and 'ignorant' were combined under 'uneducated'; and so forth. We limited the number of freelist terms for presentation to those terms mentioned three or more times for the sake of space, ease of analysis, and difficulty in determining whether those terms mentioned twice or once were idiosyncratic or outlying descriptors.

A brief examination of the above terms shows that two of the twelve terms were negative – 'dangerous' and 'uneducated'. 'Dangerous', however, potentially has a dual meaning as some Albanians are 'proud'

	ITEM	FREQUENCY	RESP PCT
1	Discriminated against	14	35
2	Brave	8	20
3	Good	8	20
4	Friendly	7	17.5
5	Traditionalists	6	15
6	Dangerous	6	15
7	Best	5	12.5
8	Uneducated	5	12.5
9	Protect Identity	5	12.5
10	Proud	4	10.0
11	Survived	3	7.5
12	[Living In] Two States	3	7.5

Total no. of descriptors: 78

Figure 10.1: Albanian Responses to 'Albanians Are'

of being 'dangerous' and 'dangerous' serves as a means of keeping Macedonians at bay. 'Discriminated against', 'two states' and 'protect identity' refer to a concern over their marginalized and ambiguous social position in Macedonia and clearly reflects that they perceive themselves as not having 'full' citizen status in Macedonia and hence view themselves as members of two states. The use of these terms also lends credence to the taxi driver's metaphoric distinction.

The unambiguously good characteristics – 'brave', 'good', 'best' and 'proud' – when tied to 'traditionalists' reflect the term that is at the heart of Albanian cultural identity – *besa*.[5] Besa is the term that is the basis for the traditional Albanian code of ethics, the 'Code of Lekë Dukagjini'. With reference to *kanuni* (the code), an intellectual and agnostic Albanian student observed that 'it infects us all even when we think it is not relevant for today's society'. This chapter is not about besa, but we want to emphasize that its importance in shaping Albanian social behaviour and perceptions is difficult to overemphasize. Our best guess for why besa was itself not mentioned by respondents is that it is an action that usually results from or shapes interactions and does not grammatically fit into the elicitation frame used here. Besa is usually translated as 'peace' or 'truce' (thus it is not an attribute of people but an action or response to other people's actions). Connotatively, besa implies a blending of honour, pride and traditions that then shapes patterns of behaviour, particularly in olden times and occasionally now, during an honour killing. In summary, Albanians generally regard themselves positively, are very conscious of their second-class citizenship and as 'survivors'; they view themselves as 'dangerous', 'brave', 'good' and 'friendly' people who will treat people fairly and honourably if they perceive themselves to be treated fairly and honourably (that is, to conduct themselves according to the principles of besa).

1.2 What do Albanians say about Macedonians? There were 38 informants who undertook the survey (19 females and 19 males) all between the ages of 19 and 50. There was an average of 2.4 responses per person.

Twenty of the 68 terms (29 per cent) used by Albanians to characterize Macedonians were unambiguously positive. Besides 'educated'

	ITEM	FREQUENCY	RESP PCT
1	No Identity/No Culture	16	42
2	Take from Albanians	10	26
3	Bad	8	21
4	Don't Exist	7	18
5	Hypocrites/False	6	16
6	Good	6	16
7	Educated	5	13
8	Cowardly	5	13
9	Avaricious	3	8
10	Nationalists	3	8

Total no. of descriptors: 68

Figure 10.2: Albanian Responses to 'Macedonians Are'

and 'good' these included: 'cultural', 'quiet', 'friendly', 'calm', 'peaceful'; a few qualified terms such as 'some are good', 'not so bad'.

The overwhelming number of negative terms, however, constitutes a near-tangible cultural barricade of disrespect and mistrust. In conversations with Albanian informants in this and other contexts, Albanians presented themselves as having traditions and as possessing a strong, historically constructed identity stemming from the indigenous people of the area – the 'Illirs'.[6] Macedonians, in contrast, were most often depicted as 'stealing Slavic culture', 'copying Greece', having an 'undeveloped culture', 'stealing history', and 'not knowing [their] own identity'.[7] The conception of Macedonian identity as artificial mirrors Albanian characterizations of Macedonians as 'hypocrites' and 'false'. In fact, most of the terms Albanians use to characterize Macedonians refute the legitimacy of Macedonian national culture and identity in contrast to the 'traditionalist' Albanians.

The Albanian characterization of Macedonians fits our hypothesis that Albanians resent the sense of default entitlement claimed by Macedonians and therefore seek to delegitimize that entitlement. This entitlement is further expressed through the characterizations of Macedonians as 'taking from Albanians' and as being 'avaricious'.

While Albanians do not appear to feel physically threatened by Macedonians (they are 'cowardly' after all), 'avaricious' and 'taking' reflect an appropriation and monopolization of national resources (i.e. government jobs, educational opportunities) by virtue of birthright, law, and networks of favouritism. The chain of perceptions – a default sense of entitlement, the assessment of a weak character, and the absence of a true history and culture as well as the self-appraisal of Albanians as 'dangerous' – supports our hypothesis concerning how the ecological fallacy would manifest itself in the context of a zero-sum perception of national resources.

1.3 What do Macedonians say about Macedonians? There were 27 Macedonian respondents (12 males, 15 females) ranging in age from 19 to 50.

Thirty of the 53 terms (57 per cent) were unambiguously good terms (e.g. 'friendly', 'calm', 'know how to think', 'smart'). The terms are related in that they reveal a calm, educated, cultured, somewhat passive ethos. Some terms overlap with the qualities Albanians associated with Macedonians (e.g., 'educated', 'calm',). Interestingly, Macedonians do not attribute to themselves the qualities of pride and aggressiveness that Albanians attribute to themselves. More relevant for our study is that Macedonians perceive themselves as 'poor', hence they are likely

	ITEM	FREQUENCY	RESP PCT
1	Hardworking	7	26
2	Nice	6	22
3	Educated	6	22
4	Peaceful	6	22
5	Patient	4	15
6	Cultural	3	11
7	Poor	3	11
10	Patriots	3	11
11	Orthodox	3	11

Total no. of descriptors: 53

Figure 10.3: Macedonian Responses to 'Macedonians Are'

to see affirmative action policies for Albanians and other minorities as threatening their own precarious economic well-being (as predicted by our theory).

A few Macedonians were somewhat critical of their own ambiguous sense of social identity. One Macedonian wrote 'We don't know how to fight for our rights', another wrote 'confused over our origins', and still another wrote 'strong while standing in front of a mirror'. The sentiments of these longer responses were also reflected in a range of shorter responses that we could not aggregate: 'Slavic mix', 'Slavic', 'Serbian', 'don't fight', 'two-faced', 'confused', 'naive', 'complicated' and 'defensive'. These mixed responses point to a hesitant sense of socio-historical national identity for many Macedonians.[7] However, the characteristics of 'hard-working', 'educated', 'cultural' and 'patriot' would seem to qualify Macedonians for being entitled to economic and educational resources, and promote their own rational for why affirmative action policies are unjust.

1.4 What do Macedonians say about Albanians? Twenty-five people participated in this survey (14 females, 11 males), they were between 19 and 50 years of age.

The term *Shiptar*, as identified by Neofotistos (2010) and both Albanian and Macedonian informants, is used here as a racist term (equivalent to the use of 'nigger' by whites in the United States), although it is also

	ITEM	FREQUENCY	RESP PCT
1	Aggressive/Fight	15	60
2	Uneducated/Ignorant	12	48
3	Many Children	10	40
4	Unkind	6	24
5	Criminals	5	20
6	Vulgar	5	20
7	Muslim	3	12
8	Selfish	3	12
9	Shiptar	3	12

Total no. of descriptors: 53

Figure 10.4: Macedonians on Albanians

used as a friendly group identifier by Albanians that emphasizes solidarity and traditional values (i.e. besa). We combined two terms into the top two terms because we saw them as synonyms but were hesitant to fold one into the other. Our Macedonian informants viewed Albanians as a physical, palpable threat and as undeserving of affirmative action programmes that provide them with good jobs and educational opportunities. The logic would appear to be that if Albanians are 'uneducated', 'criminal' and 'vulgar' then the fault for their poverty lies in them and not in the 'system' or in the Macedonian people. Just as our Albanian informants saw Macedonians as undeserving of their economic and educational standing so too do our Macedonian informants see Albanians as undeserving of governmental aid; this view is underscored by their perception of themselves as 'hardworking' but 'poor'. The third term – 'many children' – resonates with Macedonians who fear that eventually they will be a minority in their 'own' country. In addition to these terms there were a number of vivid phrases that Macedonians used to describe Albanians: 'kidney extractors', 'they want to take Macedonia from us', 'for money they changed their religion and became Muslims-*wahabis*', 'sheep shearers' (meaning Albanians will shear the Macedonian sheep).

Though there were fewer respondents for this survey question there was, nonetheless, consensus among Macedonians who viewed Albanians as aggressive, uneducated, having too many kids and threatening. The Albanians' perceived lack of culture and education provides a rationale for Macedonians to argue that the affirmative action policies of the Ohrid Framework Agreement are fundamentally 'unfair', since unqualified Albanians are replacing or being hired over the more 'educated' and 'hardworking' Macedonians. If our Macedonian informants' responses reflect a general Macedonian viewpoint, then our theoretical position that each group views the other through a zero-sum game, or hydraulic lens, is supported.

In Table 10.1 we provide an overall view of the four freelists. This table provides a more holistic, comparative view from which to analyse dimensions of tolerance and prejudice. The terms have been re-organized, so that they scale from positive to negative terms. This was done to make the table more 'user-friendly' and aid in the analysis of the aggregated materials.

Table 10.1: Comparative View of the Four Freelists

	ALBANIANS	MACEDONIANS
ALBANIANS	Brave	Good
	Good	Educated
	Best	Nationalist
	Friendly	Cowardly
	Proud	No Identity/No Culture
	Traditionalists	Take From Albanians
	Protect Identity	Bad
	Survived	Don't Exist
	Discriminated against	Hypocrites/False
	[Living In] Two States	Avaricious
	Uneducated	
	Dangerous	
MACEDONIANS	Aggressive/Fight	Hardworking
	Uneducated/Ignorant	Nice
	Many Children	Educated
	Unkind	Peaceful
	Criminals	Patient
	Vulgar	Cultural
	Muslim	Patriots
	Selfish	Orthodox
	Shiptar	Poor

There is no overlap between how Albanians characterize themselves and how Macedonians characterize themselves. This is somewhat surprising since they live in the same area and one would assume that there would be some overlap in what would be considered 'good characteristics'. Albanian and Macedonian characterizations of Macedonians overlap only with 'educated'. Other than that, Albanians' characterizations focus on questioning the authenticity of Macedonian national identity and also suggest that Macedonians have a weak/false character. These characterizations express symbolic opposition to the perceived dominant status of Macedonians and question the means by which this dominance was attained.

Our analysis is developed further in Section Two where we seek to find the underlying dimensions by which the descriptive terms found in the four freelists (and a few others) are ordered. Our purpose is to see if we can reduce and also induce a few salient dimensions by which all these various characteristics are constructed and whether or not we can find distinct dimensions for Macedonians and for Albanians, respectively. We also wanted to see if, alternatively, each group reflects these dimensions in culturally distinct ways. By dimensions we are referring to a continuum semantically anchored by antonyms. Thus an evaluative dimension, good–bad, is anchored by 'good' at one end of the continuum and 'bad' at the other; the term 'neutral' would be somewhere at the centre along this continuum. The advantage of a continuum is that the descriptors are not seen as isolated, discrete containers or 'vehicles' of meaning but as continuous and relative to one another. Thus, rather than analysing terms separately, we can see them as ordered by and representing a deeper underlying dimension of meaning.

Discovering the Underlying Semantic-Cultural Dimensions of Albanian and Macedonian Perceptions of Self and Each Other

The freelisting exercise generated names and frequencies of terms. By showing where these terms lie on a two-dimensional cultural semantic grid we can discover the underlying dimensions informants probably used to make sense of these terms. Terms are theoretically presumed to lie along the intersection of these two dimensions, with the distance between terms representing semantic proximity. For example, if we give people a set of index cards with the names of dog breeds on them and ask them to sort the cards into piles on the basis of similarity, we might discover that informants rely on the dimensions of size and aggressiveness to sort terms. Thus, terms for large-sized but gentle breeds will be more proximate to each other than to large and aggressive, and most distant from small and aggressive breeds. The two measures should be independent of one another and therefore the dimensions should be orthogonal (at right angles) to each other.

Given our analysis of the freelists we expect one dimension to be good–bad and the other active–inactive. The latter dimension we inferred because words like 'calm', peaceful', and 'well-behaved' are associated with Macedonians while terms that imply action such as 'tough', 'aggressive' and 'proud' were identified with Albanians. Further, we expect that good terms will be differentiated from bad terms, but given that we didn't find much overlap between Macedonian and Albanian 'good' terms, we would expect that these might be sorted so that Albanian good terms would gravitate towards the 'active' anchor point while Macedonian good terms would gravitate towards the 'inactive' side of the 'active–inactive' dimension. If there is such a strong conceptual separation, then we would have strong support for our theory, which would abet in developing effective proposals to reduce ethnic tensions.

To obtain the data for constructing an MDS (multidimensional scale), we wrote 47 terms provided in the freelists on index cards and then asked US informants to sort them into separate piles based on their similarity. We used a US sample to pile sort the terms because we wanted native English speakers to sort the English terms, as they had been translated from the original cards which were written in Albanian and Macedonian, respectively. We also wanted the cultural–semantic grid to be constructed independent of the populations from which our respondents were drawn, in order to prevent a bias in sorting caused by culturally relevant connotative meanings. Our cultural–semantic grid should be independent of such meanings, so that the terms are sorted based on their semantic rather than their cultural content. If we had used Albanian and Macedonian informants, they would most likely not have considered the terms independent of their evaluation of whether they were characteristics of Albanians or Macedonians.[7]

The results of our task are presented in Figure 10.5. The figure is referred to as an MDS. It depicts the conceptual relationship and provides a visual image of the semantic relations between the terms that we had asked our informants to sort into piles on the basis of their similarity in meaning. It should be remembered that the terms are, in themselves, discrete items, but the dimensions of an MDS refer to the underlying continua along which these terms are ordered. One can use more than two dimensions, but it becomes increasingly more difficult to interpret the MDS (since it is presented on paper – a two-dimensional space). By convention, if the level of stress (the amount of distortion or the residual error in the relative placement of all terms) is 0.16 or less, then there is no need to search for a third dimension and one can adequately interpret the terms using two dimensions (Borgatti 1992). As noted earlier, the two dimensions are each continua anchored by antonyms, and the coordinates of the terms (left out in the figure) reflect the position of each term along both dimensions. The MDS provides a window into identifying the main criteria informants implicitly use to evaluate the semantic similarities of each term relative to all the other terms.

For ease of analysis we took out 20 terms. If we had not done so, the figure would be unreadable. Furthermore, the 20 additional terms

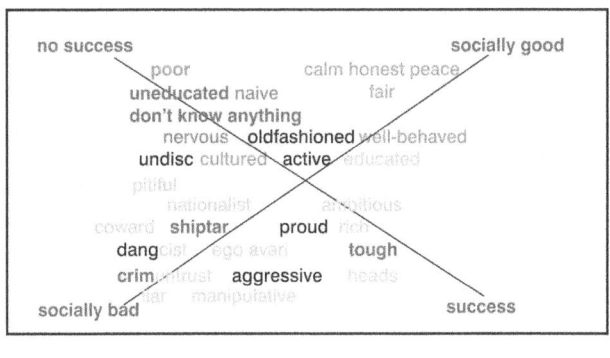

Stress in 2 dimensions is 0.151

Key:

Colors:

■ = Albanians on Albanians

■ = Macedonians on Macedonians

■ = Albanians on Macedonians

■ = Macedonians on Albanians

some shortened terms:

dang = dangerous

cist = racist

undisc = undisciplined

Ego = egocentric

Figure 10.5: Attribute Labels Along a Cultural-Semantic Two Dimensional Scale

were deleted after we analysed the MDS and made a 'best guess' as to what the two dimensions were that underlie the relative positioning of terms. The two dimensions that order these terms appear to reflect a 'success–no success' dimension and a 'socially good–socially bad' dimension.

The 'socially good–socially bad' dimension is one that we had expected to find. We added 'socially' to 'good' and 'bad' because most of the terms along this dimension refer to social aspects of this evaluative dimension (e.g. 'well-behaved', 'honest', 'peace', 'criminal', 'untrustworthy', 'liar', 'dangerous' and 'manipulative'). We could not justify the hypothesized 'active–inactive' continuum as ordering the second dimension. In our search for an 'active–inactive' dimension, we concluded that this dimension appeared to be folded into the evaluative dimension as the 'good' terms predominantly reflect 'inactivity' (e.g. 'calm', 'peace', 'well-behaved') while the bad terms reflect more active behaviour (e.g. 'criminal', 'manipulative', 'avaricious'). Also, we could not replace the anchor terms 'good–bad' with 'active-inactive' since the latter do not fit the range of terms along this dimension as well as does 'good' and 'bad'.

'Success' and 'no success' seem to correspond with the second (almost orthogonal) dimension if we keep in mind that success is generically conceived and is not infused with an ethical or ideological sensibility. That is, being 'rich' and having 'huge heads' are indices of a generic 'success' reflective of wealth and egocentrism respectively but not of 'ethical' or 'spiritual' success. For the 'success–no success' dimension we noticed that the terms 'poor', 'uneducated' and 'don't know anything' are located towards the 'no success' end of the continuum while 'rich', 'tough', 'huge heads' and 'ambitious' lie towards the other end. Terms in the centre of the MDS like 'nationalist', 'cultured', 'old-fashioned' and 'nervous' are more or less neutral in their association with success. In hindsight, given the generally poor economic situation in Macedonia, the nationalist brush that both groups use to portray the other and the centre-periphery relationship of the two groups, it is not surprising that measures of success are a primary concern for both groups and help frame the lenses for both self descriptors and descriptors of each other.

AFRICA: EUROPE: ALBANIA: MACEDONIA   251

We will point out a few interpretations that seem valid and pertinent to this study. Notice for instance that Macedonian self descriptors tend to cluster along both the 'socially good' and 'no success' ends of the two dimensions. From this we can, with confidence, infer that Macedonians view themselves as being good members of society but not being rewarded for their 'goodness'. Further, it follows that Albanians, given their minority and marginalized perspective, would view these two kinds of Macedonian self-descriptors as hypocritical, reflecting an unwarranted sense of self-entitlement. Albanian conceptions of Macedonians as 'pitiful', 'racist', 'egocentric', 'avaricious' and 'manipulative' make good sense in this light as a sort of 'other side of the coin' view of the Macedonian character. One would assume that when the majority ethnic group feels that they are good, peaceful, hardworking, educated citizens they would be upset if they are not rewarded with at least some of the cultural indicators of 'success' they feel entitled to and would be even further upset when some of these rewards are proffered to groups lacking 'socially good' characteristics. The way Albanians perceive Macedonians is the inverse of Macedonian self-perceptions. Both view Macedonians as feeling entitled to state resources by virtue of their self-evident virtues. However, the Macedonians take this assessment seriously, while Albanians view it as an illustration of Macedonian hypocrisy, racism and nationalism.

The Macedonian on Macedonian terms are distributed along the upper half of the MDS (between 'no success' and 'socially good'), while the Albanian on Macedonian terms are distributed along the lower half between 'socially bad' and 'success'. The Macedonian terms on Albanians are (except for 'tough') distributed along the 'socially bad' and 'no-success' half of the MDS and Albanian on Albanian terms are distributed across the MDS, with a slight pull towards the lower half. This shows that both have quite negative images of each other. Albanians use very few self-descriptors (other than the generic 'good' and 'best') that gravitate to the 'socially good' or 'success' anchor points. In fact, the majority of self descriptors gravitate to the 'no success' and 'socially bad' ends of the MDS. The only self-descriptors towards the 'socially good' end of the MDS are terms that reflect besa (e.g. 'proud', 'active', 'old-fashioned'). The negative Albanian self-descriptors (e.g. 'undisciplined', 'criminal', 'uneducated') are worthy of further investigation as we do not know if they are a result of a pragmatic, 'realistic' view of themselves, a product of social and material conditions, or a result of a national popular media controlled and dominated by Macedonians that portray Albanians in this negative light.[8] We can, with some hesitation, observe that Albanians were more self-reflective and not nearly as uniform in describing themselves as were Macedonians.

In general, Albanians viewed the Macedonians as 'socially bad' and 'success(ful)' while the Macedonians saw themselves as 'socially good' and '(un)successful'. In keeping with the ecological fallacy, Albanians would then assess the success of Macedonians as undeserved and due to deceitful behaviour manifested in historically unequal access to state resources such as education, jobs, and political power that further the interest of Macedonians over other ethnic groups. Macedonians would assess any success on the part of Albanians as due to their criminal, tough and cliquish familial behaviour implied in the Macedonian use of the term 'shiptar' and the importance of besa.

Concluding Remarks: Suggestions for Resolving Interethnic Conflict

The taxi driver's trope that 'across the *kamen most* is Europe, on this side is Africa' is a troubling message that must not be ignored, because too many Albanians would agree with this comment, and most Macedonians would recognize its validity. For the Macedonians, this trope reflects the recent arrival of Albanians and their aggressive, uneducated characteristics, while for the Albanians it would be a result of the following identity: Macedonia (the nation-state)=Macedonian ethnicity=Christianity=the territory of Macedonia. These symbols are visually on display in Photo 2 taken on the *kamen most*, which shows the Macedonian flag on the 'European' side of the bridge and the large cross on top of Vodno mountain.

Ferguson and Gupta (1992) have critiqued the anthropological tendency to identify territory with culture and nation, writing that: 'A certain unity of place and people has been long assumed in the anthropological concept of culture' (1992: 17). While this is a great point, one should also realize that ordinary people conflate people, place and culture on their own, without the urging of the state or cultural elite. They also note that efforts to construct 'ethnic counter nations' within a nation often use 'oppositional images' to gain support and motivate supporters for separatist movements. They suggest these homogenizing and countervailing tendencies are constructed by elites, or by those with political agendas that require the construction of an 'avaricious' and threatening 'other' to suit their needs. They further suggest that the unity of country and territory or ethnic counternational movements are a result of the 'politics of' (ibid: 11; 17) or 'fields of' (ibid: 20) power. They ask 'Who has the power to make places of spaces?' 'who contests this?' and so on (ibid: 11). In asking 'Who' they are falling into the same trap they are critiquing – that a person or group is behind it all; that there is a master hand or hands behind the scenes responsible for these conflating simplifications.

While the cultural or political elite or even the anthropologist may well promote these homogenized views, we suggest that in the case of Macedonia there are clear spatial–ethnic divisions that people themselves have no trouble labelling 'Albanian' or 'Macedonian' (here we ignore important other minority groups because they are not part of this study, but the argument can be extended to Roma, Turkish, Torbesh and probably other communities as well). We agree that the use of the term 'culture' is problematic, and that it no longer should be applied automatically across a territory much less a nation. Ferguson and Gupta (1992) as well as de Munck (2000) have noted that the rich in one country have more in common with the rich in other countries than they do with the poor in their own country. Nonetheless, their argument entails a classical Marxist assumption of the elite controlling the way the masses perceive their self-interest, thus creating a collectively held 'false conscious'. We provide a simpler argument based on the ecological fallacy, which is a general psychological tendency to view the individual as having the characteristics of the group with which she or he is identified. Thus the relevant other is typically personified and generalized. Further, we are interested in the material conditions which shape the content of the ecological fallacy by asking what are the type of characterizations that people use to divide themselves into divisive (or cooperative) groups?

Ferguson and Gupta's influential argument does not specify conditions for conflating culture with territory, nor specify the relationship between conditions and types of collective images (the content and reasoning of false consciousness). In this sense our theory is an advance over Ferguson and Gupta's theory because it presumes the psychological tendency to construct psycho-cultural profiles of others in terms of the ecological fallacy, and also specifies what types of profiles will be constructed, depending on material conditions.

The ecological fallacy refers to perceiving the actions or character of the individual as reflecting the actions or character of the group she or he represents. We can therefore say, nurse X is not very sensitive because he is a man, presuming that a feature of being a man is being insensitive. More pertinent, stories about an 'ignorant' Albanian who received a high-paying and prestigious job he didn't deserve as a result of affirmative action policies implemented by the government can be understood as a generalizing prototype of Albanians using the OFA charter to their advantage, even though all Albanians are not addressed in the above scenario.

Recognizing that the ecological fallacy is a psychological mechanism for making sense of the world is important for developing policies that counteract tendencies to generalize from the one to the many and also in influencing how the one-to-many is mapped. As it is time to 'de-territorialize' culture, it is also time to 'de-characterize' ethnicity. We suggest that one way to do this is to develop policies by which a variety of different 'types' of Albanians and Macedonians are publicly portrayed in various types of media and educational programmes and texts. We suggest a focus on deconstructing the presumed homogeneity of ethnic profiles in whatever ways possible.

We claim that the ecological fallacy is a universal cognitive tendency whose form and content are shaped by the material conditions of the society, the perceptions of relative access to the available valued resources and the perception of resources as growing, constant or decreasing. For 'Macedonian' we took as our starting point that resources were at best constant both in reality and perception, given that the unemployment rate is extraordinarily high and stable (ranging between 30 and 40 per cent for the last two decades). We also took as our starting point that the above condition led to a general nationwide perception of interethnic relations as framed by a zero-sum game calculus. Thus, material gains by one group were interpreted by the other group as leading to material losses for them. Ethnicity becomes the relevant social variable for the zero-sum game because of the ecological fallacy. In turn, Albanian and Macedonian ethnic differences are further compounded by their respective religious, linguistic, historical origins and cultural difference. We suggest that the material conditions and perceptions of them be altered, preferably by developing successful national economic strategies leading to growth, which all groups can participate in, and a means to eradicate corruption and 'old boys' networks through which both groups interpret as endemic cronyism and structural/ideological biases that favour the other group.

Finally, our data suggests that the content of the ecological fallacy shows that Albanians perceive Macedonians as insecure, cowardly, avaricious, rich and educated. From their perception Macedonians are successful because 'the system' is biased in their favour. Conversely, Macedonians view themselves as poor, hardworking, and educated, and thus justified in gaining access to the available, albeit meagre, national resources. Yet their right to these resources which, as they perceive it, is based on merit is blocked because of OFA and also the aggressive, cliquish behaviours of Albanians, who obtain jobs for which they are unqualified. Just like the Albanians, the Macedonians reason that 'the system' is unfair.

These zero-sum game effects on the ecological fallacy can be modified, first both through programmes that illustrate the falsity of these perceptions and second, through implementing a stringently implemented merit-based system of rewards. However, by far the best way to eliminate the effects of the effect of zero-sum game perceptions is to develop a growing economy in which all groups have a stake. To do this requires confidence in multicultural vectors of skills, social networks and creating alliances based on cross-cutting 'bridging' ties between ethnic communities (Granovetter 1973).

While there seems little likelihood that interethnic tensions will erupt into active separatist movements or chronic violence within Macedonia, the tensions between the groups seem to have reached a stable level of passive hostility underlain by cultural and geographic segregation. Should the homeostasis of this tension be broken by some unforeseeable series of divisive events, the stage is already set for fresh conflict. By this we mean that the pragmatic accord between Albanians and Macedonians and their current coexistence is a vast improvement over what relations were, but it is not enough to ensure political stability and full integration of Albanians into Macedonian society.

Notes

1. There are also Macedonian Muslims, Torbesh (who mostly were Slavs who converted during Ottoman rule). The Cross was built in 2002 to mark 2000 years of Christianity in Macedonia.
2. This is the main university in Macedonia.
3. Robinson (1950) coined the term 'ecological fallacy' to refer to the error of interpreting variations in environmental settings as variations among individuals.
4. Our theory is an adaptation of the 'image of the limited good' argument first laid out by George Foster (1965).
5. *Besa* is the term which frames and is the basis of the Code of Lekë Dukagjini, which as one intellectual (and agnostic) Albanian student said, 'infects us all even when we think it is not relevant for today's society'. This chapter is not about besa, but we want to emphasize that its importance in Albanian culture and, perhaps more importantly, for Albanian, is difficult to overemphasize. The reason besa was itself not mentioned here is because it is an action that usually results from or shapes interactions and not a characteristic of individuals or groups.
6. *Illirs* refers to the Illyrians who were the original people of the southeastern Balkan area. Illirs was mentioned by two Albanians in the Albanians on Albanians freelist and were more frequently alluded to but not directly mentioned.
7. As a matter of ethics, we are obligated to explain to informants the nature of our study and thus they would understand how we obtained these terms and the purpose we are using this study. This information likely would have biased Albanian and Macedonian pile sorting but they are unlikely to have affected our American informants who don't know anything about Albanian and Macedonia.
8. These descriptors were elicited from different Albanian informants in the freelist exercise, we could not combine them under one label but they clearly make the same point – that is disputing the authenticity of Macedonian identity.

9. We do not know how many Macedonians question the legitimacy of their own socio-cultural historical identity as 'officially' constructed. It could well be a minority but in any case it is not an insignificant minority.
10. This latter point is completely conjectural, as there seem to be popular media outlet for Albanians and a separate one for Albanians and we not researched whether this conjecture has any validity, but we pose it as a possible reason for the negative self imagery that does reflect popular Macedonian conceptions of Albanians as drug and sex traffickers (see the movies *Anathema* and the Western movie *Taken*).
11. The situation is I think virtually identical to the one Qadri Ishmail (1997) wonderfully describes for Sri Lankan Tamils when they were watching the Sri Lankan national cricket team beat the Australians for the 1996 World Cup.
12. We did the back translation on most of the terms but some were accidentally skipped and conducted only after it was too late.
13. This is identical to a Q-sort; it is a method described by Steve Borgatti (1992), de Munck (2009).

References

Balelvska, Kristina 2006. *Macedonian 2006: Towards Stability?* Rome: Ethnic Barometre.
Borgatti, Steve 1992. *Anthropac*. Columbia, SC: Analytical Technologies.
De Munck Victor C. 2000. *Culture, Self, and Meaning*. Prospect Heights, IL: Waveland Press.
Foster, George M. 1965. 'Peasant Society and the Image of Limited Good'. *American Anthropologist* 67(2): pp. 293–315.
Ismail, Qadri 1997. 'Batting against the break: on cricket, nationalism, and the swashbuckling Sri Lankans'. *Social Text*, 50 (1): 33–56.
Friedman, Victor 2001. 'Languages and ethnicity in Balkan politics: Macedonian, Bulgarian, and Albanian (Meeting Report #215)'. *East European Studies (EES) News*. Washington, DC: Woodrow Wilson International Centre for Scholars. pp. 4 & 11.
Granovetter, Mark 1973. 'The strength of weak ties'. *American Journal of Sociology*. 78(6): 1360–80.
Gupta, Akhil and James Ferguson 1992. 'Beyond Culture: Space, Identity and the Politics of Difference'. *Cultural Anthropology* 7 (1): 6–23.
Neofotistos, Vasiliki 2010. 'Post-socialism, social value, and identity politics among Albanians in Macedonia'. *Slavic Review* 4: 882–902.
—— 2004. 'Beyond stereotypes: violence and the porousness of ethnic boundaries in the Republic of Macedonia'. *History and Anthropology* 15 (1): 47–67.
Robinson, W.S. 1950. 'Ecological Correlations and the Behavior of Individuals'. *American Sociological Review* 15 (3): 351–357.

11

NATIONAL PURITIES, ECOLOGICAL DISASTERS: GREEK MODERNITY AND THE WAR ON NATURE

Anastasia Karakasidou

Water

It was in the early Saturday evening of 4 June 1988 when my sister and I entered the depopulated hamlet of Mavrorahi, one of the satellite communities of the Assiros Township that eventually became the centre of my first ethnographic fieldwork in Greek Macedonia. Mavrorahi was founded as a small community in the 1920s, when refugees from Pontos (the southern Black Sea area) arrived in Greece. We (meaning my sister and me) sat at the tiny coffee shop:

> And we became the audience of an ongoing loud verbal exchange between two old men: one had fashioned a pair of homemade crutches, while the other was wearing a thick mustache and the clothes of a herdsman. They were sitting on the same side of the small room, but in separate tables. I did not understand much of what they were saying, since they were conversing in their Pontic dialect; but one word sounded Greek and was repeated plenty of times: *nero* (water). *Bahcthses* (garden) and *potisma* (watering) were two other words that I could understand. (Field notes)

Later we learned that the village's few remaining stockbreeders were complaining that too much water was used for domestic and gardening purposes, making water for their animals scarce and expensive. Water was very affordable at 12 drachmas per cubic metre for each household, if no more than 50 cubic metres were consumed. Above that amount, the fees climbed to 300 drachmas per cubic metre. The domesticated village water came from an old spring that the Ottoman Turks had converted into a well. Villagers kept their vegetable gardens by the spring and water was never a problem. But, because water was brought up to Mavrorahi, and didn't have enough pressure to reach the hamlet, it has constantly been a problem: a scarce resource that has created rifts in local society. The soil in Mavrorahi also contributed to the problem since it is a kind that requires more than usual amounts of water. Accusations of stealing water, aggressive verbal exchanges between villagers and even cursing were daily occurrences.

The Ottoman Turks, who inhabited the hamlet before 1922, had water mills down by the river Bogdana or Boidana (from the Slavic Bogdan, meaning 'God given'), which drains into the Langadhas basin's two lakes (Lake Agios Vasilios and Lake Koroneia). But the river water is not clean any more; villagers told me this the very first day I entered their ethnographic space. The yogurt makers in nearby Dorkadha and the slaughtering houses of Xiloupolis threw their waste in the river. Both towns are located north and northeast of the hamlet, and the original 1922 refugee settlers and their descendants inhabit them.

Bogdana flows down the plain, and was a vital part of the life of Assiros, the township centre. 'The river had so much water in the past,' Assiros villagers also told me, 'that flooding was always expected and feared.' The Assiriotes also had their own water mills for grinding wheat by the river, and water was so abundant that the mills kept working day and night. I heard plenty of times the notorious story of how the house of a prominent Assiros family was 'taken' by the river in the 1930s and destroyed the family's economic success and prominent status. The village's policeman, an otherwise notoriously fearful man, tied himself on a rope trying to save his wife and child from drowning.

Even during the German occupation another flood that destroyed village houses and properties was remembered and narrated. Although a small dam was built upstream by the Forestry Service to control flooding, it was not very successful in keeping the river waters controlled. The delicious fish called 'boriana' were captured by nets at the river, and Assiriotes enjoyed eating them. For their First of May celebrations, they used to go to a place by the river called 'O Lakos tis Maros', (Maro's Ravine) and there they would eat, drink, sing, dance, swim and collect flowers all day long. The river's sand was also of good quality, and the Assiriotes used to transport it and sell it in Thessaloniki. An old Byzantine settlement, called Assi, was located by the river, and Assiriotes claimed that some village families originated from there. Nicknamed *Kioutsouk Stambul* (the small Istanbul), this site was much praised with local and historical pride. Now the place by the river has become an unofficial garbage dump.

Air

On 6 July 1988, I took my first excursion down the river Boidana, accompanied by my Assiros landlord. Kyrios Mitsos informed me that all the Assiros household waste gets dumped into the river. At the same time, not much water was flowing, causing stagnation and a stale smell. Local politicians kept promising that they would pipe the waters, but nobody kept their promises. 'All along the river,' I wrote in my field notes the same night, 'on our way back to the village, a smell reached my nose, a foul strong smell accompanied us.' Gone forever were the sweet smells of past life, many villagers kept telling me. 'We used to bake bread,' women told me, 'and the whole village smelled sweetness.' Women complained that although not too many bake their own bread any more, the smell of baking is not the same. Each family kept a few animals in their yards, but there was no smell. Assiros women took great pride in their cleaning activities, whitewashing their yards every week. Most village homes had outhouses, which the women cleaned every day by adding new sand. Only the wealthy villagers could afford toilets and their own septic tanks. Yet, the outhouses were clean, and there was no smell. Now, nobody keeps animals in the village, and yet the air is not fragrant. The summer heat made the smell even worse.

Fire

The summer of 1988 brought one of the first heatwaves in Greece. I remember the exhaustion on the faces of the old farmers who gathered in the coffee shops in the mornings. The day following my excursion to the river, exhausted by the heatwave, I was napping in the afternoon. The heat almost put me to sleep. But the precise moment sleep was reaching my eyelids, the village's loudspeakers brought me back to reality. The loud voice of the village's secretary announced that a fire was raging in the Lagadia site outside the village. He asked all the villagers to get out and help put the fire out. Kyrios Yiannis warned the villagers through the loudspeakers that the fire was slowly approaching the village and everybody should help. From far away, I could hear the sirens of the approaching fire engines. Maybe I was too idealistic, but I did expect villagers to run for help, an expectation that led me to disappointment. 'I could not go back to sleep,' I reported in my ethnographic notebook, 'and I went into the kitchen. Kyrios Mitsos has just returned from work and he was having his lunch. He did not seem to care much about the fire.'

When I later went down to the village *agora* (the public space with shops and offices), everything seemed to be normal, as if no big disaster was happening. Behind the hills to the northeast, I could see the blazing red and orange colour of the fire. I had been reading the town's archives during the mornings of my stay, and I knew from past township meeting minutes that rats were a repeated and notorious enemy that ravaged the fields of wheat during the summers. I had reported about them in my ethnographic notebooks a month earlier, on June 14. 'That evening, I was trying to reach the river with my car, but the winding footpaths and dirt roads were too confusing and I lost my direction. I never reached the river that evening, but I saw thousands of rats infesting the fields of wheat.'

Throughout the decades, the township would take measures to control the rats, and setting the fields (and them) on fire has been one of the most popular of such measures. This time, the fire got out of control, and the army with their fire engines worked on extinguishing the flames throughout that night. When we woke up the next morning, all signs of the disaster had vanished. The rat population was once more put under control. Nobody seemed to mind the sight of the burnt fields. Every villager seemed to have welcomed the fire, with the exception of an old man, whom I had never met. He was so sad, his friends at the coffee shop told me, that some of his trees got burnt, that he died the following Sunday. He used to go to his small garden plot with his donkey every day, and he had fruit trees and a vegetable garden there. Not too many Assiriotes kept gardens: since World War II, the vast majority of their fields had been devoted to the cultivation of wheat. Some women kept vegetable gardens in their back yards, but wheat was the crop that brought income to the villagers.

Earth

Moving up the hills to the ecologically and politically marginalized hamlet of Mavrorahi, I found only a few men still involved in agriculture and husbandry. I talked with local farmers about their crops and yields and how they marketed their products. Their land was located on hills and so less fertile than plots located on the Assiros plains. Their yields were considerably less (200 kg per stremma wheat yield in Mavrorahi, vs. 500 kg of the Assiros wheat fields). A little over a week after I established myself in the hamlet, I found a used fertilizer bag lying on the side of a path. The sign said that it was from the Cooperative Fertilizer Union and the slogan said: 'The right fertilization means good yield, quality and savings.' The few remaining farmers in Mavrorahi reminded me on many occasions that they would get even fewer yields if chemicals were not used. The farmer adds two types of fertilizers to cereals, one when they plant the seeds and another in late February to early March. They praised mechanization as another blessing that liberated them from strenuous physical labour.

That summer I spent a good part of my time with farmers, both those of the hills and those of the plains, discussing their crops, yields and the marketing of their products. My primary informant in Mavrorahi was Kyrios Yiorgos, a vivacious short man with an abundant knowledge of farming, stockbreeding and politics. He diligently told me about the kilograms of fertilizers and pesticides he bought on credit from the Agricultural Bank, and how much he had to use in order to extract an honourable yield from his crops. The township's *agrofilakas* (field warden) was also a resident and we had long discussions on herding rights. He used to go around on horseback, he told me, but recently he had bought himself a scooter and drove around the fields. Despite their marginalization, or perhaps because of it, Mavrorahi was pristine; the *topos* appeared to be pure. Reading my notes now, I cannot stop myself from feeling emotional about the fresh eggs, cheese, milk and vegetables that my friends offered me generously.

Visiting the place now, almost 20 years since that original entry in the pristine hamlet of Mavrorahi, the picture of the landscape is different. A huge garbage dump for the Thessaloniki garbage is now situated a couple of kilometres to the west of the hamlet. The news about the decision to build the dump reached the area for the first time in the spring of 1990 and a huge protest was organized. For the first time in the township's history, Assiros and Mavrorahi inhabitants united in common action: they both saw the disaster that such a site would create for the township. We closed the main road for a couple of days that spring, attracting media attention. The decision was not reversed, however, and the daily Athenian newspaper *Eleftherotypia* reported on 21 May 2009 that the mayor of Assiros, along with an environmentalist group, were protesting against the dumping of toxic substances, including medical waste, in Mavrorahi.

The people in the hamlet have also experienced changes: Kyrios Yiorgos, my primary informant and dear friend, died of lung cancer over a dozen years ago. His wife, Maria, died a few months after him from colon cancer. The *agrofilakas* (field warden) also died a rather quick death from liver cancer in 1997. Everybody was taken by surprise with his sudden illness and death. He never drank, he never smoked, his wife kept telling me in 1997, when I visited the hamlet again after a long absence. 'He lost weight, he turned yellow, and he died quickly,' she told me. My landlady in Mavrorahi was operated on for colon cancer, but as of autumn 2006, she is fine.

Nation

The ethnographic antennas of the pedestrian graduate student that I was then received the waves and messages of changing patterns in agriculture, environment and health. Cancer was already an experience close-to-heart, since my father died from Hodgkin's disease in 1982. But the politics of the modern nation-state were the focus of my research. Cancer was still a dreaded disease mantled in a 'conspiracy of silence' (Patterson 1987). Environmental disasters, like Chernobyl, were feared, but also marginal in the quest of modern development. Modernity was imprinted in my own sense of what constituted proper and timely research at that time. Inspired by Eugene Weber's *Peasants into Frenchmen* (1976), with a strong background in Marxist theory and European national and labour movements, I read, observed, listened and analysed the narratives of political and ethnic difference within the territorial landscape of the nation. When I entered this ethnographic space, I wanted to investigate the relation between local and refugee populations as they, since the 1920s, were forced to construct a culture of coexistence that nevertheless now binds them together in an imaginative, yet, viable Greek national community. State and party politics governed our lives then: political parties, ideological divisions, the Left and the Right, the politics of class and social change were the themes researched and discussed. Most of our colleagues were close to the poor and the disenfranchised. As anthropologists, we followed the lives of those that society had not been very gracious to. To this intellectual armour of the times, we anthropologists introduced the local politics of ethnicity and identity. We insisted on recognizing the socially constructed everyday essence of the nation, and nationalism was scrutinized to an unprecedented degree.

In the course of the summer of 1988 when I moved down from Mavrorahi to Assiros – from the hills to the plains – and took residence in the town of Assiros, I researched the animosity between the two communities as it was manifested in their ethnic cultures and identities. But since the old Mavrorahi Pontian refugees addressed the Assiriotes as 'Bulgarian', I shifted my research's centre of gravity to local ethnic and national history. I investigated as many aspects of the local manifestations of the nation-state as I could. Along with other colleagues investigating similar themes (Danforth 1995), we went beyond the school version of the master narrative of national history and we historicized, contextualized and deconstructed the nation. We spent ink and brainpower on how to discuss and analyse the social construction of nationality and the sense of belonging, both in real and imaginative ways. We lamented on how the original revolutionary and emancipatory nationalist movements led to the creation of hierarchical and stratified national societies. Nationalism bothered us, and we wished it to wither away. But, as the ongoing debate between Greece and the Republic of Macedonia regarding the latter's name indicates, nationalism is well and alive. It seems that it not only imprints the national to the personal, but it appropriates almost everything personal and transcends it to the national. Who imagined, 'what and when' was what kept us intellectually busy for the last two decades?

The State

Nevertheless, heatwaves and forest fires, polluted riverbeds and air pollution have been ravaging Greece for the past two decades. I reread my 1988 field notes about the field fire I witnessed, and I am reminded of the story of anthropologist Robert Redfield who was so involved in the study of the peasant urban continuum in rural Mexico that he ignored the revolutionary flames that dotted his research space. I was studying politics and nationalism, and the ill side effects of modernization were only marginally addressed. As ethnographers, we are not quite the distanced spectators that those of other disciplines proudly and stubbornly fashion themselves to be. We admit that we have our own binoculars but, although we have spent great effort in reflecting on our capacity to observe and interpret the operatic occurrences in the cultures of the 'others', we are still in tune with the fundamental necessity and irreversibility of the modernization project. We would like to shape and strive for a humane and fair modernity; our gaze towards it continues to have a cosmopolitan grace that tends to ignore the natural and venerate the cultural and the political.

In the course of my stay in the hamlet of Mavrorahi, I researched the myriad ways the Greek nation-state was present or absent in the lives of the destitute original refugees and their descendants. I collected stories about their journey of dislocation to Greek Macedonia after 1922, their settlement, their poverty and hardships. I reconstructed the land redistribution projects of the 1920s and drew charts with family, marriage and kinship relations that linked the few families in residence. In the abandoned and ruined schoolhouse, I found the school's archives and read diligently the files that revealed how education was a tool in the hands of the state to convert these disparate refugees into Greek nationals. I concentrated my discussions on issues of ethnic antagonisms and politics with the *endopioi* (local) population of Assiros. Since the latter was the seat of the local government and the largest of the three communities that made up the township, I indulged in uncovering the politics of the local within the context of the national. I wanted to capture the presence, the machinations and the manifestations of the state in creating national homogeneity in Greece's 'New Lands'. I searched for both the overt and covert presence of the state in local life in this marginalized community. These feelings are revealed in my field notes on the night of June 10:

> I am in Mavrorahi, alone, and I am wondering in this marginal hamlet, is the Greek state present here? Where is the taxman? Where is the community's secretary? The *lixiarhos* (public record keeper)? Who keeps the records? No church bells were heard on the Sunday morning. There is no priest to perform the ceremony. No newspapers and no buses come to the village. Only the state doctor comes regularly, mainly to fill out prescriptions and hear the complaints of the elderly former farmers. The coffee shop is closed most of the times and opens on demand.

Modern

In the township centre of Assiros, Greek politics are played out in the coffee shops. In the mornings, elderly men crowded the village's two coffee shops and debated both local and national politics. But in my

Assiros field notes, the politics of environmental pollution popped up constantly. No matter how many times I tried to change the topic to ethnic and local history, the men and women, the young and the old, the rich and the poor related their concern to me. Since water and electricity were brought to their homes in 1969–70, the lives of the Assiriotes changed. The water fountains that each village neighbourhood enjoyed were shut off. Gone is the main fountain located in the *aghora* with its Greek inscription dating back to 1894. One hundred years later, the piped domesticated water comes from three different locations, drawing water from under the bedrock using advanced Japanese machinery. In the summer of 1988, the local government was proposing to search for a new water source: one did not need a prolonged stay in the village to recognize that the children were suffering from dental problems. Thorium was traced in the local water, a chemical that turned the children's teeth brown, and township leaders sought alternative sources for their running water.

The two small creeks that defined the town's topography in Ottoman times (Ambelolakkos and Tourkolakkos) have practically no water any more and the few drops that trickle down from the hills are polluted. 'Our village used to be like a small island between those smalls rivers that always had water,' one of the coffee-shop owners in the *aghora* told me. The industrial waste from the above-mentioned slaughterhouses situated upstream had contaminated them, villagers claimed. With the post-junta and PASOK incentives for small businesses and industries in the 1980s, the number of polluting production units in the Langhadhas basin increased dramatically. One can see the small industries lining the road that connects the town to Thessaloniki. Greenhouses also contributed to the industrial scene. The government subsidized these industrial-farming places and had farmers attend free seminars on greenhouse production. I spoke to a couple of men involved in greenhouse production: it appears in my notes that their main concern was not the effects the chemicals used would have on their bodies, but whether or not the plastic covers would endure gusty winds.

Agricultural practices also contributed to the near destruction of the topsoil. 'We keep adding fertilizers,' farmers told me, 'and what do we expect the earth to do?' Having turned to the monocultivation of wheat since the advent of the mechanization of agriculture in the 1950s, the Assiriotes claim that there would be no yield if chemicals were not used. 'We cannot go back,' a *manavis* (vegetable monger) told me, 'we will starve.' They also claim that nothing else can grow in their fields because of the Vardaris north wind. The land now appears tired. Chemical and mechanized agriculture was what saved them from servitude to the town's *tsorbatzidhes*, the elite Greek-speaking socio-economic class that even during Ottoman times held the majority of land and stock in their hands. But, at the same time, it created new conditions for nature and human bodies.

I was slowly beginning to understand how much modern agriculture and the economy were not only related to state politics but also how the latter either helped or neglected the farmers. The study of modern chemical and mechanized agriculture is not only about the agricultural bank and the cooperatives; it is also about the local politics of unequal access to land. The land reforms of the 1920s might have created a country of smallholders, but it also created a new mode of food production that eventually made agriculture dependent on chemicals. The Greek nation-state promoted, encouraged and subsidized a good deal of polluting activities in the hopes that it would 'develop' the country. This also planted the seeds for environmental degradation and potential carcinogenesis in the human body. 'By constructing this sewage channel under the *aghora*, they created a disaster, and they brought cancer to the village. They made our village ugly, dirty and smelly,' Kyria Nitsa told me.

In our conversations about local history, Kyria Nitsa was an honest narrator. She was one of the few villagers who openly used Slavic words and sentences. Her ancestral house still stands in the *aghora*, but she died of colon cancer more than a decade ago. As far as I know, several men who had small shops in the *aghora* also died of cancer, including the tailor, and a coffee-shop owner, who were brothers. Several of the elderly men with whom I spent hours discussing local politics and history in the coffee shops also died of cancer. Prostate cancer seems to be the most common form they suffer from. My landlord, Kyrios Mitsos, who accompanied me to the polluted river that very first summer in the field also died of prostate cancer, a mutual friend told me.

Cancer

Kyrios Mitsos came face to face with cancer when, in the 1960s, his ten-year-old daughter died of leukaemia. I saw a photograph of Katerina and I still remember her big eyes, her serious lips, and no sign of a smile on the face of this unfortunate girl. There was no treatment available then and she lived 40 days after diagnosis. 'She got weaker and weaker,' her mother told me, 'and she died. She was plump and beautiful. We did not understand where her sickness came from.' I visited her grave in the village's cemetrey, a simple monument with a wooden cross in memory of one of the first victims of leukaemia in the village. Leukaemia struck Vasoula, the daughter of our next-door neighbour, who was diagnosed during my second year in residence in Assiros. She received treatment in Thessaloniki and, as far as I know, she survived it to lead a normal life and got engaged. Throughout my stay in Assiros, there was almost daily talk about the rising cancer incidents in the village. I had a good friend who generously treated me to lunch on many occasions who lived in constant fear of the disease. Her neighbour died from bone cancer and another friend had breast cancer. The priest's wife was also diagnosed while I was in the village, while another man was having chemotherapy treatments for bone cancer. A well-to-do family took the woman with uterine cancer to Memorial Hospital in New York City for treatment. These were a few of the cancer cases narrated in my field notes. Kyrios Steryios, the village's lottery-ticket seller, provided some sense of humour about the disease: he had lost his wife to leukaemia and had also had a cancerous tumour removed from his vocal chords. The doctor told him not to smoke, not to drink, to watch out for colds but not to be afraid. He did not seem particularly afraid and was a regular customer at the local coffee shops drinking his favourite *retsina* wine and smoking cigarettes.

When I started a second research project on the Slav Macedonian minority in the Florina border region of northwestern Greece in the 1990s, the theme of cancer and mortality in minority communities also was evident. A Slav Macedonian activist group began to demand human rights in practising and performing their non-Greek culture, and sentiments were growing high and debates were heated, taking much of our attention, but still cancer in the field appeared constantly. I remember in the summer of 1995, when I made a hurried trip to the provincial town of Florina, in rural northwestern Greece, to interview a Slav Macedonian political activist who was dying from a recently diagnosed liver cancer, without knowing himself from what he suffered. In Greece, it is not uncommon for physicians to keep terminally ill patients ignorant of the full extent of their ailments; disclosure is often left to the discretion of family members. I had learned of his condition through a mutual acquaintance, and I admit to feeling rather anxious at the time; disturbed by his affliction and hoping for the opportunity of an interview before he passed away.

He was frail and weak the day I visited him. His nurse had just stopped by and given him a 'shot' he told me, and he felt better that day. He was able to discuss with me how he became involved in minority politics. He recounted how he migrated to Western Europe in the 1960s to search for work, escaping local unemployment and police repression. He eventually returned to northern Greece and began his project of speaking out to his non-Greek culture and identity. During the interview it was as if the cancer was absent, he did not know what he was suffering from and I pretended I did not know either. We both performed the 'conspiracy of silence' roles, a fascinating cross-cultural human response to cancer. But the 'absence of cancer' in our conversation also signified that what mattered to us both was this man's activism and leadership in giving the Slav minority of the region a voice. That was the story I wanted to transcribe and present to the world of scholarship. Kostas Gotsis died a few weeks after my visit, and I will find the courage sometime to publish that interview. His brother also suffered from throat cancer, but as far as I know, he survived the ailment.

In the new millennium, it is certain that cancer strikes Greeks and Slavs, Vlachs and Gypsies, Christians and Muslims indiscriminately. One needs little scholarship to appreciate that cancer strikes globally, afflicting men and women, young and old, rich and poor alike. It was on the basis of observations made originally in the field, particularly the concerns local residents expressed about the spread of cancer in their community, that I started in the late 1990s to think of how I could redirect my research to the study of chemical pollution and this disease.

Modern National Bliss

The study of cancer took me to urban and rural China, to the island of Crete (Karakasidou 2008), and to the tobacco-producing hamlet of Paliambela in northern Greece. Information regarding carcinogenesis was also collected in the town of Wellesley, Massachusetts. I revisited the border region of Florina and researched the new electricity-producing unit built in Ahlada, an industrial unit that some Slav activists claim brought an end to the ethnic politics that created rifts in the local community. My study compares carcinogenesis in different cultures and aspires to find commonalities in the cultures of cancer in the global village. The most common theme links carcinogenesis to modernity. In addition, my new and old field data reveals that the process of nation building across cultures has also been a process of scientific modernization, during which clean air, pure water, and soil pollution paled in importance. Nationalism played an important role in this process, and served as a cultural mechanism at the service of man's scientific quest and domination over nature.

As a major force and a by-product of the political project of modernity, nationalism appropriated designated landscapes and transformed them into polluted environments. Through a strong alliance between state and industry, the pure and the pristine have mutated into the polluted and the contaminated. The sacred life of the state, its nation and genealogy, along with the promise of progress and affluence overtook the hearts and minds of citizens. The profanity of the state, however, manifested itself in the ways it appropriated landscapes and dominates nature. The desire for modernity and national pride rendered the early voices of protest against the world war on nature marginal. The Assiriotes and Mavrorahiotes warned the anthropology student of the changes occurring around them and their worries. It took almost 20 years for their voices to be brought out. It is now time to uncover the modernity-associated risks that both nature and the human body suffer in the hands of scientific modernity.

For Urlich Beck, the production of modernization risks follows the boomerang curve; a circularity of social endangering that renders the perpetrator and the victim identical (Beck 1992: 37–38). The Italian philosopher, Giorgio Agamben (1995), suggests that this politicization of 'bare life', the decisive event of modernity and the Enlightenment, occurs in a 'zone of indistinction', where living beings are transformed from the objects to the subjects of bio-political power. I have dealt with these issues elsewhere (Karakasidou 2007), where I analysed the modern cancer patient and his dependence on Western biomedicine for survival of the individual body. Science has taken over the decisive role of helping some to survive: it creates the possibility for a new quest of the 'survival of the fittest'. It is doing so, however, through a new 'conspiracy of silence', trying to underplay the morbid and dread character of the disease.

For this reason, we find that the discussion of cancer causality is always laden with doubts and uncertainties: we prefer to talk about risk, rather than danger (Lock 1998). If the dangers of scientific modernity are not openly acknowledged, then we can continue performing and enjoying it. In this way, we deflect our attention from any discussion of accountability. In the habitat and habitus of modern humans, an avoidance relation to danger has been constructed. Anthropologists are no exception to this rule.

I have been aware of how my work on the social history of cancer sounded unfamiliar to some colleagues. Others rushed to label it as scaremongering, since it does indicate a conviction that an impending universal catastrophe in the face of cancer is slowly appearing in the picture of humanity. Downplaying the dangers of the ecological destruction that modernity has inflicted upon the planet is the task of those in power, not us social scientists who are trying to interpret and change the world. Their concern is to keep the status quo of industrial (or post-industrial) societies. Our concern is to create safety and equality in the new global world.

And, yet, we observe in some post-postmodern theorists a tendency to underplay the dangers of industrial society. Zizek (1999), for example, seems to be wary of risk theory because it 'underestimates the impact of the emerging new societal logic on the very fundamental status of subjectivity (Zizek 1999: 341). Although he acknowledges the theory's central position that we live in a society that comes after nature and tradition (Beck 1992; Giddens 1990), he cannot see how the subject of the risk society can be 'held accountable for decisions which he was forced to make without proper knowledge of the situation' (Zizek 1999: 338). While the 'risk society' and 'second enlightenment' theorists call for the subject to make decisions that will affect our survival on the planet, Zizek and other postmodernists bring to the forefront the essential role of reflexivity and subjectivity. Risk theory, Zizek maintains, does not take into account 'all the consequences of global reflexivization' (ibid: 343). And, since reflexivity exists at the core of the Freudian subject, the subject of a risk society remains unequivocally a modern subject, albeit with new anxieties generated by risk. It is precisely on those anxieties of the narcissistic personality that we should concentrate our efforts, Zizek argues. In a sense, the reflexive subject of the Enlightenment that Kant called for over two centuries ago survives intact in risk society. Therefore, according to the postmodern (or rather the reflexive modern trend), risk society theory should be dismissed because it poses a risk on the 'performative dimension of symbolic trust and commitment'. In this vein, we can endlessly reflect on the reflective and look at the ecological disasters around us as only a hypothesis that has not yet been granted scientific proof (Zizek 1999: 335).

Responsibility

As much as our past emphasis on national politics and identity overshadowed early local concerns for environmental pollution, illness and death, postmodernism now appears to overshadow attempts to undo the wrongs of modernity. One could argue that the cultural wrongs of modernity had been targeted for potential change. Despite attacks from the materialist front, the 'cultural left', for example, acquired a strong and elegant voice in defending its agenda and finding a legitimate place in the intellectual space (Butler 1998). The theoretical abstractions as to whether the material or the cultural left is legitimate deflect our attention once more from confronting the dangers of modernity. At the same time, it forgets one basic Marxist premise: that there is no cultural without the material and vice versa. There is no opposition between the two, just a complementary relationship that anthropologists such as Robert Murphy (1971), have recognized. At this point of human history, however, the dimension of the natural should reappear in our thought: there can be no material/cultural without the natural. By bringing into the debate this additional 'ground zero' materiality, so to speak, I leave no space for parody. I ask for action.

As a way of concluding, I would like to urge us to reflect on the recent attempts by 'risk society' social theorists and pragmatist philosophers to shake this lethargy and probe the intellectual world of reflexive modernity (or postmodernism) to think about the catastrophe happening around us (Beck et al. 1994; Giddens 1990; Jonas 1966). With the globalization of science, technology and modernity, the same cultural mechanisms of domination over nature are available and practised throughout the world. Nature has been transformed into a marginalized environment, as the pure and the pristine have mutated into the polluted and contaminated. The ecological peculiarity of the twentieth century is perhaps an unintended consequence of the intellectual and political patterns of state capitalism. The environmental, climate and health peculiarities we have experienced in the last decade are unintended consequences of the scientific, political and intellectual patterns associated with the process of modernization. The mantle of nationalism can be held accountable for the miasmatic geographies that modernity created, threatening nations with pollution and the vulnerable bodies of its citizens with dreadful diseases and ailments, such as cancer.

For Michel Foucault, modernity was also connected to the physicality of the individual. Bio-political power was part of the strategy and mechanisms of control associated with the modern nation-state. The physical life of our species is not absent from the politics of modernity, with bio-power being the most fundamental and unique paradigm of modern society. It was towards that direction that the Assiriotes wanted our discussions to go; that modernity brought them a better life than their forefathers could even imagine. Modernity was good because it destroyed the somewhat feudal structure of the past agricultural society. It created a flock of equal smallholders. At the same time, however, it quietly planted the seeds for the destruction of nature and the environmental balance. Earth, air, water and fire are all now different. An obligation of our reflexive modernism is to at least reflect and recognize the ills we have done to nature, then, join the voices of those who want to bring an end to the global war that humans had declared on nature.

Every time I reread my field notes from that original research in the summer of 1988, I am impressed at the local wisdom of the people of Assiros and Mavrorahi, who saw from first-hand experience the destructions that modernity was inflicting upon them and their habitat. The Chernobyl nuclear disaster that happened only two years before was also discussed; villagers worried because the rate of cancer incidences had doubled in their community in the last decade: in their eyes, cancer was becoming an epidemic. When I challenge myself to go back to my field notes and see how much information about cancer and environmental destruction I had inadvertently collected that first summer, I am impressed. Thanks to the methodology of the ethnographer, I was absorbing and transcribing every minute detail of life that my ears were catching. Twenty years later, I bring out those voices, with the hope that we recognize our next task. It is the responsibility and obligation of those anthropologists with a holistic view of humanity – those who can acknowledge that the cultural, the subjective and the reflexive are not the only manifestations of humanity that bring essence to human existence – to enter the debate and the wave of activism to save life on this planet.

References

Agamben, Giorgio 1995. *Homo Sacer: Sovereign Power and Bare Life*. Stanford, CA: Stanford University Press.
Beck, Ulrich 1992. *Risk Society: Towards a New Modernity*. London; Newbury Park, CA: Sage Publications.
Beck, Ulrich, A. Giddens and S. Lash 1994. *Reflexive Modernization: Politics, Tradition and Aesthetics in the Modern Social Order*. Stanford, CA: Stanford University Press.
Butler, Judith 1998. 'Merely Cultural'. *New Left Review* 227: 33–44.
Danforth, Loring 1995. *The Macedonian Conflict: Ethnic Nationalism in a Transnational World*. Princeton, NJ: Princeton University Press.

Fotopoulos, Nikos 2009. 'Dangerous toxic chemicals in the Mavrorahi dump'. *Eleftherotypia*, Thursday 21 May, p.21 (in Greek).

Giddens, Anthony 1990. *The Consequences of Modernity*. Stanford, CA: Stanford University Press.

Jonas, Hans 1966. *The Phenomenon of Life: Toward a Philosophical Biology*. New York, NY: Harper & Row.

Karakasidou, Anastasia 2007. 'Humanizing cancer and the biopolitics of the disease in Crete'. *Patient Embodiment*, Christina Lammer, (ed.) Wien: Locker, 169–86.

——2008. 'The elusive subversion of order: cancer and the human experience in modern Crete, Greece'. *Cultural Perspectives on Cancer: From Metaphor to Advocacy*, Juliet McMullin and Diane Weiner (eds), Santa Fe, New Mexico: School for American Research Press, 83–102.

Lock, Margaret 1998. 'Breast cancer: reading the omens.' *Anthropology Today*, 14 (4): 7–17.

Murphy, Robert F. 1971. *The Dialectics of Social Life: Alarms and Excursions in Anthropological Theory*. New York: Columbia University Press.

Patterson, James T. 1987. *The Dread Disease: Cancer and Modern American Culture*. Cambridge, MA: Harvard University Press.

Weber, Eugene 1976. *Peasants into Frenchmen: The Modernization of Rural France, 1870–1914*. Stanford, CA: Stanford University Press.

Zizek, Slavoj 1999. *The Ticklish Subject: The Absent Centre of Poilitical Ontology*. London: Verso.

12

'KAPKA PO KAPKA' (DROP BY DROP): CIVIL SOCIETY AND RURAL ECOLOGY IN THE PRESPA LAKE REGION OF MACEDONIA

Jonathan Matthew Schwartz

Prespa Lake as Field, Region and Blessing

Prespa Lake in the Balkan region of Europe is an anthropological and geopolitical site, as well as a geological phenomenon. There are actually two interlocking Prespa Lakes, one, 'Mikro' (47 sq. km.), the other, 'Makro' (260 sq. km.). Both have international borders. Mikro Prespa borders on Albania and Greece; Makro Prespa has three bordering countries: Albania, Greece and Macedonia, the last having the largest portion of the lake. This chapter will concentrate on Large Prespa Lake, and especially on the Macedonian territory in that water basin.

Prespa's uniqueness as a site does not obviate its qualities for comparison with other landlocked water basins on the globe. If fresh water is unpolluted and abundant, it both gives and receives the blessing of its inhabitants. Water is both a subject and an object of seasonal ritual. The local site for the blessing of water on Saint John the Baptist's Day in January is the beach in Oteshevo, on the western shore of Prespa Lake. As in other towns in the Balkans, and in the diaspora communities, the Orthodox priest tosses a crucifix into the water and boys race into the cold to retrieve it (Schwartz 2000). The winner receives a blessing for his accomplishment. On Gjurgjovden (Saint George's Day, 6 May), water from the lake or from Golema Reka (Big River) is taken for spiritual cleansing. Moreover, sprigs of willow trees along the shore are cut and hung on the doorways and window frames of homes. Both Orthodox and Muslim households can practise this annual vernal ritual, but the Roma communities in Macedonia are surely the most enthusiastic celebrants of Gjurgjovden.

A glacier, a lake, even a small pond or a tiny stream becomes, as it were, a living person in the minds of the beholders and neighbours (Cruikshank 2005). A body of water is a key topic in folklore, song, poetry and, last but not least, philosophy. Herakleitos of Epheus gave the keynote utterance that expresses how water becomes a body, a near relative. In all its constant changes: 'You cannot step twice into the same rivers, for fresh waters are ever flowing in upon you' (Burnet 1958: 136).

Bodies of water also suffer and need to be healed. Fresh water, an essential resource for life, can be threatened. Lakes and ponds can dry up and rivers can 'die'. This chapter will address such a condition in the Prespa Lake region: both the diagnoses by various actors and their efforts for curing it. Over a 35-year period, from 1975 to 2010, the water in Large Lake Prespa has severely receded. With a current mean average depth of about 18 metres, three serious recessions have occured: 1975–77 (1.2 metres), 1987–90 (3.7 metres), and 2000–02 (2.2 metres). That is a total of 7.1 metres during the three most critical periods. The water's quality has also declined along with its quantity (2009 UNDP).

Prespa Lake lies on the periphery of three national territories and evokes a sense of remoteness for all three countries. There is no permissible border crossing between the Macedonian and Greek territories on the southeastern shore of Prespa Lake. Such rights of passage, however, are now permitted between the Albanian and Macedonian shores on the eastern edge of the lake. The uncordial relations between

Greece and Macedonia typically stem from ideological disputes over the name, Macedonia, and the hero, Alexander the Great, but this international conflict appears to be more easily resolved when the two opponents turn their attention to their shared environmental crisis in Prespa Lake. This value placed upon the environment is one of the hopeful contentions of the following chapter, which can merely poke the surface of the Lake's problem.

One ominous question, therefore, loomed again in my brief, recent fieldwork in Spring 2010. 'Why does Prespa Lake fall?' This question, of course, called for many corollary questions and several sorts of explanations. Was the decline in the lake's volume an 'act of Nature', or was it the result of human actions? Or, as you might guess: 'Both of the above.' Then came the troubling social questions, such as: Whose actions? Whose inactions? Who, if anybody, is doing something about the condition? What is being done? The situation of Prespa Lake, to be sure, is more suited for a PhD dissertation than a summary essay by a retired anthropologist.

Prespa Lake has an altitude of 850 metres above sea level and is connected by a sub-mountain stream with Ohrid Lake to the west; this lake has an altitude of 600 metres above sea level. Thus, between the two lakes of nearly equal size, Prespa towers over its neighbour. In contrast to Ohrid and Struga Lakes, Prespa has no urban centres on its shores. Prespa is a feminine name, and in the folklore connected with her name she is one who sought to preserve her virginal innocence. The Macedonian word 'Prespa' refers, philologically, to two ostensibly different experiences: 'avalanche' and 'hibernate'. In the actual setting of steep mountain slopes, one might sense the notion of a glacier that 'sleeps', that is, until it awakens to descend as an avalanche.

The simple, well-known, legend about the maiden Prespa goes something like this: A (much older) rich man (in some versions identified as a Turk) wanted to marry the lovely young Prespa. She was forced into the marriage but, immediately after the ceremony, threw her golden wedding ring far into the lake, which subsequently got her name. Several years later a fish was caught in Ohrid Lake, and in its belly was found Prespa's wedding band. It was likely that a fish in Prespa Lake swallowed the ring and swam into Ohrid Lake. This discovery of the wedding band inside the fish testified to two things: first, that Prespa was primordially and hierarchically pure, in short, sublime; second, that Prespa Lake's water fell into Ohrid Lake through a deep channel in the mountain named Galicica, entering Ohrid Lake in a clear, cold stream at the monastery SvEti Naum, one of the holiest sites in the Macedonian Orthodox Church.

In order to test empirically the flow of Prespa Lake into Ohrid Lake, upon which the fable of Prespa's wedding ring was based, a team of German geologists in the 1920s poured a powerful red dye into Prespa Lake near Oteshevo, near the probable source of the underground channel and later found traces of this same chemical in Ohrid Lake, near SvEti Naum. This experiment proved that the lakes were connected and that the force of gravity carried water from Prespa to Ohrid.

As a region, Prespa is thought of as 'essentially' clean. Her waters are fed by the melted snow and ice from the peak of Mount Pelister (2,600 metres above sea level). In the Prespa region, Mount Pelister is spoken of as 'Baba', grandmother, and at the peak are two small glacial lakes called 'the two eyes'. Both Baba and Prespa are 'people'. Streams from 'Baba's' top provide generous supplies of fresh water to the Greek and Macedonian villages on the eastern uplands and shoreline of Lake Prespa.

On the Greek side of the border there is intensive cultivation of tall (3 metres high) 'Prespa' bean plants. On the Macedonian side of the border, the biggest, and nearly exclusive, cash crop is apples. Though the two neighbouring districts have highly different agricultural produce both, nevertheless, consume immense volumes of water in various irrigation systems, and herein resides a partial explanation for the Prespa Lakes' recession. I have often heard though, that it was the neighbour's excesses, 'not one's own', that caused Prespa's problem. The two border areas, neighbours as they are, stand back to back. The distance by existing roads from the Macedonian village, Brajcino, to the Greek village, (Saint) German, is nearly 100 kilometres via the two large cities Bitola and Florina. A 4-kilometre walk along the lake, which could cross the international border, as noted above, is strictly prohibited.[1]

Instead of one's own actions another common, 'natural' explanation for Prespa's falling level involved an under-mountain earthquake between Prespa and Ohrid Lakes. This earthquake resulted, it was said, in a huge cavern that swelled with Prespa's water. Prespa Lake therefore dropped. The flaw in this explanation was that Ohrid Lake did not recede, as it would have, had it lost out on Prespa's underground tributary. Earthquakes are frequent and memorable in the region. Seismic phenomena, for many inhabitants, seem to epitomize and punctuate nature and history.

Earthquakes might also be 'mythical' explanations, not because they are grounded in falsehood, but rather they assume causal power beyond the extant evidence. Such is the quasi-explanation of a seismic event that opened a huge cavern inside Mount Galicica for storing Prespa's water. When a NATO-led research team studied the issue in 2005, it could find no evidence for the seismic episode (Tanevska: 14 July 2010, personal communication). Climate change and global warming, which are also the consequence of human intervention, cannot be ascertained from the existing research.

The villagers in the three countries around Prespa Lake can be monolingual, bilingual or trilingual. Albanian, Greek, Macedonian, Romi, Serbian, and Turkish are spoken within a radius of 30 kilometres, from the centre point of the lake. Many of the villagers, moreover, have family members living abroad in North America, northern Europe and Australia, and many have themselves lived and worked abroad. English, French, German and Scandinavian languages, then, are also part of the region's rich linguistic repertoire.

The Prespa Lake region has maintained its multi-ethnic composition since the last turbulent decades of the Ottoman Empire and the subsequent wars of the twentieth century: World War II, the Greek Civil War, and, most recently, the wars within the former Yugoslavia. The 'multicultural mosaic' quality of the region may fascinate an ethnographer's imagination, but the hard fact is that this diversity is beyond the reach of solo fieldwork research. Crossing borders was out of the question, and it was often problematic to conduct research within the multi-ethnic villages, or in the mono-ethnic villages, a few kilometres away. If rivalry and envy were apparent – as they were occasionally – informants from one group might suspect the ethnographer of supporting another group. Few scholars, if any, are capable of doing intensive research in the numerous, diverse Prespa tongues. What gives the Prespa region its coherence, however, is not 'culture' but agriculture combined with, and funded by, widespread labour migration.

Since the 1960s, villagers from every ethnic community in the Macedonian Prespa municipal district (numbering about 20,000 persons) have engaged in the cultivation, harvesting and marketing of apples. In former Yugoslavia, 'Prespa' was almost synonymous with apples. One proud resident told me in 1979 that his region was 'Yugoslavia's California'. The socialist regime led by Marshall Tito, in contrast to the Soviet command economy, allowed families to develop their own agricultural production and marketing. Tito's government moreover encouraged temporary emigration with the explicit obligation to send remittances to the native villages.

Pecalba is the native Slavic term for labour migration, remittance and return. Etymologically, pecalba is rooted in the Orthodox religious term for sacrifice and redemption. The experience of pecalba has been a common element in the family histories of virtually every ethnic group in the Prespa Lake region. Under the repressive Albanian government during the Cold War, emigration was strictly forbidden, causing more bitterness than the actual suffering of migration. Emigration flourished in Greece, especially during the 1950s and 1960s. The Greek and Macedonian border areas of Prespa Lake bear clear traces of extensive emigration. The Greek border villages, which I visited in 1992 and 1993, were depopulated during and after the Civil War (1947–49). The villages consisted primarily of abandoned, old stone houses, whereas the Macedonian villages were, and still are, dotted with white stucco houses built during the 1970s, the peak period of pecalba. Many of these new homes, though, are unoccupied because the owners live most of the time in Australia, Sweden, Denmark, Canada or the United States.

The conflicts of the 1990s inhibited travelling between the other regions and republics of the erstwhile Yugoslavia. The *pecalbari* (labour migrants) were joined by exiles and refugees from the war-ridden country. While one could meet impassioned spokesmen for national, religious and cultural purity in diaspora, one could also hear the voices of newly founded NGOs. 'Civil society' was to become a key actor in ex-Yugoslavia. To conclude this many-faceted introduction, I could point to at least three discrete, yet interconnected, parametres: Prespa, pecalba and apples. All of these can tell more about a shared regional livelihood than pristine ethnic culture.

From Soros to Selo: Civil Society's Path to the Mountain Village[2]

Professor Ernest Gellner, whose birthplace was in Prague and whose primary teaching post was in Cambridge (England), was one of anthropology's most sceptical talents. His critical, learned wit undid any dogma it came into contact with. After the collapse of the Soviet system, and in the final seven years of his life, Ernest Gellner became an eloquent advocate of 'civil society', an activist of, by and for non-governmental organizations. He both described civil society and pre-scribed its curative powers. The concept of civil society emerged in the European Enlightenment. This concept he wrote, 'seemed distinctly covered with dust...all of a sudden (it) has been taken out and thoroughly dusted and has become a shining emblem' (Gellner 1994: 1). The author himself was probably the chief duster. Gellner's advocacy convinced a number of social anthropologists, myself included, that civil society activism and ethnographic research could make a loving couple.

I proposed the courtship as 'NGOgraphy', where the ethnographer and the NGO accompanied each other in field projects (Schwartz 1996, 2000a). NGOers became a new sort of informant and close associates. NGOers were the new gatekeepers to the field, who could help circumvent the restrictive local and national government officials. NGOs, moreover, had Land Rovers for their ascents into remote mountain villages. NGOers were bi- or trilingual, so they could interpret what the villagers said during the meetings.

George Soros, whose birthplace was Budapest and whose residence was in New York, became civil society's indisputably most generous and tireless financier during the same years as Gellner established educational institutions in central European cities. The former Austro-Hungarian Empire's ethnic and linguistic plurality represented for both men a prototypical civil society. The cosmopolitan, urban spirit in the early years of the twentieth century could be rejuvenated at the very end of that century, after the fall of the Berlin Wall.

The brutal siege of Sarajevo and the violence of ethnic cleansing came as a shock, splintering the multi-ethnic confederation in Yugoslavia, the country which also had served as a bridge between East and West during the Cold War period. It quickly became evident that ex-Yugoslavian peoples were as much in need of civil society as the people in former Soviet bloc countries. Armed combat is hardly the context for the growth of a free civil society. The Republic of Macedonia had a precarious position in the former Yugoslavia: it was a country in quotation marks (Schwartz 1993). Neighbours did not believe in its existence as a 'real nation'. Like Bosnia, Macedonia was multi-ethnic and had differing religious affiliations. Macedonia's citizens, moreover, were also divided linguistically. The majority, an estimated two-thirds of the population (totalling around 2 million), were Orthodox Christians, with their mother tongue being Macedonian.

Because the Republic of Macedonia won its independence from the regime in Belgrade without armed conflict, and remained tense but peaceable during the neighbouring war in Croatia and Bosnia, the fragile country became a destination for a UN peace-keeping mission and several civil society projects that aimed at maintaining multicultural coexistence. The Soros Foundation established an 'Open Society' office in Skopje that financed a variety of educational and media initiatives. Local radio stations which broadcast news and music from the different linguistic communities were among the most frequent recipients of Soros funding (Schwartz 1996; Mursic 2005).

Anthropologists, most of whom had conducted their fieldwork in sites on the Greek side of the border, were drawn into the 'Macedonian Conflict' (Danforth 1995) as it intensified following the independence of the Republic of Macedonia. If one is allowed a measure of professional pride, anthropologists and ethnologists who did research into the knotty Macedonian issues also became engaged in defusing potential conflagrations. Perhaps this engagement actually helped in maintaining peace by diverting some of the antagonisms. On occasions, the wrath of extreme nationalists from one ethnic group was aimed at an

CIVIL SOCIETY AND RURAL ECOLOGY   285

anthropologist who, according to the nationalists, always seemed to take the cause of the undeserving 'Others' in a conflict. In the nationalist rhetoric of every Balkan society, the native anthropologist who advocated ethnic coexistence and mutuality was guilty of nothing short of treason. The outsider anthropologist who likewise advocated the same goals was considered a dupe of the other side's propaganda.

In 1994, an ad-hoc group of anthropologists in Great Britain organized a Forum Against Ethnic Violence (FAEV); one of its first activities was a conference held at the University of London in November of that year with the provocative theme: 'Macedonia: the Next Balkan Tragedy, or a Model for Multi-culturalism?' (cf. Cowan 2000: x–xii). Many of the anthropologists who presented papers at that conference later contributed chapters to Jane Cowan's collection. Anthropologists took a stand for moderation and mediation. We were unanimous in our dread of tragic 'ethnic cleansing', but we were also doubtful whether Macedonia could be considered a 'model of multiculturalism'. Our hope for Macedonia was better put in a traditional Muslim admonition for caution: *'Machallah!'*, an exclamation that has much less finality than the Judeo-Christian 'Amen!'.

The organizers of the FAEV in London invited several representatives of NGOs from the Republic of Macedonia, including Sasho Klikovski, a young physician who led an organization with the name: Macedonian Center for International Cooperation (MCIC). Klikovski's presentation and subsequent discussions with him persuaded me to place 'civil society' as the keystone of my coming research, a three-month project in early 1995 that I began soon after returning from the FAEV conference in London: in what specific ways, if any, has the metropolitan civil society as embodied in the Soros Foundation, reached the remote mountain villages of Macedonia?

The Prespa Lake region was to remain my home base from February until May 1995. Was the Prespa region a site for civil society programmes? I soon found that it took a Sherlock Holmesian feel for clues in order to find any traces of civil society projects. At the main office for the Soros' Open Society Foundation in Skopje, staff people said that Prespa, because of its valuable apple orchards, was neither poor enough, nor marginalized enough, to be a site for projects. Yet the lake's recession, the river's industrial pollution from Prespatex (the local textile plant in Resen), and the excessive use of toxic pesticides in the apple orchards were ample reasons, I thought, for environmental NGOs to locate in the Prespa region.

Multi-ethnic though it was – and that can be said for virtually every municipality in the Republic – Resen was not regarded to be in need of assistance. However, one night while listening to a local radio station, 'Radio Delicious' (the trade name of the sweet apple), I heard a music programme called 'Balkan Blues Cafe'. The name of the announcer was Nehru, a journalist and secretary at Resen's town hall. I visited him at the town hall the next morning. Nehru said that he had applied for funding from the Soros Foundation, and because the station broadcast multicultural and multilinguistic programmes, the foundation provided him with the transmitter, which he installed in a tiny radio shack in his backyard. (When I spoke with him recently, Nehru said that 'Radio Delicious' had closed down in 1998.) The only other Soros' contribution in 1995 was two copy machines for the secondary school in Resen. It was partially due to my intervention on behalf of the school's teachers that the copy machines arrived from Skopje's Soros office in Autumn 1995. Otherwise, organized 'civil society' had left no discernible traces in the Prespa Lake region during the 1990s.

Much more tangible was civil society's entry into rural Macedonia through the development projects of the MCIC. My fieldwork in 1995, and again in September 1998, to a very arid, tobacco-growing district near Prilep was in the company of project organizers, whose efforts were aimed at creating fresh water supply and sewage control. The separation of waste from fresh water in the villages was a top priority. Cooperation between the residents of the villages was a precondition for the MCIC action. If a project reached completion in one village, the example could be readily followed by the neighbouring villages, a beneficiary contagion.

In April 1995, Herbie, a villager, took me along on one of his tours in the border area to Albania in western Macedonia, which included a cluster of multi-ethnic villages in the Dolna Reka (Lower River) district. Herbie, who had studied engineering, spoke Albanian and Macedonian.

Some of the villagers were Macedonian Muslims, so there were three ethnic communities in the region. On occasion negotiations took place with a single ethnic group's members; sometimes the meetings included two groups, rarely all three at one time. He then could coordinate the concrete programmes for digging trenches for pipes lines that kept dangerous waste separate from households, gardens and pastures.

After a cordial planning meeting in a village with Muslim and Orthodox Macedonians, as we drove away in the Land Rover Herbie made this memorable comment, 'Too much talk about multi-culturalism is no way to help a project.' The pragmatic spirit, said my inner American voice, has to shine through civil society's translucent ideology. Accomplishment in programmes for solving environmental problems is far more likely than projects aimed at the maintenance of cultural plurality.

The village committees had shown us their completed work with much deserved pride. The men thanked Herbie again and again for his *pomoc* (help). One of the verbal changes that takes place in the transition from Soros Foundation to mountain village is that MCIC's 'cooperation' is transposed as 'assistance'. The change is subtle but significant. 'Civil society' assumes a cosmopolitan perspective in which mutuality and cooperation constitute the ultimate morality of actions. The villager, the project leader and the donor 'cooperate' with each other, but the villager tends to perceive the project as a gift, as help, from the urban office (cf. Sampson 1996 for an analysis of the donor/recipient in civil society projects). MCIC's 'cooperation' ('*sorobotka*' in Macedonian) and 'assistance' (*pomoc*) to the villagers in water resource projects, however, precipitated ethnic coexistence as an indirect consequence.

I puzzled over this shift in meaning for years, and it was an important item for research in my recent revisit to Macedonia. Of course I was curious as to my hopes for better control of water resources in the Prespa region. Had 'civil society' in the past ten years got access to the water that flowed through Prespa's villages? Was the improvement, if any, felt as 'help from the outside'? To venture answers to these questions, I shall now turn, in the concluding section, to 'the present' of Prespa, in an attempt to bring 'up to date' the water level and quality of Prespa Lake's basin.

'Drop by Drop' (Kapka po Kapka): Some Good News from the Field

'Kapka po kapka' was a new phrase I heard numerous times during recent fieldwork in Macedonia. The phrase refers to a relatively new, and now widely used method for irrigating fruit orchards. Several Prespa apple growers ascribed the invention to Israeli engineers. Scarcity of fresh water and intensive agriculture in Israel led to this technical development. As adapted to Prespa's orchards six years ago, a long black synthetic rubber hose is tied to each side of a fruit tree and continues to connect the trees in the entire orchard, dripping, or sometimes finely spraying, the roots with water pumped from a well dug in the orchard. The drop by drop method is practised in many of the family-owned orchards in Prespa, and growers from the three largest ethnic groups (Albanian, Macedonian and Turkish) have started to use the drop by drop watering system. One also sees huge coils of the black hosing stacked in Resen's agricultural supplies stores, along with crates of diverse pesticides.

I asked a first-year English class at the high school in Resen – a section with Albanian as mother tongue – if their families had apple orchards. Nearly all of them did. How many of them, I then asked, incorporated drop by drop in their orchards? A sizable majority of the students raised their hands. The innovation, 'kapka po kapka', replaced the variety of channelling systems for irrigation, which required intensive labour both within each orchard and between the orchards. Digging, repairing and clearing the channels added to the summer months' workload, a time of year when pecalbari returned from abroad and when elaborate weddings were celebrated.

If the water had to be channelled from mountain streams, its use had to be carefully negotiated, so that all the farmers got a share of it at least one night a week. Such were the situations in 1982 and 1993 that I observed in Krani, a village with both Albanian and Macdedonian inhabitants (Schwartz 1996: 37–39). To dam up and steer the flow of water, the men made use of empty plastic sacks, many that had once contained pesticides. Heavy stones and shovels of mud kept the plastic sacks in place. The system worked something like railroad switches that shunted the direction of the flow. Both the digging of relay channels and the distribution rights to the water meant that a village's residents had to maintain a measure of trust for one another, across ethnic, as well as across property lines.

The drop by drop method, however, shifted the irrigation of orchards to the efforts and expense of each individual owner, who had to have a well dug for the electric pump that brought ground water to the hoses. Drop by drop was highly costly for the apple grower to install, but it was preferred. The ground water level under the orchards sank, so in the past five years the wells have become deeper and deeper, dropping down to 80, and even to 100 metres in some orchards. The efficiency of the new system, however, resulted in less water spillage. It also meant that some of the water from the mountain streams could actually run into Prespa Lake. The volume of water that flows into the lake is not known.

Ljupco Tanevski, my host in April–May 2010, was showing me his orchard and that of his neighbours'. He pointed out a bend in the Golema River, south of Resen, where he and the other local owners, Turkish and Macedonian, used to work together to reinforce the feeder channels to their orchards. He now misses the former communal spirit, which is lost because of drop by drop. He has not installed this method himself, but he has a small gasoline-driven pump and moves by hand the 100 metre hose from row to row of his admittedly small orchard of 120 trees.

The drop by drop apparatus has replaced another major source of water for orchard irrigation. I discovered this other system quite by accident. I was hiking alone on the lake shore of Prespa in 1993. Just north of the village beach resort of Pretor, I heard in the distance something like the drone of electric turbines. It was indeed a large-scale electric pumping station that drew water from the lake and sent it far up the gradual slope in concrete conduits to many apple orchards.

No one had previously mentioned this pumping station when I had inquired as to why the lake was falling in level. I kept asking the question in my subsequent fieldwork trips. I heard from several men that a comparable pumping plant was on the Greek side of the border, one that pumped water from Mikro Prespa to the bean farms. Mikro

Prespa's level had likewise fallen through the years, and its water in the spring months was said to flow into Makro Prespa. There were also two pumping stations in the Albanian territory, which were operative until 1990, but compared to Greek and Macedonian agriculture in the region, Albanian farming was on a modest scale.

The enigma of Prespa's long-term recession was beginning to be solved. I recently learned from Liljana Tanevska that there had been two pumping stations in the Macedonian territory: both of them opened in 1956; one near Pretor on the eastern shore, and the other in Surlenci on the western shore. They both stopped operations in 2006, seemingly not for ecological reasons, but because of the transition to economic privatization. Economic explanations trump ecological explanations. The company that had purchased the pumping stations went bankrupt. An estimated 20 per cent of water for irrigation purposes in the Prespa region came from the two pumping stations (Tanevska personal communication 14 July 2010).

The shutting down of Prespa's largest workplace, 'Prespatex' in Resen, was a similar 'economic' cause for an environmental improvement. Prespatex was a Yugoslavian textile firm that could not make the transition from socialism to capitalism. The industrial waste from this textile factory ran directly into the Golema River and then, in much diminished volume, entered Prespa Lake, 15 kilometres to the south. Its water, I was told, had different colours, depending on which dyes were used that day. The river, as mentioned, was also the source of irrigation to many apple orchards along the way.

Perhaps because my recent, brief fieldwork was concentrated on Prespa's water basin – trying to achieve what I call the 'laser beam method' of current anthropology – I found that my inquiries into ecology were very often diverted into problems of economy. Informants and friends had, as always in the past, the production and price of apples as the main topic on the agenda. The falling of Prespa Lake was important, but not as important as the falling of the price of apples. Where and when could one sell the crates of apples picked in October and stored, perhaps until April, the following year? Growers said that the hybrid, Ida Red, was selected because of its long-term resilience. Ida Reds can survive the winter in the crates and can, hopefully, be sold at Easter time. The last of the 2009 crop was trucked away at the end of April 2010, when the orchards were in full blossom. The prices were, many said, historically low, and the apples were difficult to sell. Expenditures exceeded returns. Whereas in the past, Prespa farmers grew many sorts of apples, a monoculture of Ida Reds is now synchronized with the addition of 'kapka po kapka'.

The European Community, which holds out the promise of a new wealthy market for Macedonia, already produces apples in abundance and in many varieties. Naumi, a high-school teacher in agriculture, said that Poland and Italy have many times the number of trees that Macedonia has, and these large EU countries have better facilities for sizing, packing and storage. They can even stick labels on every apple! Shoppers in the EU need not wait until October to buy fresh apples. In March they arrive from Argentina, South Africa, etc., and they are sold for 20 times the price of what a Prespa grower receives, if the apples ever enter the EU countries. I heard two men say that some Prespa apples were bought by Greek merchants for mere pennies per kilo and exported at higher EU prices as 'Greek apples'. Economic resentment and envy keep political fires burning, and nationalist politics postpones ecological improvements. After this dire aside into political economy I return to the main and more affirmative thesis of the chapter.

The electro-driven pumping stations in Greece and Macedonia, one can infer, were a factor in the vector sum of human causes for the lakes' recession. Pumping water from the lake and channel irrigation from the mountain streams are both likely explanations for the substantial reduction of Prespa Lake's volume in the period 1975–2010. Economic causes, usually failures in privatization schemes, however, had unexpected, but favourable, consequences on the environment in Macedonia after the dissolution of Yugoslavia.

The recently published brochure by **UNDP** (United Nations Development Programs) contains a tentative, modest summary of Prespa's current condition and its causes. Its conclusion points more to 'natural' causality than to 'human interventions':

> The causes of this phenomenon have not been fully investigated. However, it has been estimated that lost water volumes

> are by factors 2 to 6 higher than the estimated amount of water abstracted through human interventions. Perametres that could explain this are natural karstic underground outflows and the inflows that are in turn affected by the rainfall/snowfall pattern.
> (UNDP 2009: 8)

Social anthropologists inquire into the variety and complexity of 'human interventions', so my inclination tends towards the UNDP factor of two, which would suggest that half the water loss is 'abstracted to human interventions', including political conflicts. (Geo)politically, the abuses of the lake were attributed to the other party across the border, what in American slang is known as 'passing the buck'. The 'others' make the mess and don't care about it. Indifference can be the result of sharply felt differences. The ethnographer in such disputes can only read between the lines, and often there is no printed page to read from. We have to interpolate the possible causes, and we also have to listen to the informants' own explanations and take them seriously. We must listen likewise to narratives in which people account for a crisis through the strange agency of 'Destiny' (Herzfeld 1992). Destiny, as it were, becomes the superlative of nature's force: the unpredictable earthquake, volcano or tsunami.

When I bring 'up to date' my long durational interest in Prespa Lake's crisis, the most impressive change is the availability of reliable knowledge and the awakened public interest in that knowledge. In this respect, the civil society organizations (and the anthropologists) have brought the metropoles and the villages into cooperative, de-colonized relations. The shared ecological consciousness is the virtual link in the process.

The issue of pesticide spraying, its dangers for the environment and for the farmer who does the job, is finally on the agenda, but it is hardly enacted upon to the degree it deserves. Practice has not caught up with consciousness. I have always asked about spraying when I spoke with apple growers and the answers were, and still are, pervaded by the fatal choice of risks. 'What if I don't spray?' is the question that invariably answers my questioning. To lose an entire crop of Ida Reds, to find one's trees barren of leaves, chewed away by tiny spiders, was a risk of not spraying. Were not a sudden frost in April, a prolonged drought in July, a wind and rainstorm in September enough of nature's ways to ruin a harvest? So the famers said, and did, 'Keep on spraying.'

The apple growers insist that they have reduced the number and quantity of spray applications. Ljupco sketched in my notebook, while seated at the table in his orchard, the dates of his spraying. The period ran from mid-April's blossoms until mid-August's unripened fruit. Every 15 or 20 days he sprayed the orchards, that is, a total of 12 or 13 'therapies', which was his own vivid choice of a word. Because it rained heavily soon after his first spraying in April, Ljupco had to spray again soon afterwards. Other farmers, I recall, said they sprayed the orchards between 20 and 30 times during a season. One of the reasons for a reduction in the number of applications was the economic expense of the pesticides. Economic rationality trumps ecological practice. The environmental organizations of the civil society have had better luck with protection of water resources than with the elimination of toxic chemicals.

'Civil society' was, and is, an actor in the field, serving as a catalyst for local, national and 'trans-boundary' initiatives. I noticed that the predicate, 'trans-boundary', was used in several documents and interviews, for it diplomatically circumvents the assertion of 'international' recognition for Macedonia. Access to printed documents with information about Prespa Lake was itself a welcome novelty for my recent research. In the past I depended on vague estimates of falling water: my own and those of informants. Qualified research has begun to supplant guesswork. Even more laudable is that public awareness has become manifest. UNDP has office space in the town hall in Resen, and it was there I could meet with the three staff persons who gave me copies of the printed documents with the statistical survey of the lake's falling level, cited above. The group was going to test water quality in the lake the following week. Non-governmental organizations (NGOs), international government organizations (IGOs), local and national authorities, and individual citizens have discovered common ground in the lake basin's environment.

Every one of the qualified persons from the region whom I asked about the pumping stations confirmed that they have not been operative since 2006. I had known of only one of them as late as 1993! The introduction of 'drop by drop' irrigation in the region dates from about the same year the lake pumping stopped. The UNDP programmes likewise were under way as well. In Nakolec, a multi-ethnic village at the lake's edge, a UNDP-sponsored water filtration project is under construction. Piping is paid for by the Environmental Ministry of the Republic. Thus, the potential of cooperation, which civil society evoked, is gradually being implemented in governmental agencies. Most significant in the conduct of projects are the local activists, who are salaried, albeit temporarily, for their work.

I am acknowledging here Liljana Tanevska and her colleagues, Sevda Jahna and Engin Baktjiar, all three of whom were born (in 1977) and had grown up in Resen. I met Sevda and Engin in 1979 when they were just toddlers. All three were young informants, high-school graduates, described in my book, *Pieces of Mosaic* (1996).

These young activists' approach to the environmental projects in the past decade was similar to that of MCIC in the 1990s. The fact that they were local residents is a significant difference. They laid the groundwork for a cooperative project in Krani, also a multi-ethnic village, by coordinating plans for the construction of a cement causeway through the town and a campaign for better sanitation. The stream water now runs unimpeded towards the lake, 2 kilometres down the slope. A village committee sees that garbage is collected regularly. These changes resulted from town-meeting discussions and cooperative action by the residents. The egalitarian participation of women in the public work project was also an item in MCIC's agenda and is a key to Krani's achievement. Municipal, as well as national funding, for these projects gathered momentum in the new millennium. The practical experience of civil society organizations in the more remote and marginalized regions of Macedonia did therefore arrive in the 'prosperous' Prespa, and, as in the western border district, the concrete results of an environmental improvement also proved of value for ethnic coexistence. If families had once cooperated in the work of digging irrigation channels and dividing the supply of water, they could also cooperate on vital issues of the environment.

Step by step, drop by drop, changes are under way to reverse the past decades' indifference and abuse. Liljana Tanevska, who has been a staff member for several NGO-led water projects in the Prespa and Ohrid Lakes region, advised me against being too jubilant when I praised the results of these efforts. Her scepticism, however, could not dampen my enthusiasm. I witnessed a spontaneous joy on her part at least once, when we visited a familiar site on the lake. Liljana drove her parents and I to the beach at Pretor on the evening of 28 April at 6P.M. The sun was going down over Mount Galicica. Liljana knew there was a vertical water-level marker sunk in the bottom a dozen or so metres from the beach line. She had read the metre level on 14 March, when the water was at the 40 cm. point. I waded out into the lake, making sure I had my glasses on, to read the almost illegible measuring post. The level was at the 67 cm. mark. There had been a rise of 27 cm. in the lake!

We mentioned this good news to Suleyman when we met him in Krani the next day. He too had noticed the recent rise of the lake because he often paced the distance on the beach to the water's edge. The distance was getting shorter. Critical anthropologists are seldom prone to tell good tidings. To celebrate the reversal of decades' recessions might be premature. Nevertheless, an empirically based blessing of the rising water is fully in order. The water-level marker in Pretor is, I will conclude, a key 'summarizing symbol' (Ortner 1973) for identifying cultural and natural changes in the Prespa region, and it is part of an entire narrative that includes the termination of the pump station in Pretor. Drop by drop serves likewise as a metaphor for the slow, but certain 'irrigation' of the Prespa region's local infrastructure in projects initiated by civil society NGOs, and subsequently by United Nations and European Union organizations. The local activists and staff persons, who helped me with this quick, incisive study, may shake their heads in wonderment at my appreciation for their accomplishments, something like students who are surprised at receiving a high grade for a term paper.

Civil society is a concept that encompasses some of modern humanity's best intentions, not least the safeguarding of nature from human recklessness. As Kay Milton writes, with reference to Arne Næss' concept 'deep ecology', the concern with nature is 'loving', drawn by more persuasive interests than duties: 'We act protectively towards nature, not because, for various reasons, we think we ought to, but because we feel inclined to' (Milton 2002: 74).

I have attempted in this chapter to stretch the category of 'informant' to include a lovely body of water that found herself in a difficult situation, like the figure of Prespa in folklore. Whether Prespa is rescued from her fate will only be evident in the coming years. The good news, thus far, is that the inhabitants of the Prespa Lake region are concerned with that fate and are taking steps to protect her.

Acknowledgements

I want to express once again special thanks to the members of the entire Tanevski family in Resen for their hospitality and for providing thoughtful answers to my constant questioning. Anthropologists who return to the field also can feel they are returning home.

Afterword: My latest report from Prespa Lake (via Liljana Tanevska) is that the lake is rising in level. Small trees that were last year on the beach are now under water. Prespa water's quality is found better than Ohrid's, where there are several cities and large tourist hotels on the shore line. In short, my slightly optimistic conclusion to the chapter 'holds water'.

Notes

1. The possibility for active vacationing and 'eco-tourism', for hiking, swimming, canoeing, mountain biking and camping would be enhanced by tri-national, mutual policies, including free passage across the borders on automobile-free trails. Prespa Lake is also a relatively protected habitat for water birds, especially rare pelicans and storks. Several non-governmental organizations have already been engaged in 'eco-tourism' programmes. An environmental organization from Switzerland, for example, has financed a woodland trail for hiking up Mount Pelister (2,600 metres above sea level) from the village of Brajcino (1,100 metres above sea level). The completed project has a shelter for staying overnight near the mountain's peak. Two streams run through the village, and the banks of these streams are no longer dumping places.

2. This section of the chapter builds upon the second of two lectures I gave at the Institute of Ethnology and Anthropology, Kyril and Methodius University, Skopje, 23 April, 2010. The first lecture, 22 April, was called: 'Anthropologists Meet Macedonia'. Thanks to Professor Ljupco Risteski, his colleagues and students for their generous attention.

References

Burnet, John 1958 (1930). *Early Greek Philosophy*. New York. Meridian Books.
Cowan, Jane 2000. *Macedonia: the Politics of Identity and Difference*. London. Pluto Press.
Cruikshank, Julie 2005. *Do Glaciers Listen?: Local Knowledge, Colonial Encounters, and Social Imagination*. Vancouver: UBC Press.
Danforth, Loring 1995. *The Macedonian Conflict: Ethnic Nationalism in a Transnational World*. Princeton: Princeton University Press.
Gellner, Ernest 1994. *Conditions of Liberty: Civil Society and its Rivals*. London: Hamish Hamilton.
Herzfeld, Michael 1992. *The Social Production of Indifference: Exploring the Symbolic Roots of Western Bureaucracy*. Chicago: University of Chicago Press.
Milton, Kay 2002. *Loving Nature: Towards an Ecology of Emotion*. London: Routledge.
Mursic, Rajko 2005. 'The colorful air over Skopje: on Macedonian radio broadcast and its perspectives'. Z. Smitek and A. Svetieva (ed), *Post-Yugoslav Lifeworlds. Between Tradition and Modernity*. Ljubljana: Zupanicera knjiznica.
Ortner, Sherry 1973. 'On Key Symbols', *American Anthropologist*. 75, (5): 1338–46.
Sampson, Steven 1996. 'The social life of projects: importing civil society to Albania. C. Hann and E. Dunn (eds.) *Civil Society: Rethinking Western Models*. London: Routledge.
Schwartz, Jonathan 1993. 'Macedonia: A Country in Quotation Marks'. *The Anthropology of East Europe Review*. Vol 2, 1–2: 93–99.
—— 1996. *Pieces of Mosaic: An Essay on the Making of Makedonija*. Højbjerg Denmark: Intervention Press. (See acknowledgements.)
—— 2000a. 'Blessing the Water the Macedonian Way. J. Cowan ed. *Macedonia: the Politics of Identity and Difference*. London. Pluto Press, 104–121.
—— 2000b. 'Civil society and ethnic conflcit in the Republic of Macedonia'. Joel M. Halpern and David A. Kideckel (eds.), *Neighbors at War*. Universitt Park: Pennsylvania State University Press, 382–400.
UNDP: 2009. *Water. Prespa Park Facts and Figures*. Skopje. Biografika.

INDEX

Adam of Macedonia, 94, 105–106n.2
Aegean Macedonians, 4, 26, 31, 34, 39n.19, 266, 269–270
Albania, 18, 32, 47, 59, 141, 199, 215, 277, 286, 290
Albanians in Macedonia
 identity of, 56, 241–242
 language of, 27, 78, 195
 Ohrid Framework Agreement and, 12, 146–147, 235–236, 245
 politics of, 235
 relations with Macedonians. See Macedonian-Albanian relations.
 women, 56, 60, 222
 see also Besa; Shiptar; Albanian-Yugoslav relations; Muslims in Ottoman Empire.
Albanian-Yugoslav relations, 90, 140–142, 147, 165, 169, 185n.10, 219
Alexander the Great, 47, 96–97, 100, 279
America, United States of, 24, 29–30, 33
Anderson, Benedict, 90–91
Architecture
 historical use of, 15, 19, 227–228
 Kumanovo, 212, 227, 231n.12,
 modernist, 218, 220, 230n.7

Ottoman, 137, 156, 212, 218–220
socialist (Yugoslavian), 156, 219–220, 228
see also Skopje architecture
Aromanian, 33, 37n.4
Ataturk, 150
Athens, 10, 22–25

Balkans
 boundaries of, 48, 52–53, 56, 61, 115
 Ottoman, 141, 148–149, 156
Balkan Wars, 1, 31, 48, 75, 141, 150, 193, 216, 218
Bektashi dervishes, 163. *See* also Dervishes.
Benjamin, Walter, 15, 17, 213, 224, 228
Besa, 241, 245, 252, 256n.5
Birlik, 16,
Bit Pazar 16, 233–234
Bitola, 9, 27, 100, 146, 280
Brown, Keith, 1–2, 7, 33–34
Bulgaria, 45, 47, 55, 59, 72–74, 141, 199, 238
Bulgarian claims to Macedonian language, 10, 34, 38n.13, 38n.16
Burushi language. *See* Macedonian language and Burushi.

INDEX

Civil society, 89, 138–139, 157, 195, 197, 199, 201, 205, 282–287, 292–295
Consensus analysis (MDS), 114–115
Cowan, Jane, 1–2, 7, 80, 285
Cross cultural
  studies, 127, 239
  survey, 109, 110–113
Cyrillics, 69, 103

Danforth, Loring, 1, 6, 39n.20, 265, 284
Decade of Roma Inclusion, 191, 193, 199–205
Dervishes, 15, 162–184. *See also* Roma Shaykhs; Sufis; Tekkes; Zikir;
  Ottoman, 163–164
  Yugoslav, 164–165, 169
Dervishluk 162, 174, 181,
Diasporas, 66, 90, 159, 225, 278, 282

Ecological fallacy, 17–18, 236–239, 243, 252–255, 256n.3
Ecology, 290, 295
Environmental action, 263, 286–287, 292–294, 296n.1
Environmental degradation, 5–6, 267–268, 271, 274–275, 279, 290, 291
EU (European Union)
  Macedonia as part of, 2, 45, 48–50, 53, 59, 158
  Turkey and, 50, 139, 158

Familija. *See* Macedonian kinship.
Florina, 27, 269–271, 280,
Freelist, 239–240, 245–248

Gender
  conceptualizing, 124–132
  literature, 109–111
  roles, 78, 109, 111, 116, 131–132
  survey, 112–114
Gevgelija, 27

Golab, Zbigniew, 22
Golden Dawn. *See* Hrisi Avgi
Gostivar, 153, 157
Gradski Trgovski Centre, 233
Greece
  national policy of 'One Nation' in, 10–11, 23, 25, 31, 35, 39n.19, 39n.21
  Macedonians in. See Aegean Macedonians
  see also Greece-Macedonia name disputes; Metaksas; Hrisi Avgi
Greece claims to Macedonian language, 10–11, 24–27, 34–35
Greece-Macedonia name disputes, 11, 35–36, 39n.20, 47, 83, 105, 149, 265, 279
Gypsy, 165–168. *See* also Roma

Hadith, 172
Helsinki Watch, 31
Herzfeld, Michael 36, 38n.12, 84, 292
Hrisi Avgi (Golden Dawn), 28–29, 35–37

Interethnic
  politics, 147
  relations, 136, 235, 255
  tensions, 2, 18, 234–235, 238–239
Islamic reform, 172–174, 178–179, 186n.15
Islamic Religious Community (IRC), 54

Kadare, Ismail, 15
Kamen Most (Stone Bridge), 16, 233–234, 252
Karadča, Vasko, 10, 23–24, 26, 37
Kavafis, Constantine, 24
Keck, Margaret, 197–198
Kosovo, 11, 63n.6, 150, 156, 165, 169, 191–192, 226–227
  crisis in, 11, 150, 156, 191–192

Kumanovo
  architecture of, 211–213, 219–222, 227–228,
  demographics of, 16, 226
  history of, 214–218, 229n.1,230n.4, 230n.6
Kyril and Metodi, 8, 66, 68–69, 71

Lekë Dukagjini, Code Of, 241, 256n.5

Macedonia
  ageing bachelors in, 77, 79–82
  constitution of, 12, 73, 146, 165, 193, 197
  democracy building in, 193
  independence of, 34, 36, 50, 73–74, 76, 237, 284
  multicultural, 1– 4, 11–12, 35, 235, 281, 284–285
  multi-ethnic, 136, 143, 152, 192–193; 196, 281, 284, 286
  parliament of, 80, 147, 235
  as part of EU 23, 45–46, 49–50, 53, 55–56, 59–60
  rural, 78–79, 110, 131
  studies of, 30, 34
  unemployment in, 9, 126, 193, 236–237, 255
  see also Greece-Macedonia name disputes
Macedonian diaspora, 66, 90
Macedonian identity, 9–10, 32–35, 45, 47–48, 52–53, 55–56, 65–69, 73–85, 93, 105, 244
Macedonian women status, 56–58, 79–80, 110–111, 131–133n.7
Macedonian language
  formation of, 31–32, 69
  dialects in Greece, 27
  Burushi language and, 93, 103–106n.5
  Rosetta Stone and, 100–105
  see also Greece claims to Macedonian language; Bulgarian claims to Macedonian language

Macedonian Orthodox Church
  as Autocephalous, 76, 106n.3
  as 'Cultural guardian', 65
  early history of, 68–71
  national identity and, 8–9, 65–67, 73–74, 77–85
  in Ottoman Empire, 71–74
  in Yugoslavia, 75–76
Macedonian kinship (*also* Familija), 66–67, 77–85
  nationalist rhetoric and, 91–92
Macedonian question, 6–7
Macedonian-Albanian Relations, 8, 17–18, 56, 225, 229, 233–236, 242–245, 252, 255–256
MATUKAT. See Turkish Community in Macedonia
Memedova, Azbija, 200
Metaksas, 25
Millennium Cross, 8, 17, 53–54, 63n.9, 233
Misirkov, Krste, 32,
MTUSITEB (Union of Macedonian Turkish Nongovernmental Organizations), 157
Multidimensional analysis (MDS), 247–252, 115–116
Muslim women, 128, 154–155, 157–158
Muslims
  in Ottoman Empire, 139,167, 184n.6
  in Yugoslavia, 140, 169, 185n.10

National character
  comparison of Albanian and Macedonian 246–249
  of Albanians 240–241, 244–245
  of Macedonians 66, 241–244
NATO, 31, 63n.16, 142, 281
NGOs, 235; 237; 282–283; 285–286; 293, 295
Roma, 14, 197–198
Soros, 193; 199; 202–203, 207n.11, 283–287
Turkish, 13, 156–158

Index

Ohrid Framework Agreement, 12, 146–147, 235–236, 245
  see also Albanians in Macedonia and Ohrid Framework Agreement; Turks in Macedonia and Ohrid Framework Agreement.
Ohrid, 66, 69–71, 76
  Patriarchate, 71
Ottoman Empire
  legacy of 72, 137–138, 156, 158, 219
  Macedonia as part of, 32, 141, 148, 163, 165
  millet system and, 71–72, 184n.5
  see also Roma in Ottoman Empire; Architecture (Ottoman); Ottoman dervishes; Ottoman Balkans; Muslims in Ottoman Empire; Macedonian Orthodox Church in Ottoman Empire.

Patriarchy (in kinship), 110–112, 130
Performative failure 162, 184n.2
Political activism, 14, 18, 193, 198–200, 283, 294–295
Pollution, 4–6, 20, 265, 267, 271, 273–274, 286
Pulevski, Gjorgji, 32, 34

Quran, 171–174, 176, 178–179, 182

Rainbow Party, 24
Roma
  Albanians and, 12–13, 53, 194, 206n.6
  Macedonia government and, 12, 14, 192–197, 201–204
  marginalization of, 12–14, 193–197, 202, 205n.3,206n.9
  in Ottoman Empire 167
  education, 195, 200–207n.13
  NGO's 14, 56, 195, 202, 207n.13
  studies, 195–197, 206n.9
  women, 202–203, 205n.3

shaykhs, 14–15, 168–183
  in Yugoslavia, 14, 56, 172, 206n.9
  see also Roma Education Fund
Roma Education Fund, 200, 203
Rosetta Stone. See Macedonian language and Rosetta Stone.

Salonica, 24, 30
Serbia, 47, 51, 59, 63n.6, 66, 72–74, 199, 218, 221, 226
Serbian Orthodox Church, 9, 66, 71, 76, 164
Shaykhs. See Roma shaykhs.
Shiptar, 225, 234, 244, 252
Sikkink, Kathryn
  see Keck, Margaret
Skopje, 16, 52, 58, 61, 233–234, 284
  architecture of, 227–228, 231n.11
  See also Millennium Cross; Stone Bridge.
Slavs in history, 8–9, 68–72
Socialism, 8, 45, 49, 51, 58–59, 141, 193, 197, 217,
  architecture of , 16, 220–222, 223, 225, 228
Soros Foundation. See NGOs
Stone Bridge in Skopje. See Kamen Most
Sufis, 165, 168, 173–176, 179–181

Tekkes (sufi lodges), 14–15,162, 168–170, 172, 175–176, 180, 182
Tetovo, 153, 155,
Tetraglosson, 23,
Tito, 10, 32, 75, 141,172, 228, 282
Treaty of Bucharest, 31, 35
Turkey-Macedonia relations, 12–13, 136–138, 148–153, 156
Turkish language, 136, 141–144, 147, 152–155
Turks in Macedonia 137, 140–141, 147–148, 151
  education of, 147, 152–154
  heritage of, 139; 156

history of, 140–146;
identity of, 12–13, 151–155,156, 159, 184n.6
in Yugoslavia, 12, 140–142, 144, 156, 169, 185n.10–186n.11
MATUKAT and, 157
migration to Turkey, 143–146
Ohrid Framework Agreement and, 147
Roma and, 194
Rumelia and, 149
Turkey relationship with, 148–151

UNESCO, 27

Vakif, 156
Vlachs, 23, 28, 73,165, 215, 230, 270

VMRO, 53, 63n.9, 93
Vrapcishte, 143, 153, 159

World Bank, 193, 196, 199, 201–202

Yoruk, 140–141, 150
Yucelciler, 141
Yugoslavia
ethno-national politics of, 12, 75–76, 140, 143
See also Roma in Yugoslavia; Turks in Yugoslavia; Muslims in Yugoslavia; Macedonian Orthodox Church in Yugoslavia; Architecture (Socialist).

Zero–sum game, 17, 235–238, 245, 255
Zikir, 171–172, 176–178

Photo 1. Victor de Munck with taxi driver

Photo 2. Skopje Plaza with Millennium Cross

Photo 3. View of Old Town from the Stone Bridge

Photo 4. Vendor at Bit Pazar

Photo 5. Victor Friedman and thug – eye to eye

Photo 6. Street in the Old Town

Photo 7. Local grocery store

Photo 8. Mother and daughter baking bread

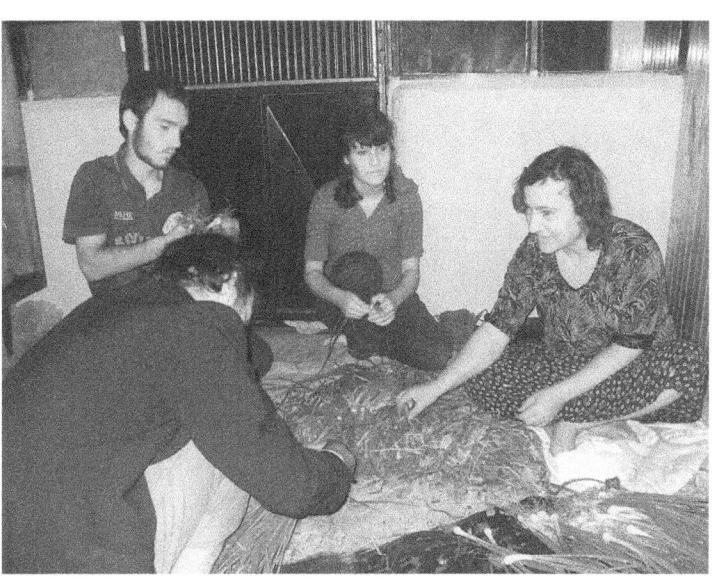
Photo 9. Family cleaning onion harvest

www.ingramcontent.com/pod-product-compliance
Lightning Source LLC
Chambersburg PA
CBHW070015010526
44117CB00011B/1586